PRENTICE HALL · LITERATURE LIBRARY

Nonfiction Readings Across the Curriculum

PRENTICE HALL
Upper Saddle River, New Jersey
Needham, Massachusetts

ISBN 0-13-437204-2

20 V054 14 13

PRENTICE HALL

Acknowledgments

Grateful acknowledgment is made to the following for copyrighted material:

Artisan, a division of Workman Publishing Company, Inc.
From "A Sense of Horses" by Michael J. Rosen, from the introduction to *Horse People: Writers and Artists on the Horses They Love*, edited by Michael J. Rosen. Published in 1998 by Artisan, a division of Workman Publishing Company, Inc. Reprinted by permission.

Ballantine Books, a division of Random House, Inc.
"The Importance of the Computer" from *Number* by John McLeish. Copyright © 1991 by John McLeish. Reprinted by permission of Ballantine Books, a division of Random House, Inc.

Julie Checkoway
From "The Writer in the Family: Civics Lessons for Kindred Spirits" by Julie Checkoway from *Poets & Writers Magazine*, vol. 26, issue 3, May/June 1998. Reprinted by permission of the author.

Cirque du Soleil and Sonya St-Martin
"My First Experience in a Circus" by Sonya St-Martin from *Cirque du Soleil*. Copyright © 1993 by Productions du Cirque du Soleil Inc. Reprinted by permission of Cirque du Soleil and the author.

Cobblehill Books, an affiliate of Dutton Children's Books, a div. of Penguin Putnam Inc.
"Brady and Lincoln," from *Mathew Brady: His Life and Photographs* by George Sullivan. Copyright © 1994 by George Sullivan. Used by permission of Cobblehill Books, an affiliate of Dutton Children's Books, a div. of Penguin Putnam Inc.

Ruth Cohen Literary Agency for the author
"Lensey Namioka, Outsider," "Music," "Writing" and "Mathematics" by Lensey Namioka. Copyright © 1997 Lensey Namioka. Used by permission of Ruth Cohen Literary Agency for the author.

(Acknowledgments continue on p. 284.)

Contents

Contents

Contents

Contents

Introduction

Many of us are accustomed to the excitement of reading fiction—whether it's mystery, romance, or adventure. However, nonfiction offers an excitement all its own, because we have the opportunity to read about real people and real events. Nonfiction writing has the power to motivate us and make us want to learn more about the world. It also gives us some understanding about the power of good writing. As poet Rita Dove says, " . . . there is simply a deep and basic pleasure in seeing words come alive . . . words are amazingly compact; they carry so much power in such a small package."

In the section of this book that concerns itself with writing, author Beverly Cleary—whose popular books you may have read in elementary school—talks about how she got started as a writer. She discusses how she got ideas for the characters we have come to know and love, such as Henry and Ribsy. From her we discover the ways in which real life can spark a writer's creativity.

Sometimes we expand our comprehension by exploring the familiar; sometimes we delve into the unknown. Barry Lopez takes us to the vast Arctic and makes us feel the frozen wonder of this unusual terrain, as he observers the behavior of adult wolves in the wild. We journey further with Linda Leuzzi, who exposes us to the important work of archaeologists—as she offers a window into the culture of the Anasazi of the far West—and naturalists—as she explains the fragile and varied ecology of the Chesapeake Bay and a forest in Brooklyn, New York.

We also learn and become stimulated by reading about the experience of famous people—often distinguished but still very human. This book contains insights both humorous and poignant about presidents Abe Lincoln and George Bush; musicians Duke Ellington and the Beatles; baseball slugger Mickey Mantle; and two victims of hate who lived in vastly different worlds, Anne Frank and Martin Luther King, Jr. By reading about well-known figures, we become affected by how they lived, perhaps adopting some of their goals or principles as our own.

In addition to reading these selections for their inherent value, you may find that some spur a particular interest. Maybe you will get some ideas for a future profession or activity. But even if you don't become a scientist or a musician, you will have gained a larger context for your own experience. For example, if you think about your own heritage and compare it to some of the writing in this book—such as the works by Lensey Namioka—you will find intriguing similarities and differences. In today's complex world, it's especially important to have an appreciation and respect for the perspective of others' cultures.

As you read from almost every part of the school curriculum—Literature, Science, Social Studies, Math, Sports, and the Arts— you may get an idea of why these subjects captured the attention and imagination of their authors. You may even find some of their enthusiasm rubbing off on you. Most importantly, you may discover that the best thing to do with any subject is to think about it, explore it, enjoy it—and perhaps, someday, write about it. You will have gained a new vantage point on the world you inhabit and how it works, on the beauties and joys to be found here, and on the mysteries still waiting to be solved.

Literature

from
I Know What the Red Clay Looks Like

Rita Dove

A WRITER is a writer all the time. I am always thinking as a writer and trying to approach the world as a writer, which means using all of my senses all of the time—being open for the breeze that comes through the window, what it smells like, and what the trees look like when the breeze touches them. It can make for a pretty scattered impression on others. But that's how a writer lives—by being deeply in the world and being attuned to it a great deal of the time, while the rest of the time is spent in the actual writing and recollection of that interaction with the world.

When I was a kid I listened to stories—the women in the kitchen, Fourth of July cookouts, folks on the porch talking—I would eavesdrop really. Listening to these stories being told and how they would affect their listeners was quite an influence on my own desire to tell stories. I also did a lot of reading. As a child, my parents really opened me and my siblings up to the glory of reading and the infinite possibilities when you open a book. It was an activity that we could do practically any time—except at the dinner table. The library was the one place we could go to without asking permission. As long as we had finished the books we had taken out from our last trip there, we could go. And we always had.

My entire childhood was imbued with reading—afternoons of curling up with a book, and the pleasure of not knowing what was going to be in it until I opened it and began to read its words. The love I felt for the words on those pages made me want to create some words of my own, and to write the stories that I had not yet found.

When I began writing at maybe ten or eleven years old, it was wonderful, because I discovered that I could go wherever I wanted to go and do whatever I wanted to do. I didn't really tell anyone about it. My brother, who is a few years older than me, and I were very close as children. Every summer, we would have a newspaper, which I would usually quit about halfway through the summer to start my own newspaper. The title of my own newspaper usually made some reference to poetry. I remember one summer it was called *Poet's Delight*. Other than my brother, I really didn't show anyone what I wrote, not even my friends. It wasn't shame, it was just that writing was such an intimate act for me that it didn't really occur to me to bring it out into the world all that much.

When I got to high school, my English teacher brought a few of us to a book signing one afternoon. I hadn't shown her any of my writing either, beyond my English papers. The writer at the book signing was John Ciardi, the poet and translator. I was so amazed that writers were really *people*. At that moment, I realized that this "activity" I had been doing, that I had been thinking of as somewhat of a game—some game that I would one day have to put away in order to become an adult—that this activity was really something adults did and were respected for. And it was called writing.

I did not make the conscious decision to become a writer until I was in college. It wasn't until I realized that I was rearranging my schedule to fit in creative writing courses that I thought, Well, maybe I should make a go of this, because writing had obviously become the most important thing to me. I was then able to recognize the yearning that I felt inside, the joy that I got when I wrote something I felt was halfway decent. When I was able to understand that the joy could somehow satisfy the yearning, I realized that the yearning, the joy, and the satisfaction were about wanting to write. I think I had the yearning for a long time before recognizing it; I just didn't know what it was.

In my poetry, I write about what the weather is like, or what the sand feels like under a sandal—that kind of thing—and it may be drawn from an experience that I have had, or that someone I know has had. I draw from other people quite a lot, particularly family members. *Thomas and Beulah* is a good example of that because it began with a story that my grandmother told me about my grandfather. As I began to re-create the scene, the event that she told me about, imagination came in. I hadn't been there, and she hadn't been there either—only my grandfather had been there, and he had long since passed away—so by necessity I had to use my imagination. In imagining, I also put my own feelings into it—how I would have felt had I actually been there—all the while trying to slip into my grandfather's skin.

As that book of poetry grew, I went to the library and did research to find out things—like what Akron, Ohio, was like in the twenties. I also talked with my mother and drew on her memories, and then I sometimes just plain made things up. That's how I work. I did the same thing with my novel *Through the Ivory Gate*—I have played the cello, but I've never been a puppeteer—so it becomes a wonderful kind of mix, and I really don't try and sort it out that much.

I do think quite a few writers work in this same way; when we try to talk about that magical moment when the poem or the story or the scene takes off and comes alive, I know that for me it's a feeling of trying to write just to keep up with that moment. This moment is the point when all of the things I just mentioned—the memories, the imagination, the stories I've heard—all come together in such a unified piece that I don't know where the energy is coming from and all I can do is ride with it. It feels terrific. It is so exhilarating, I feel like I could write forever, that I am inexhaustible. The ideas and the words come faster than I can write them down. Although sometimes, right before that happens, there is a moment of great despair when things don't seem to be clicking; but the faith that it will come together takes me there. I learn so much in the process; it is profound discovery.

There is some truth to the whole notion that something strikes the poet like a thunderbolt and she is then inspired. Inspiration is part of the writing process, and I think of it as being much more visceral than cerebral. I also think that there is a different kind of inspiration that comes when one is working and things begin to click together. I'll leave it up to all the scientists and psychologists to come up with the right terminology for it, but I do think that I try to engage all of my senses when I write. Absolutely and completely. I try to get *in* it. And then I need to find a word that will best describe being in it, which is very cerebral. The mind, the soul, the heart, and the heartbeat try to get into sync, and when they do, it is very difficult to say which takes precedence, in fact I don't think any one thing does.

When the writing doesn't gel together, I just keep working. For example, since I am both a poet and a fiction writer, let me try to explain the differences I feel between both mediums. I find that the rhythms are very different between these two genres. With poetry, very often there are the days and hours of a lot of frustration when things are not coming together. When things finally do click, I find the moments of connection are usually much more brilliant and unequivocal. With prose, I find that the periods when things are not clicking are not quite as depressing because there is so much to do in prose besides working on those connections. I guess you could call it housekeeping—tidying up ragged paragraphs, creating an atmosphere, checking dialogue—so that I can keep active in the work and not despair that it won't come together. Maybe it is because I consider myself more of a poet than a fiction writer, but I also find the moments that come together in prose are not as epiphanal as those in poetry. So it's a trade-off. I prefer the higher highs and the deeper depths in poetry.

For me, there is simply a deep and basic pleasure in seeing words come alive. The simpler the word, the better. Because words are amazingly compact; they carry so much power in such a small package. I think the simpler the word, the more power it contains, because our first words were very simple, one-syllable words. If I can find a way to bring back all the power of the word *bread,* not Wonder bread, but *bread*—the stuff that gives us life—if I can restore the freshness and magic to that word in a prose passage or in a poem, then I've got it all. What an incredible power—I smell it, I feel it, I am alive.

I run through all the different attributes of a word when I am trying to find the right one. A word not only has a meaning—it also has a sound, a feeling in the mouth, a texture, a history. Very often, if a word has the right meaning, but not the sense, the deeper sense I need, I try to think of words that rhyme, or I look up its etymology. Writing for me means that intense pleasure of dealing with language, working with the language like a potter works with clay. I think most writers have an almost shameless love of language, of words and the way they work.

When we are children, we love to play with language; we like feeling sounds in our mouth. Then as we start to grow up, what begins to happen is that the pleasure of mouthing words has to be compromised because words are also used for daily interactions. Using charcoal or paint to create art is an activity that can be kept discrete. But the use of words can't be. We have to use them to talk and to communicate. Many people forget the pleasure of words for the purpose of expediency—they have to get on with their lives. I also think that this is why a lot of poets and writers are not great conversationalists. We are not the kind of people who sit around at the party spouting off witty and glib repartee. And a lot of that has to do with this intense love of words. To constantly make the switch between honoring every word and using them just to get on with things is very difficult. It's almost schizophrenia.

I've recently been named poet laureate of the nation, and I am still trying to decide what that title means. It is a kind of public or outward affirmation, not so much that I'm a good writer, but that the writing reaches an audience. And that is gratifying. Unless you do a lot of public readings, every time you sit down to write or finish a piece, there is that fear of being misunderstood. You say to yourself: What I'm writing is *really* crazy; no one is going to relate to this. So to have this sort of official recognition not only as a poet and writer, but also as someone who can stand forward and be a channel for literature in this country, is marvelous.

It doesn't really matter to me what kind of validation the title may give me as a poet—I don't really worry about that kind of stuff. Every time I sit down to write, it's a new ball game. The poem, or the story, or the scene, that I'm working on has its own problems, and there is always the fear that the poem or passage will not work or mean anything to anyone else. The intensity of this sort of hand-to-hand combat never goes away.

It is very exciting to think that the country thinks enough about literature to appoint a younger poet laureate, which may encourage the idea of writing in children and engage our youth by saying in effect: See? This can be done. That the country chose to honor a black woman is also tremendously exciting. On the one hand, it declares that there is value and richness in diversity. But it also shows that multiculturalism and diversity do not mean being separate. My ultimate desire is to be considered as part of the human family—to be recognized and respected as a black woman, but not to have that fact make any earth-shaking difference. It is significant that I am a black woman, but it is not the end-all-be-all in terms of being poet laureate.

A Celebration of Libraries

Richard Lederer

JUST about everyone has seen the blue highway signs with the big white *H* and an arrow pointing the way to the nearest hospital. Some state library associations have suggested that our roads be fringed by a similar kind of road marker with a prominently displayed *L* and an arrow pointing in the direction of another local institution: the public library. Such a sign would remind us that librarians serve us in much the same way as doctors and nurses and that books are just as vital to our health as bandages and medicine.

Elinor Lander Horwitz once wrote in *The Washington Post,* "There are numerous men and women perambulating the earth—in appearance much like ordinary respectable citizens—who have warm, loving, passionate—even sensuous—feelings about libraries." After I published a column tracing the history of libraries in the United States, Gertrude King Ramstrom, of Nashua, New Hampshire, sent me her "warm, loving, passionate—even sensuous—feelings" about her childhood adventures in a New England town library. Her testimonial makes vivid Shakespeare's claim that "my library was dukedom large enough."

Dear Sir:

Your article about libraries whisked me back in time and place to the 1920s and the little village of Haydenville, Massachusetts, where I grew up. Its tiny library, which is still in use, was our only avenue of adventure to the wonders of the outside world, and my brothers and I, along with our friends, made good use of it.

It is not a very imposing building either in architecture or size, and a traveler probably would not even realize one was there. Although it is on Main Street, it is tucked back at an angle to the road and has a mien of withdrawal, or shyness, as if aware of its insignificance among the libraries of the world. But to us it was a structure of great importance.

Its single room is shaped like the letter *H* with the crosspiece widened to include almost the entire area. Wonderful little nooks, furnished with stools and chairs, are formed by the extensions of the vertical bars of the *H*, and that was where we acquired a glimpse of the world, had our curiosity aroused, and met with our friends. It was open every Friday evening, and directly after supper Mother made us wash up and comb our hair so we would look respectable and be clean enough to inspect books without leaving fingerprints. Most of our friends were doing the same, and about 7 P.M. we congregated on the wide stone step of the building.

On summer evenings we lingered outside to talk, but in winter it was nice to push into the room and stand over the one-pipe register and allow the heat to blow up around us. There were no rules about talking, except when we became too boisterous, so the boys jostled and joked in one nook while we girls squeezed into another to whisper and giggle.

In our little library was born my love of history, which became my major in college. From *The Colonial Twins*, *The Puritan Twins*, and *The Twins of the American Revolution* through *The Red Badge of Courage* and *With Malice Toward None* I read, and am still reading, every historical novel available. By corroborating their assertions with the facts of history, I have found a never-ending source of enlightenment.

While my brothers read *The Bobbsey Twins*, *Tom Swift*, and *Huck Finn*, I read *Pollyanna*, *Bambi*, and *The Yearling*. As we grew, my older brother turned to *Twenty Thousand Leagues Under the Sea* and almost wore out Lindbergh's *We*. I can still picture the blue binding of the book with a silver airplane etched on the cover and my brother slouched in a big easy chair with his leg dangling over its arm. Both socks wrinkled around his ankles showing bare legs below the cuffs of his knicker pants, and his hand rumpled his hair as he soared high over the earth with his hero.

As he traveled the skies and seas, I traversed America with Willa Cather, learned to love animals through Albert Payson Terhune stories, found goodness in life with A. J. Cronin, and whisked away on the whimsy of Elizabeth Goudge. It was a wonderful experience, and because of it I would add another beatitude to the ones we learned back in our Sunday School days: Blessed are they who can read and enjoy a good book for theirs is the world and its kingdoms.

I firmly believe that children are influenced by what they read and that the books we took home from the library impressed upon us what Mother and Dad tried to teach—that good character and high moral values are to be desired above all other attributes. We heard it, we read it, and so we lived it. There is no greater endowment that can be given a child than an ideal and a hero, and our little library did just that for us.

Gertrude Ramstrom's paean inspires me to share a dozen of my favorite quotable quotations about libraries:

• Libraries are user-friendly.—*American Library Association*

• A library implies an act of faith which generations, still in darkness hid, sign in their night in witness of the dawn.—*Victor Hugo*

• I have always imagined that Paradise will be a kind of library!—*John Cheever*

• Take one brisk walk to the library. Take out any book by a tried-and-true writer. Take a brisk walk home and read with all attention. The exercise plus the tonic of the book will provide all physical and mental requirements for good health. —*Helen Hayes, at age eighty-six*

• I am a self-confessed library buff, drawn to them like others are drawn to theaters, art galleries, bars, or football games. I am proud to say that I have more library cards than credit cards in my wallet and that I know where all the coffee machines are located at the Library of Congress.—*Paul Dickson*

• Libraries will get you through times of no money better than money will get you through times of no libraries.—*Library poster*

• Perhaps no place in any community is so totally democratic as the town library. The only entrance requirement is interest.—*Lady Bird Johnson*

• In an era when millions more Americans can identify Boy George than George Eliot, it is gratifying to know that there is still a place where making acquaintance with Eliot and other literary giants is as easy as a walk or a drive to that spectacular intellectual galaxy, the local public library.—*Michael Birkner*

• Call it impiety, but to me the very word *library* has a sanctity that *church* cannot gain. The sacredness is my own association, of course. It is thick walls and tall windows. It is quiet rustling pages that whisper of knowledge. It is cool and smelly with that exciting odor that can only be got from aging glue, printers ink, paper, leather, and ideas together.—*A. C. Greene*

• A great library contains the diary of the human race.— *George Dawson*

- Libraries remain the meccas of self-help, the most open of open universities . . . where there are no entrance examinations and no diplomas, and where one can enter at any age.
—*Daniel J. Boorstin*
- In a library it's hard to avoid reading.—*From a student essay*

The Case for Short Words

Richard Lederer

WHEN you speak and write, there is no law that says you have to use big words. Short words are as good as long ones, and short, old words—like *sun* and *grass* and *home*—are best of all. A lot of small words, more than you might think, can meet your needs with a strength, grace, and charm that large words do not have.

Big words can make the way dark for those who read what you write and hear what you say. Small words cast their clear light on big things—night and day, love and hate, war and peace, and life and death. Big words at times seem strange to the eye and the ear and the mind and the heart. Small words are the ones we seem to have known from the time we were born, like the hearth fire that warms the home.

Short words are bright like sparks that glow in the night, prompt like the dawn that greets the day, sharp like the blade of a knife, hot like salt tears that scald the cheek, quick like moths that flit from flame to flame, and terse like the dart and sting of a bee.

Here is a sound rule: Use small, old words where you can. If a long word says just what you want to say, do not fear to use it. But know that our tongue is rich in crisp, brisk, swift, short words. Make them the spine and the heart of what you speak and write. Short words are like fast friends. They will not let you down.

The title of this chapter and the four paragraphs that you have just read are wrought entirely of words of one syllable. In setting myself this task, I did not feel especially cabined, cribbed, or confined. In fact, the structure helped me to focus on the power of the message I was trying to put across.

One study shows that twenty words account for twenty-five percent of all spoken English words, and all twenty are mono-syllabic. In order of frequency they are: *I, you, the, a, to, is, it, that, of, and, in, what, he, this, have, do, she, not, on,* and *they.* Other studies indicate that the fifty most common words in written English are each made of a single syllable.

For centuries our finest poets and orators have recognized and employed the power of small words to make a straight point between two minds. A great many of our proverbs punch home their points with pithy monosyllables: "Where there's a will, there's a way," "A stitch in time saves nine," "Spare the rod and spoil the child," "A bird in the hand is worth two in the bush."

Nobody used the short word more skillfully than William Shakespeare, whose dying King Lear laments:

> And my poor fool is hang'd! No, no, no life!
> Why should a dog, a horse, a rat have life,
> And thou no breath at all? . . .
> Do you see this? Look on her, look, her lips.
> Look there, look there!

Shakespeare's contemporaries made the King James Bible a centerpiece of short words—"And God said, Let there be light: and there was light. And God saw the light, that it was good." The descendants of such mighty lines live on in the twentieth century. When asked to explain his policy to Parliament, Winston Churchill responded with these ringing monosyllables: "I will say: it is to wage war, by sea, land, and air, with all our might and with all the strength that God can give us." In his "Death of the Hired Man" Robert Frost observes that "Home is the place where, when you go there,/They have to take you in." And William H. Johnson uses ten two-letter words to explain his secret of success: "If it is to be,/It is up to me."

You don't have to be a great author, statesman, or philosopher to tap the energy and eloquence of small words. Each winter I ask my ninth graders at St. Paul's School to write a composition composed entirely of one-syllable words. My students greet my request with obligatory moans and groans, but, when they return to class with their essays, most feel that, with the pressure to produce high-sounding polysyllables relieved, they have created some of their most powerful and luminous prose. Here are submissions from two of my ninth graders:

> What can you say to a boy who has left home? You can say
> that he has done wrong, but he does not care. He has left
> home so that he will not have to deal with what you say. He
> wants to go as far as he can. He will do what he wants to do.
> This boy does not want to be forced to go to church, to
> comb his hair, or to be on time. A good time for this boy does
> not lie in your reach, for what you have he does not want. He
> dreams of ripped jeans, shorts with no starch, and old socks.

So now this boy is on a bus to a place he dreams of, a place with no rules. This boy now walks a strange street, his long hair blown back by the wind. He wears no coat or tie, just jeans and an old shirt. He hates your world, and he has left it.—*Charles Shaffer*

For a long time we cruised by the coast and at last came to a wide bay past the curve of a hill, at the end of which lay a small town. Our long boat ride at an end, we all stretched and stood up to watch as the boat nosed its way in.

The town climbed up the hill that rose from the shore, a space in front of it left bare for the port. Each house was a clean white with sky blue or grey trim; in front of each one was a small yard, edged by a white stone wall strewn with green vines.

As the town basked in the heat of noon, not a thing stirred in the streets or by the shore. The sun beat down on the sea, the land, and the back of our necks, so that, in spite of the breeze that made the vines sway, we all wished we could hide from the glare in a cool, white house. But, as there was no one to help dock the boat, we had to stand and wait.

At last the head of the crew leaped from the side and strode to a large house on the right. He shoved the door wide, poked his head through the gloom, and roared with a fierce voice. Five or six men came out, and soon the port was loud with the clank of chains and creak of planks as the men caught ropes thrown by the crew, pulled them taut, and tied them to posts. Then they set up a rough plank so we could cross from the deck to the shore. We all made for the large house while the crew watched, glad to be rid of us.—*Celia Wren*

You too can tap into the vitality and vigor of compact expression. Take a suggestion from the highway department. At the boundaries of your speech and prose place a sign that reads "Caution: Small Words at Work."

from

My Own Two Feet: A Memoir

Beverly Cleary

ON January 2, 1949, I gathered up my typewriter, freshly sharpened pencils, and the pile of paper and sat down at the kitchen table we had stored in the back bedroom. *Write* and no backing out, I told myself. In all my years of dreaming about writing, I had never thought about what it was I wanted to say. I stared out the window at the fine-leafed eucalyptus tree leaning into the canyon and filled with tiny twittering birds. I looked out the other window at a glimpse of the bay when the wind parted the trees. There *must* be something I could write about. The cat, always interested in what I was doing, jumped up on the table and sat on my typing paper. Could I write about Kitty? He had a charming way of walking along the top of the picket fence to sniff the Shasta daisies, but children demanded stories. A daisy-sniffing cat would not interest them. I thought about the usual first book about a maturing of a young girl. This did not inspire me. I chewed a pencil, watched the birds, thought about how stupid I had been all those years when I aspired to write without giving a thought to what I wanted to say, petted the cat, who decided he wanted to go out. I let him out and sat down at the typewriter once more. The cat wanted in. I let him in, held him on my lap, petted him, and found myself thinking of the procession of nonreading boys who had come to the library once a week when I was a children's librarian, boys who wanted books about "kids like us."

Why not write an easy-reading book for kids like them? Good idea! All I needed was a story. How was I going to pull a story about boys from my imagination when I had spent so much of my childhood reading or embroidering? I recalled the Hancock Street neighborhood in Portland where I had lived when I was the age of the Yakima boys, a neighborhood where boys teased girls even though they played with them, where boys built scooters out of roller skates and apple boxes, wooden in those days, and where dogs, before the advent of leash laws, followed the children to school.

These musings were interrupted by a memory that sprang from my days at the hospital. A harried office worker whose husband was overseas asked if her two children, a well-behaved boy and girl, could come to the library after school. I agreed. Once they brought their dog with them, which pleased men who missed their own dogs. The next day their mother told me that a neighbor had driven the children and their dog to the hospital. When the family started home, they learned a dog was not allowed on a streetcar unless it was in a box. Rain was pouring down, the nearest grocery store that might have a box was several blocks away—by the time the woman finished her tale, she looked even more harried than usual.

Aha, I thought, the germ of a plot just right for little boys. The trouble was, I soon discovered, I did not know how to write a story. It had been thirteen years since I had written anything but letters, radio talks, and tiresome papers with footnotes. Although I had received excellent grades and complimentary comments on both high school and junior college writing, the only corrections were on spelling, punctuation, and syntax, the sort of thing dear to English teachers. No teacher ever told me how I could improve my stories or suggested any changes at all.

If, in the 1940s, there had been writers' groups, I probably would have joined one. Fortunately, they did not exist, or if they did, I did not know about them. I believe a writer's work should spring from one person's imagination, unassisted by a group of friends who may be helpful but who also may be of questionable judgment.

As I sat listening to twittering in the eucalyptus tree and thinking of the boys from St. Joseph's, my story-hour audiences, and classes I had visited, it occurred to me that even though I was uncertain about writing, I knew how to tell a story. What was writing for children but written storytelling? So in my imagination I stood once more before Yakima's story-hour crowd as I typed the first sentence: "Henry Huggins was in the third grade." Where Henry's name came from I do not know. It was just there, waiting to be written, but I do know Henry was inspired by the boys on Hancock Street, who seemed eager to jump onto the page. Hancock Street became Klickitat Street because I had always liked the sound of the name when I had lived nearby. I moved Claudine's house from Thirty-seventh Street to renamed Hancock Street to become Henry's house. When I came to the skinny dog who found Henry, I needed a name. We happened to have spareribs waiting in the refrigerator, so I named the dog Spareribs and continued the story, based on the family who took their dog home on a streetcar. I changed the family to one boy, and the streetcar into a bus.

Writing without research, bibliography, or footnotes was a pleasure. So was rearranging life. If I needed a character or incident, all I had to do was pull it out of my memory or imagination without searching a card catalog or waiting in a crowd of pressured students at a circulation desk. What freedom!

When I finished the story I thought I was pleased with it, but I was not sure anyone else would be, so I invited a bookstore friend, Sara, who was both knowledgeable and sardonic about children's books, to come to dinner and read my story. I knew she would not try to meddle with it, and she would be honest. While I tossed the salad, Sara read "Spareribs and Henry" and gave her opinion in her no-nonsense way: "They'll be glad to get it." That was her only comment, but it gave me the assurance I needed and was the last time I asked anyone other than Clarence to read a manuscript.

What to do next? I doubted that Elisabeth Hamilton would be interested in such a slight story. To inquire about publishers I wrote to Siri Andrews, who by then had left the University of Washington to become children's editor at Holt and then librarian in Concord, New Hampshire. She suggested Abingdon-Cokesbury Press, and I sent my story on its way. As I walked down the steps of the post office, I found I was having more ideas about Henry.

The story quickly came back semirejected. The editor wrote saying, "I enjoyed reading this story very much—which is something I cannot say of all the manuscripts that come in here! It has humor, action, and realism, and I think that both boys and girls, but particularly boys from eight to eleven or so, would enjoy reading it very much." She went on to point out that a short story for this age group did not work into book format easily except as one of a collection of short stories and that this age group preferred a book-length story. She was kind enough to say that perhaps I could write a number of these "short incident" stories and submit them to magazines. "Then perhaps you could weave these stories about a plot which would carry its own suspense and climax and have a book-length manuscript to offer." If this worked out, she hoped I would send the manuscript to her, for "it seems to me it might very well fit into our publishing program."

Well! I reread the letter half a dozen times, and went to work telling/writing my other stories about Henry, which had an assortment of inspirations. One story, "The Green Christmas," was a new version of a story I had written when I was a freshman in high school, a story based on a newspaper clipping about some boys who had gone swimming downriver from a dye works that had dumped dye into the river. The boys had come out dyed green. In my high school story I had the accident save a boy from playing the part of an angel in a Christmas pageant. This turned into a story about Henry trying to get out of playing the part of a little boy in a school PTA program. (I had once been a tin soldier in such a play.) He was saved when green paint was dumped on him when he helped paint scenery.

Another chapter was based on an incident that happened to the boy next door when I lived on Thirty-seventh Street. He was passing a football to another boy across the street when a car came speeding around the corner. The football flew into the car and was never seen again—a good beginning for a story but not a satisfactory ending. Of course the boy who owned the football blamed Henry and demanded his football back. How? I recalled a summer vacation during college when some friends were talking about catching night crawlers to use for bait on a fishing trip. When I said I had never heard of night crawlers, we went on a hunting expedition. Armed with flashlights and two quart jars, we went to dimly lit Grant Park, where the lawn was damp from recent watering. In a short time we pulled from the grass two quarts of writhing worms each eight or nine inches long, a disgusting sight. Having caught them, we felt they should serve some useful purpose. What to do with two quarts of worms? "Waste not, want not," we were often reminded during the Depression.

Someone had an inspiration—we drove to a fire station that had a large fishpond. We dumped our worms into the water, which was instantly full of churning, leaping, apparently grateful fish. This incident helped me solve Henry's problems. He caught, with the help of his parents, enough night crawlers to sell to neighborhood fishermen to pay for the football. Today, in my old neighborhood, I see childish signs that say: NIGHT CRAWLERS FOR SALE.

I continued to work, combining my writing with birdwatching, letting the cat in and our, and an added activity, bread baking. After Clarence drove down the hill to the university, I often mixed a batch of bread and set it to rise over the pilot light on the gas stove. Then I sat down at the kitchen table to battle my typewriter. About the time I was ready to stretch my legs, the bread had risen, filling the house with yeasty fragrance, ready to be punched down and divided into loaves to rise again. On my next leg stretch, I put the bread into bake and inhaled the lovely fragrance. By the time the bread was done, the cat felt neglected and sat on my paper. I pushed him off, took the bread out of the oven, buttered the crisp brown crust, and stopped writing for the day.

Hannah's company and her garden made a soothing change after a morning with my enemy the typewriter, an enemy I finally abandoned for first drafts. Ideas flowed much more easily in long-hand. I continued happily inventing stories about Henry from reality and imagination, and as I wrote, Mother's words, whenever I had to write a composition in high school, came back to me: "Make it funny. People always like to read something funny," and "Keep it simple. The best writing is simple writing." Some of Professor Lehman's words also echoed through my mind: "The minutiae of life," and "The proper subject of the novel is universal human experience." I remembered Mr. Palmer's three-hundred-words-a-day assignment and disciplined myself to write every day.

Then one morning as I wrote, it occurred to me that all the children in the stories were only children. Someone should have a sibling, so I tossed in a little sister to explain Beezus's nickname. When it came time to name the sister, I overheard a neighbor call out to another whose name was Ramona. I wrote in "Ramona," made several references to her, gave her one brief scene, and thought that was the end of her. Little did I dream, to use a trite expression from books of my childhood, that she would take over books of her own, that she would grow and become a well-known and loved character.

The group of short stories needed one last chapter. I mulled over my childhood on Hancock Street, and for some reason recalled circus posters along Sandy Boulevard when the circus was coming to town. Why not have Spareribs be a lost circus dog? I did not much like the idea, but it was all I could come up with. More mulling did not help, so that was the way I ended the book. I was not really satisfied with that last chapter. Having a clown turn up on Klickitat Street could hardly be called universal human experience, at least not in Portland, but since I had never written anything longer than those twenty-four pages on "Plato: Teacher and Theorist," the seventy or eighty pages I had written about Henry seemed as long as the novels I had studied at Cal.

What was the next step? I knew from bookstore talk and conversations at Quail's house that I was under no obligation to Abingdon-Cokesbury because the editor had not sent a contract. While I was grateful for her words of encouragement, I felt I should try a larger publisher. I thought of Elisabeth Hamilton in her handsome hat and liked the idea of my manuscripts in the hands of someone I could visualize. I also recalled that she wrote a letter when she rejected a manuscript if she felt it revealed the author showed talent.

Unfortunately, I had some reservations about Morrow as a publisher because I had met the West Coast rep several times at Quail's house and heard him express his dislike of children's books and how unnecessary he thought they were. On the other hand, at one of Quail's parties I had also heard two Morrow adult authors, Harvey Ferguson and Oregon author H. L. Davis, agree that Morrow was fair to authors. That is what I wanted, a publisher who was fair to authors. They also said that, although the rep had made much of being a talent scout, his strong point was getting books into bookstores. I could understand this because I had watched him selling to Quail at Sather Gate, where he was always kind, gentlemanly, and knowledgeable about the books on his list. I liked him; I just didn't like his attitude toward children's books, which, however, I decided to overlook. After all, he had been denied the experience of working with Yakima's nonreaders, so how could he understand?

I also heard H. L. Davis remark that when he sold his first manuscript he had walked through the middle door of the post office when he mailed it. He felt this had brought him luck, and ever afterward he had walked through the middle door of the post office whenever he mailed a manuscript. What worked for a Pulitzer Prize-winning author might work for me, even though I was uneasy about that last chapter. I sent my manuscript to Elisabeth Hamilton with my maiden name as author and my married name and address typed on the title page but without a covering letter. What could I say except the obvious: I hope you buy my book.

I had often heard Quail tell would-be authors that if a publisher did not report on a manuscript within six weeks, sending a letter of inquiry was acceptable. Morrow, kind to authors, thoughtfully sent a postcard saying my manuscript had been received, so at least I knew it wasn't lost in the mail. After several weeks went by, I began to watch the mailman while clipping off dead roses to disguise my true purpose. Since he had never seen me in the garden, he became curious and wanted to know what I was waiting for. When I explained, he began to watch for my mail as eagerly as I, and at the end of six weeks, left his heavy mailbag by the hedge and came running down the steps waving an airmail letter. "It's here!" he shouted as I ran to meet him. A letter, not a returned manuscript! I went into the house to read it.

I tore open the envelope and read the first sentence of Elisabeth Hamilton's letter dated July 25, 1949. "Several of us have read your story, 'Spareribs and Henry,' and we are very much interested in it as a possibility for the Morrow list." She went on to praise the story and to say that "the last chapter, 'Finders Keepers,' was not up to the previous chapters." How right she was. She then asked if I would be willing to make revisions. Of course I would, in my own blood, if necessary. She closed by saying she was going on vacation until shortly after the middle of August, and if I would undertake revisions, she would send criticisms and suggestions on her return. I flopped into a chair and, smiling at the whole world, read and reread the letter. Then I telephoned Clarence to give him the news and wrote a letter saying I would be pleased to make revisions.

The middle of August, I started pulling weeds in the garden, but this time confessed to the mailman my motive, other than getting rid of weeds. "Not today," he said every day until the middle of September, when I had pulled a lot of weeds. He ran down the steps once more, this time waving a big brown envelope, as pleased as if he were giving me a personal gift. I tore it open and read Mrs. Hamilton's first paragraph, which concluded with: "...my ideas of what I hope you will do with it are very definite indeed." That sentence had a do-it-or-else ring.

The suggestions began, "1. Is it important to you to use the pen name Beverly Bunn? We all like Beverly B. Cleary better." This gave me pause. I liked my maiden name because it was a name people remembered. I finally agreed to the change provided the middle initial was dropped, an initial that had been foisted on me by the U.S. Government even though my middle name was Atlee. When I wrote home, Mother was indignant. "Bunn is a fine old pioneer name," she wrote. A number of books later, Elisabeth, as I called Mrs. Hamilton by then, apologized for being so presumptuous.

Mrs. Hamilton also disliked the dog's name and suggested Ribs or Ribsy as sounding more like one a boy would choose. She was right. Why couldn't I have seen that? Then came her most valuable suggestions: "There are several highly dramatic spots in the story, which should be developed better. These incidents are now described very briefly, and the value of the story is partly thrown away." She listed five sentences, all of them easy to expand. And then there was the last chapter. Mrs. Hamilton was blunt: "We don't like the last chapter at all." She went on to say it could be left out altogether; on the other hand, parts were too good to drop. "The circus idea is so threadbare that I would much prefer to have no reference to a circus at all in the story." She was right, and I have recalled this sentence many times over the years whenever I see another circus story or toy. Mrs. Hamilton went on to say I could make the dog's former owner an ordinary person and develop the best parts of the chapter. She closed by saying that the book would probably be priced at $2.00 and they could offer 8 percent on the first 10,000 copies and 10 percent thereafter, with an advance against royalties of $500. If I would agree with the suggestions, she would have a contract drawn up. I was so naïve I hadn't known how many details a contract would cover.

After I had studied Mrs. Hamilton's suggestions, I saw that they actually involved very little work. They were easily made and sent off; a contract and check arrived, as well as a letter saying, "We all think this is going to be one of the exciting publications of the fall." The book was now titled *Henry Huggins*. After all my years of ambition to write, of aiming both consciously and unconsciously toward writing, I had actually written. I was a real live author. I was most grateful to Elisabeth Hamilton for the first instruction in writing fiction I had ever received.

I telephoned the bookstore to tell Sara, who spread the news. Then I told other friends. Everyone was surprised and congratulated me with varying degrees of enthusiasm. One neighbor said, "I think it's just great that you sat quietly at home and cracked that New York crowd. *Now* you can be eccentric." Harvey Fergusson said, "Why don't you quit fooling around with children's books and write for adults? I have a hunch you could write like Katherine Mansfield." Hannah was pleased for me, but she was also indignant because I had not given my manuscript to the Morrow rep to submit for me. "Don't you want to be a feather in his cap?" she asked. No, I didn't want to be a feather in anyone's cap, especially the cap of a man who had so vigorously expressed a dislike for children's books. The rep, the next time he was in Berkeley, said, "Don't go out and buy a yacht, but this book will sell." He did very well by it, and so did Sather Gate because Quail offered it to every customer who came in. She sold five hundred copies during the Christmas rush of 1950. Mother wrote that Dad was proud of me and that she was telephoning everyone with the news. Clarence said he knew all along I could do it.

After keeping the advance royalty check for a few days to admire, I took it to the bank to deposit. As I walked down the winding road, the sky shone blue through the gray-green eucalyptus leaves, but because eucalyptus buds tend to roll underfoot, I watched my step. Half-hidden by a sickle-shaped leaf was a nickel. I picked it up and put it in my pocket, and as I walked, my fingers played with that worn nickel while my mental pump, having been primed by *Henry Huggins,* was at work on a story about a girl named Ellen Tebbits who had trouble hiding her woolen underwear at ballet class.

I was confident that a satisfying life of writing lay ahead, that ideas would continue to flow. As I walked, I thought about all the bits of knowledge about children, reading, and writing that had clung to me like burrs or dandelion fluff all though childhood, college, the Yakima children's room, and the bookstore. As I mulled over my past, I made two resolutions: I would ignore all trends, and I would not let money influence any decisions I would make about my books.

I was so happy, the day was so bright and fragrant, that I did not bother to take the bus at the bottom of the hill but walked on down Euclid Avenue, across the campus, past buildings where I had attended classes, the building that brought painful memories of the English Comprehensive, the library where I had spent so many evenings with Clarence, the Sather Gate Book Shop, to the bank next door. There I deposited the check and one worn nickel for luck.

In my years of writing I have often thought of that nickel and now see it as a talisman of all the good fortune that has come to me: friends, readers, awards, travel, children of my own, financial security that has allowed me to return the generosity extended to me when times were hard for everyone. It was indeed a lucky nickel.

The Writer in the Family
Civics Lessons for Kindred Spirits
Julie Checkoway

ABOUT 12 years ago, when I lived in the Midwest and was studying at the Iowa Writers' Workshop, my friend Carole and I traveled together to hear Maxine Hong Kingston speak at a small Jesuit college on the banks of the upper Mississippi. It was February and gray. The auditorium was peopled largely by nuns in habits and women with blue hair and hardshelled pocketbooks. Had they read *The Woman Warrior* and *China Men?* I wondered as I took my seat. Did they know what they were in for?

Kingston had a new book out—*Tripmaster Monkey*—and she read passages from it. The book was wise and funny, and she was funny and sweet and puckish, her long gray-black hair parted in the middle and tucked behind her ears. Kingston had just returned from China—her first trip there, to visit the village of her ancestors, and she spoke some about that too that day, about how in China she had felt both at home and not at home and how those two feelings seemed just right.

It was my second and last year in graduate school, and I wasn't having a terribly easy time. I had found the workshops brutally cold. In Iowa, I hadn't really felt like much of a writer and hadn't found too many other people who seemed to believe I would ever be one. I was so miserable, in fact, that I had decided to leave the entire United States behind and go to China myself for a couple of years. If you spun the globe around, China was about as far as a person could get from Iowa City.

On that day that I heard Maxine Hong Kingston read from *Tripmaster Monkey* I was a rather desperate soul.

After the others in the room had finished having their copies of *The Woman Warrior* signed, I snuck up to the front, to the dim corner of the stage where Maxine Hong Kingston stood. I breathed deeply and looked her straight in the eye.

She looked back at me with anticipation.

"I'm a writer," I blurted out. "I'm leaving for China soon. Do you have any advice that you could give?"

Maxine Hong Kingston took her hands out of her pockets and put them on her hips. She cocked her head to one side and thought for a moment, then she smiled. She put her hands back in her pockets and said with absolute seriousness:

"Keep your eyes open."

And I got it. I went away happy. I took Maxine Hong Kingston's simple advice to heart.

In China I kept my writer's eyes wide open.

And my first book came from that. An entire book arose from that one moment of straightforward, writerly kindness.

Writing

Lensey Namioka

I WROTE my first book when I was eight, and it was a swash-buckler titled *Princess with a Bamboo Sword*. I illustrated the book, drawing pictures of the heroine wearing a long, flowing traditional Chinese gown held together by a flapping sash. Maybe the book should be described as a "swashsash" or a "sashbuckler." Anyway, it was full of derring-do and sword fights, interspersed with acrobatic kung fu.

You might think that an eight-year-old girl would write about dolls having tea parties with cuddly teddy bears. The fact is, we write what we read, and action stories formed the bulk of my childhood reading. Our house was filled with piles of paperback novels, and their covers always featured a leaping swordsman wearing the traditional Chinese costume of baggy pants and cloth boots. Almost as often, they featured a woman warrior wearing the sort of gown and sash that were in my illustrations.

Who read these books in our family? Chiefly my mother and my elder sisters. My father held to the traditional belief that a gentleman and a scholar wasn't supposed to read fiction. In the old days, an educated man read history, philosophy, and maybe some poetry—of the Tang dynasty. Fiction was written by people who had failed the state examinations and were ineligible to get a job as an official. To make a living with their hard-earned education, many took up the sordid occupation of writing novels. Novels were called *xiao sh uo,* or "small talk," and they were considered a low form of literature read only by womenfolk and servants. If a man was caught buying a novel at a bookstore, he would claim he was buying it for one of his wives or daughters. Today, some of these novels have finally been recognized as masterpieces of Chinese literature, but in the old days men had to read fiction in secret.

One great novel, written in the Ming dynasty, was *Shui Hu,* sometimes translated as "Outlaws of the Marsh." It has delighted readers to this day with its action-packed pages and gave rise to a whole genre of action novels. In the twentieth century, many men finally came out of the closet and began to read novels openly. Among people of my parents' generation, men and women both enjoyed action stories, especially those filled with sword fights and kung fu. My mother and her friends often exchanged piles of these paperback novels, the way kids today exchange comic books.

I grew up surrounded by action novels. In addition to my mother's paperback books, I started to read translations of Western adventure stories, such as *The Three Musketeers* and *Treasure Island.*

Predictably enough, when I started writing fiction my first work was an action novel. *The Princess with the Bamboo Sword* had no sequels, however, and many years passed before I tried to write fiction again. I started seriously writing for children in the early 1970s. My first thought was to write about a band of Chinese outlaws. But the Cultural Revolution was still sweeping through China, and books such as *Outlaws of the Marsh* were banned. I was afraid that if word got out that I had written an action novel about outlaws, my relatives in China could get into real trouble.

I decided to write about a couple of unemployed Japanese samurai instead. Those of you who have seen Japanese television or the movies of directors like Kurosawa know that there is a genre of stories, called *chambara,* about the wandering samurai (the term *chambara* comes from the sound of clashing swords). Our family spent a year in Japan from 1968 to 1969, and during that time I saw my fill of samurai movies and TV programs, with enough sword fights to fill buckets of blood and to send hundreds of severed limbs flying off into space.

My father-in-law encouraged my interest in feudal Japan. My husband's hometown was Himeji, noted for its White Heron Castle, the most beautiful castle in the country still in its original state. I made repeated visits to the castle, learned about its construction, and heard stories about the ghosts that haunted the place. When I eventually started writing novels, my first work was *White Serpent Castle,* and the castle scenes were based on what I had seen at Himeji.

Altogether I've written seven books in the samurai series. When the Cultural Revolution ended in China, I finally decided to writ an action story about a band of outlaws in China. *Phantom of Tiger Mountain* incorporated all the things I loved most in my childhood reading: kung fu, sword fights, humor, pathos, suspense, and horror. Among all my books, it was the easiest to write. It almost wrote itself.

But this book and my samurai series are different in one respect from the Chinese paperback novels and the Japanese *chambara.* My books are mysteries as well. The reason is that in addition to action stories, my youthful reading included a lot of mystery stories. One of my sisters always had her nose in a book about a detective called "Fuermosi." He was an odd look-ing man who wore a funny wool hat and smoked a pipe. But he was very clever at solving mysteries and was always miles ahead of his bumbling doctor friend.

I became addicted to these stories, too. Years later, I discov-ered that "Fuermosi" was the way Fujian people pronounced "Holmes." The first Chinese translator of the Sherlock Holmes stories was a man from Fujian!

Today I'm still a fan of mystery stories, and I belong to the Mystery Writers of America. It's hard to decide which is more fun: reading or writing mysteries.

Actually I hadn't seriously considered writing as a career until rather late in life. It was something that started creeping up on me when I was nearly forty years old. True, I had written *Princess with a Bamboo Sword,* but that was something half-forgotten from my childhood.

Things changed when my daughters were born and I had to find day care for them if I was to continue teaching. We were liv-ing in Ithaca, a small town in upstate New York at the time, and in those days there weren't many reliable day-care centers. For a while we hired nannies for the girls. One was not very good, and a second one was well-intentioned, but absolute putty in the hands of the children.

When the children kept getting sick, I decided to give up teaching and stay home. For a while I worked at translating pa-pers by Chinese mathematicians into English. Then during the Cultural Revolution, mathematical research ceased in China, and the only papers I received were written by academicians beating their breasts and confessing their political sins. Trans-lating these papers was not a rewarding occupation.

About this time, my mother was writing a book about Chi-nese restaurants. She had written a successful Chinese cook-book, and her publisher, Random House, asked her to write a short work on how to order a good meal in a Chinese restau-rant. My eldest sister had translated the cookbook, but she was too busy to work on the present one. Mother asked if I would like to do the translation. It was enjoyable work, and it whetted my appetite for writing.

My next attempts at writing were short articles for a Seattle newspaper on local Asian activities. One of my articles was about Japanese toilets and how to use them. It created a stir, and for a while I achieved some local notoriety and became known as the "Toilet Lady." I wasn't paid much for these articles, but they were fun to write. The first real money I received was for a humorous article I sent to one of the two major Seattle newspapers. It was about squirrels. We had a peach tree in our yard that produced luscious peaches every summer. But before they could ripen, pesky squirrels would come and take bites from the green peaches. Finding the peaches bitter, the squirrels would fling them on the ground. Our lawn would be covered with green peaches, each with a bite taken out of it.

There is a recipe for squirrel stew in our edition of *The Joy of Cooking,* together with an illustration of how to skin the animal. At that time, however, it was illegal in Seattle to kill squirrels. The only thing we could do was to trap them and release them somewhere else. Accordingly we bought a trap, placed a couple of peanuts in it, and set it under our peach tree. It worked! In no time we had an angry, spitting, foulmouthed squirrel inside. We drove the squirrel across the canal and released it on the campus of the university. It was a humane procedure, since hundreds of students would be feeding the little beast.

But the number of squirrels did not decrease and green peaches with bites in them continued to litter our lawn. Finally we found out why. People on the other side of the canal were trapping squirrels and releasing them on our side. All we did by our trapping was to exchange squirrels.

I wrote up the squirrel article, and it was accepted for the tabloid section of the newspaper. I've kept the yellowing pages of the article ever since.

I continued to write articles and started to aim at the magazine market. My next big sale was an article about Japanese castles, which I sold to the magazine *Travel.* It began to seem that a career in writing might be possible after all.

Isaac heartily encouraged me. He said it was through my April Fools' jokes that he first became convinced I had real creativity. When we were graduate students together, I had printed a fake notice that circulated around the math department on April 1, telling everybody that an eminent mathematician was coming to give a talk. The title of the talk was so absurd that I was sure nobody would be fooled for long. I was a little scared when many people took it seriously and made elaborate plans to welcome the famous man.

This didn't prevent me from continuing my April Fools' activities. When Isaac was a visiting scholar at the Institute of Advanced Studies at Princeton, we all received an invitation to the annual banquet from the director, Robert Oppenheimer. The invitation stipulated black tie. Since very few visiting scholars owned a tuxedo, I circulated a fake notice about an E-Z Fit Tuxedo Rental Company. Again, more people than I expected fell for the hoax. I was badly frightened by a letter from Dr. Oppenheimer, asking Isaac to go to the director's office and explain the fake notice. The letter was, of course, another hoax!

Still, I continued my nefarious activities. But gradually, Isaac became my only victim because I was spending most of my time at home. That was why he was so eager for me to exercise my creativity on writing fiction.

As I mentioned earlier, the story about the White Serpent Castle was my first juvenile novel (not counting the one about the princess with the bamboo sword). It was not the first one to be published, however. All the characters in it are Japanese, and I was told that I couldn't hope to sell a book with Asian characters. This was before the interest in multicultural literature.

After falling off a horse, one should get right back on again, and failing to sell a book, one should start another one right away. Therefore I wrote another book about my two Japanese samurai, but this time I was careful to include a Portuguese soldier of fortune called Pedro as one of the main characters. The book was titled *The Samurai and the Long-Nosed Devils*. Pedro was called a long-nosed devil because when the Japanese saw their first Europeans, what struck them the most were the amazingly long noses of the Caucasians.

It's ironical that I had to add a Caucasian character, Pedro, to get my first novel published. Years later, I wrote a science-fiction story, "LAFFF," which featured a girl called Angela. My editor suggested making her Asian American, although there was nothing whatever in the story to require that she should belong to an ethnic minority. After some soul-searching, I finally decided to make the girl Chinese American and added some ethnic touches such as egg rolls and bean sprouts.

There is no question that my writing career received a big boost because of the growing interest in multicultural literature. More and more publishers asked for books about ethnic minority groups, including Asians. I was certainly standing in the right place at the right time.

Before cultural diversity became fashionable, marketing my books was hard. Selling a few newspaper and magazine articles was one thing, selling a full-length book was a different matter altogether. It hadn't occurred to me at first that writing was a craft that had to be learned, like playing a musical instrument. Unless you have a hopelessly bad ear, like Yang the Youngest, you can improve your writing by hard work, namely study and practice.

I learned this vital fact in Seattle through a writing teacher who read my manuscript for *White Serpent Castle*. Very tactfully, she suggested that I attend writing classes. I had taken freshman English in college, but the course was more concerned with great literature than with the nitty-gritty aspects of writing.

By attending my first adult writing course, I found out that, as a writer, I was a beginner. I also had the good fortune to join a support group of writers who read their current work to each other and gave frank but constructive criticism. I owe an immense debt to this group, and I still go to meetings regularly. We call ourselves the Rejects because we get many rejections from editors and from agents, although we are all published writers.

Getting published, in my case, would not have been possible without the help of a literary agent. If you're a beginning writer, it's not easy to find an agent willing to take you as a client. On the advice of my friends, I submitted sample chapters of *The Samurai and the Long-Nosed Devils* to a contest sponsored by the Pacific Northwest Writers Conference. It won a prize in the juvenile division, and on this basis I was able to interest an agent from New York, Patricia Lewis. Within a couple of months, she sold the book to David McKay.

After David McKay bought the book about the long-nosed devils, my agent asked whether I had another book with the same setting and characters. I was able to hand her *White Serpent Castle*, already typed up. Therefore the first novel I wrote was the second one to be published.

I confess that when I wrote *White Serpent Castle*, I had intended it to be a mystery novel for adults. After all, those Chinese books about outlaws and flying swordsmen were enjoyed by young and old alike. Moreover, people of all ages loved mysteries.

But everybody who read my manuscript—family, friends, writing teacher, literary agent—immediately saw it as a book for young people. At first I was a little offended. "You mean my book isn't good enough for grown-ups?" I asked.

The answer is even more unflattering. It took some years for me to accept the fact that my writing is suited to young people because in some ways I have never grown up. I had more fun when I visited Disneyland and Disney World than the children who were there!

Two of my books were written for adults, however. One is *Japan: A Traveler's Companion*, a guide for the foreign tourist in Japan. It took a lot of nerve to write about Japan when I barely mumble enough of the language to get around. Actually, the book developed out of my earlier newspaper article about Japanese toilets. The whole book is from the point of view of a foreigner who faces daunting and embarrassing situations while struggling to get around Japan. There are chapters about inns, trains, food, museums, and, of course, castles. But readers and reviewers still like the toilet chapter best.

My agent sold the book to Vanguard Press, a small independent house which was later bought by Random House. Vanguard wanted me to do another travel book, and I wrote one about traveling in China. This time, it was not from the point of view of a foreigner, but of a native returning after many years. Yes, there is a section on toilets in this book, too.

So far, my writing has been either mystery-adventure stories set in feudal Japan or adult nonfiction. Again, it was Vanguard Press that suggested a juvenile book with a contemporary setting. I wasn't enthusiastic about the idea at first. I preferred flashing swords and eerie castles.

But it was around this time that my daughters were taking advanced math courses, and I began to remember my own experiences in school. I wrote *Who's Hu?* which is about a girl being thought a freak when she likes mathematics. It is also the first of my contemporary books about the experiences of Chinese immigrant families in America.

Over the years, a number of people have helped me to develop as a writer. The Rejects, of course, have had the greatest influence. So did my literary agents. After Pat Lewis died, I tried to manage on my own for a couple of years, but without success. Through a friend, I found another agent, Ruth Cohen. She was the one who suggested more books about Asian Americans, and that led to the series about the Yang family. A couple of my editors worked very hard on transforming me from a storyteller to a novelist.

Many people ask me whether my books are autobiographical. Is Emma Hu, the math whiz, my alter ego? The answer is no, unfortunately. Emma is a much better mathematician than I am, and the book contains some wishful thinking. True, some of the characters in that book are taken from life. Friends of the family immediately recognized Emma's father as my father, but most of the other characters are made up from an arm here and a leg there. Nor do I usually write about real incidents. My books are fictional, and so are the characters. Many of them are outsiders, like myself, but they are not real people.

Some of the books contain themes that are important to me, such as women in mathematics and science. But I don't write books primarily because I have a crusade or a wish to right a social wrong.

I write books because it's fun. There's nothing else I enjoy more.

A Story Rescued from the Ashes

Jim Trelease

NOT all stories are published as soon as they are written, and some take longer to write than others. Robert McCloskey spent a full year writing the 1,142 words in *Make Way for Ducklings*. E. B. White thought about and revised *Stuart Little* for nearly fifteen years. But *Where the Red Fern Grows*, by Wilson Rawls, is the only children's book I know that was completely burned before publication because the author was ashamed of it.

Along with *Call of the Wild*, by Jack London, and *Lassie Come-Home*, by Eric Knight, *Where the Red Fern Grows* is one of the great American dog stories. And like those other books, *Red Fern* is about far more than just a dog. It's about a boy and his overwhelming dream to own a dog. It's about family life in the Ozark Mountains in the early part of this century. And it's about hunting—which means it's about death, too.

But as much as anything, it is about (Woodrow) Wilson Rawls, who said that the book—with one or two exceptions—is his boyhood in dirt-poor Scraper, Oklahoma. There was no school, so Rawls's mother taught her sons and daughters at home as best she could. When the family moved to an area that had schools, "Woody" attended for a few years until the Great Depression struck, and then dropped out in the eighth grade.

But during those years when his mother taught him at home, she'd made a practice of reading to her children. At first young "Woody" wasn't too interested in the books. "I thought all books were about 'Little Red Riding Hood' and 'Chicken Little'—GIRL stories!" he said. "Then one day Mama brought home a book that changed my life. It was a story about a man and a dog—Jack London's *Call of the Wild*. After we finished reading the book, Mama gave it to me. It was my first real treasure and I carried it with me wherever I went and read it every chance I got."

Climbing riverbanks and chasing raccoons through the woods, he began to dream of writing a book like *Call of the Wild*. But being too poor even to buy paper and pencils, he never thought that someday there would be thousands of children who would carry *his* book around as though it were a treasure.

As a teenager, Rawls bounced from place to place working as an itinerant carpenter and handyman. He worked on construction jobs in South America and Canada, and on the Alcan Highway in Alaska. Along the way he began to write stories, but not having had any formal classroom training in spelling and grammar, he could not bring himself to offer them for publication. Each one represented a broken dream and was hidden away in a trunk.

And then, just before he married, and not wanting his new wife, Sophie, to know about his failures, he took the old stories from the trunk and burned them. Eventually his wife learned of the burned manuscripts and asked him to write one of them again. Hesitantly, he rewrote *Where the Red Fern Grows*—35,000 words—in three weeks of nonstop, unpunctuated writing. When he was done, he left the house, unable to witness Sophie's disappointment. Hours later, he telephoned for her opinion. "Woody, this is marvelous. Come home and work on it some more and we'll send it to a publisher," she said. Since Sophie had had a formal education, she polished up Rawls's spelling and grammar, and together they ventured into publishing.

On their first attempt they sold it to the *Saturday Evening Post* (where *Lassie Come-Home* had been serialized twenty years earlier). Editors at Doubleday spotted it and recognized the potential for a book. At first it sold very slowly, and it almost went out of print. But teachers and students began a word-of-mouth publicity campaign about it in the late sixties that boosted sales, and with the arrival of the Bantam paperback edition, it has become a perennial favorite.

from

The Faces of Science Fiction

RAY BRADBURY

I AM one of those fortunate people who were born to be joyful writers and discovered the fact early on. It began to surface when I was eight and fell deeply in love with *Amazing Stories* and *Wonder Stories*. It really burst apart in me when I was twelve and started writing sequels to Edgar Rice Burroughs Martian novels. I have written every single day of my life since then, with no dry spells and no stopping for anything. I am not so much a science fiction writer (which many deny) as I am an Idea Beast. Any idea that nags or bites or waves at me I respond to with a yell and a dash for the typewriter. Large or small, any fancy, notion, concept or revelation is welcome. The History of Ideas as a pageant of dreams fashioning themselves into three dimensional machines, is certainly my quiet madness. Mysteries in abundance surround us. Trying to solve some of them to survive, is the business of all of us writers and the people who jog along ahead of us, the scientists. I have at least ten thousand more days in me, which means a few million more words to go. I can hardly wait to get to them.

from

The Faces of Science Fiction

C. J. CHERRYH

I'M a technologist. My scholastic study was classics/ archaeology, which is a study of how humanity got from picking up a rock to wondering (eventually) how to find a more efficient rock. Humanity tried to find a more efficient way to produce food and other ordinary and extraordinary things; and as often as ancient humanity got bored with mundanity, the band gathered round the fire and told tales about someone finding a more efficient rock/firemaker/sword/ship—whatever. Which inspired someone to dissatisfaction with the rock/firemaker/sword/canoe at hand. And that someone went out and made a better one.

One thing you learn in archaeology is that there weren't any good old days . . . compared to now. With local blips and dips and peaks in the chart of human affairs, the steady trend has been uphill and better. I'd rather live today than thirty years ago or three hundred or three thousand. And I'd rather live in the future than now. I want to get to space. Maybe somebody will take my books where I can't go—that being the nature of books. Somebody took Homer, who wrote one of the first voyage stories—to a new world beyond a sea he never saw; and here- after they'll carry him to Mars and further across a sea he never imagined. It's my ambition first to write a book that will push someone to go where I'll never get the chance to—and second to write a book someone will carry along on a voyage I'd like to have made.

Of course—if someone gives me a shuttle ticket . . .

The Attic: A Family Museum

Susan Power

THE attic in Grandmother Power's home was a world of dust, cobweb curtains, bashful spiders, and family history. In 1973 I was eleven years old and unable to get a good night's sleep in that house. The few times I was alone on the second floor, I had the feeling I was being watched. *Don't be stupid,* I hissed to myself. But moments later I would run downstairs to join the others just the same. Now I think it was the attic that unnerved me. Perhaps I could feel it pressing down on the rest of the house, burdened with the family archives and memories, a museum gone to ruin. My mother, however, was intrigued by the idea of an attic. As a child she had lived in a log cabin, single story, where room was scarce, and no one ever accumulated enough objects to need storage.

"We'll check out the attic tomorrow," Mom told me, the night of our arrival.

The next day as my father settled his ailing mother in a nursing home just a few doors away from her own address, I followed my mother up a narrow flight of stairs. Our hands brushed Oriental rugs that had been rolled so tightly they resembled columns tipped on their sides—they lined the stair railing, wedged between the wooden rail and the wall. Mom and I stepped carefully across the floor, so blanketed by dust it felt as though we were walking through powdery snow. We left tracks. We skirted the stout trunks and leaning stacks of books to stand together in a space free of clutter. We moved in a circle, a dance of confusion.

"Where should we begin," Mom said. It sounded more like a decision than a question. So we set to poking through the contents of as many trunks and boxes as we could reach. With eager hands we unearthed the only stories my mother didn't already know.

"Your father's people sure are pack rats," Mom said, sounding both critical and delighted. I smiled because she had said *Your father's people,* rather than *Your people*—a distinction of some importance to me.

All my life my mother had told me that I was late being born, I really took my time. I think I was just postponing the confusion. Half Yanktonnai Dakota (Sioux) and half white, I tortured myself with the obvious question: Whose side am I on anyway? We lived in Chicago, halfway between my two grandmothers, midway between two worlds. Grandmother Kelly lived on the Standing Rock Sioux Reservation in North Dakota, and Grandmother Power lived in Albany, New York. Grandmother Kelly was three years old when Sitting Bull was killed, and remembered seeing the wagon that brought his body to the agency for burial. Grandmother Power graduated from Smith College and was later invited to join the Daughters of the American Revolution, though she declined. They were never brought together while they were alive, so they could meet only in me.

I felt distinctly Indian as my mother and I toiled in the attic, uncovering old secrets in letters, treasured mementos, faces in tintypes, names in Bibles, unread books. It was all so unfamiliar to us it was completely fascinating.

Among the pages my mother rescued from oblivion was a legal document that recorded the events surrounding the murder of my ancestor John M'Gilmore:

> *From the Plea Roll, in the reign of King Edward II, 1319:*
> *Robert Walsh was indicted at Waterford for killing John, son of Ivor M'Gilmore, and pledged that the said John was Irish, and that it was no felony to kill an Irishman.*
>
> *The King's attorney (John Fitz Robert le Poer) replied that M'Gilmore was an Ostman of Waterford, descended of Gerald M'Gilmore and that all his posterity and kinsmen were entitled to the law of Englishmen by the grant of Henry Fitz Empress, which he (the attorney) produced.*
>
> *And issue being joined, the jury found that on the first invasion of the English, Reginald the Dane, then ruler of Waterford, drew three great iron chains across the river to bar the passage of the King's fleet; but being conquered and taken by the English, he was for this tried and hanged by sentence of the King's court at Waterford with all his officers.*
>
> *They further found that King Henry the Second [who reigned in 1154–1189] banished all the then inhabitants of the town except Gerald M'Gilmore, who joined the English, and dwelt at that time in a tower over against the Church of the Friars.*

Mom chuckled to herself as she read the form. "People are crazy, aren't they? It was no felony to kill an Irishman, so they proved he was an Ostman. Well, we can certainly relate. There have been times when it wasn't a felony to kill an Indian, either."

My mother was mesmerized; she had released a legion of ghosts, a chain of lives. Our faces were smudged and our hair was powdered with dust; we began to perspire as the afternoon heat gathered in the room, although we couldn't be sure it was solely the work of the sun. Together my mother and I had invoked the spirits of my white ancestors—they heard their names spoken aloud for the first time in centuries. And who could blame them for thronging to that cluttered garret, jostling for elbow room and a comfortable perch? Their lonely breath filled the gabled space, leaving us less air to breathe, less room to maneuver. I can smile now at the irony: The Indians were prowling through the attic on a voyage of discovery, exhuming my dead Pilgrim fathers. Several of my ancestors had helped form the original colony in Massachusetts, one of them had signed the Declaration of Independence, a number of them had fought as patriots in the American Revolution, and one crafty collector had diligently acquired the autographs of the main players in the Civil War.

My mother was overwhelmed by the stories and the artifacts; she called out to me again and again: "Come take a look! *This* is your heritage too."

But in the end we were seduced by the memory of a young woman who had not gone to battle, been elected to public office, or founded an institution of higher learning, as had so many of the others. It was late in the day when we came across the plain wooden box that contained her life. Her name was Josephine Parkhurst Gilmore, and she was born on October 8, 1841. She had been taken in as a child by the Parkhursts, who later adopted her when she was eighteen. She lived with her adoptive parents in Newton Centre, Massachusetts; her father was a minister, and she would marry Joseph Henry Gilmore (my great-great-grandfather), pastor of the Baptist Church of Fisherville (now Penacook), New Hampshire. The wooden box contained a packet of letters Josephine had written to her parents and a lock of her red-brown hair—the same dark shade as my own. Later we would find her wedding dress, crumpled inside a paper bag. I think it had been ivory silk trimmed with creamy white lace, but now it was the color of weak tea. We uncovered her tiny matching slippers—the satin covers and ribbon laces were still intact, and the soles unblemished. She must have worn them just the one time. The wedding shoes were so small and narrow my mother and I could barely manage to slip our hands inside them.

My mother studied the letters right there in the attic, beneath the faint light of a single bulb. She read me her favorite passages aloud, and I peered over her shoulder at the magnificent loops of Josephine's artful script.

"I wish I could write like that," I murmured.

Josephine's character seemed to us sunny and fine. She aspired to goodness, and confided to her mother at age seventeen: *Sometimes I can hardly believe that I am indeed a child of God. For when I consider all His benefits and how unmindful I am of them—it seems only just that He should cut me off.*

Josephine was deeply grateful to her parents for taking her in as a small child and raising her as their own. She told them: *I think much of you and dear Father. You don't know how I feel toward you both when I think of all of your kindness for me, my heart is big with gratitude often times when I can't speak. I often shudder when I think of what I might have been if you had not had compassion for me. God will reward you for it. I never can.*

Mom was tickled to learn that Josephine and her husband honeymooned in Niagara Falls, like so many couples after them. Josephine was nineteen years old and "Harry" twenty-seven when they married, and their wedding trip was "glorious":

In the short time I have been here I have got quite tanned up. I have not as yet ascended any of the mountains about here. I don't think I shall feel in any hurry about it—while there is so much to be seen at the foot of them.

Harry, myself and a Mr. and Mrs. Thompson, a very pleasant couple from Boston, went together to the Flume, Pool and Basin. We had a charming excursion—such scenery and such climbing I never saw. We went clear through the Flume as far as we could go and came down outside of it. Then we took a charming walk through the woods, part of the way logs serving us for bridges and after going down a very steep pair of stairs we came to the Pool. I never enjoyed anything more. Everything was so wild, so grand and so wonderful. Everything said as plain as could be said: Behold the works of God.

There was a great old man at the Pool who paddled us about in his boat. He is quite a philosopher in his way, and contends that the earth is hollow and has a map to explain to people his theory. Some wicked wag who knew the old man's eccentricities wrote a letter purporting to be from Queen Victoria and sent it to him—the most ridiculous letter it is that ever was seen, but he takes it for truth and has

*facsimile copies of it for sale. I'll send you pretty soon. The
original he keeps in a glass case.*

I laughed at the mention of the elderly gentleman and his grand
theory, but my mother said, "I wish we had that letter." He was
clearly the sort of person she would enjoy meeting. Mom gasped
as she read the paragraph a few lines farther down: *General
Peirce and Hawthorne, the author of "Marble Faun," have been
here. Harry seemed to be quite a pet with them. They wanted him
to go fishing with them, so he went early this morning.*
   "That's Nathaniel Hawthorne she's talking about!" Mom told
me. "And he considered your great-great-grandfather a pet."
   It was hard for me to imagine the stern, bewhiskered Joseph
Henry Gilmore I had seen in photographs as anything but a
solemn cleric, though there were indications of poetry in his blood,
for he penned the lyrics to my favorite hymn, "He Leadeth Me."
   During the next year my great-great-grandparents traveled extensively, and in her letters Josephine described trips to Brooklyn and Philadelphia. She was greatly impressed with the Liberty
Bell. In all her travels Josephine's parents were never far from
her thoughts. From Philadelphia she wrote: *Evening finds me in
Mr. Watson's office to write just a little to my dear ones at home. I
have been showing your daguerrotypes to the Watsons today and
I shouldn't want to tell you the compliments which were paid you.
I would like so much to see the dear originals tonight. I hope you
are well and happy. I think of you many times a day.*
   Finally, in 1862, Josephine was home in New Hampshire for
a time. My mother's voice softened as she read a letter from this
period: *I wish you could look out of my window for a few minutes
and see the clouds come sailing up the north. Yesterday I went on
a delightful jaunt to see some cattails—on the way I picked and
had picked for me over fifty Indian pipe flowers which are very
rare. Then I picked a lot of myrtle, wild myrtle; it is like ours only
more graceful, and with these I trimmed my hair and Aunt
Nancy's. I have my hair trimmed with one thing and another,
every night. I wish you might have seen the leaves I had the other
night—maple they were—some of them were a deep green with
red spots and stripes in them, others pure red, etc., beautifully
turned by the frost. There are quantities of beautiful things here
to dress my hair with—if one will look for them.*
   The attic was growing dark and I was suddenly weary of my
great-great-grandmother's reasonable voice. *Was she never per-
snickety?* I wondered. *Was she never cross?*

"Listen to this," Mom said, laughing. With great relief I heard the following censure: *Sallie Smith and I hardly speak to each other now. She snubbed me in the most pointed manner when I first came, until she found I was getting more attention paid me than she was, but then it was too late and I had had enough of her ways, and I just avoid her. I treat her politely, but no more. She is generally disliked and no wonder; her "stuckupishness" don't go down with anyone. She is a great hypocrite and a mischief maker.* Josephine Parkhurst Gilmore wasn't perfect after all. This was an ancestor I could accept as family.

Shortly before leaving my grandmother's attic Mom reached the last letters at the bottom of the box. They had been written in 1863. We quickly learned that Josephine was pregnant and her baby due at the end of September. In August she caught a cold she couldn't shake, and the girl begged her mother to come for a visit: *In addition to my cold I have the old complaint that summer brings. Of course I am weak, very. I try to keep up good courage and I haven't fairly broken down yet, but it is hard work. I have sent a telegram to father this morning and Lucy is still in Concord waiting for an answer to it. The Browns are all at home now. So you may feel safe about me I shall have good care.*

I wish you could be with me my last month. I think I need you as much then as at the time, and perhaps more. I don't seem to have any heart to take hold and get things ready. I may feel differently when I get better though. It would be so nice to have you here to arrange with me.

Two days later she mailed another entreaty:

I don't want to alarm you but I feel as if I must have you with me. I wanted to send for you but felt as if it would be perhaps foolish to do so, but Mrs. John Brown thinks I ought to. She has been with me all the afternoon rubbing and bathing me and wants me to send for the doctor but I had rather not, but I will send for you. Harry can't get back before the last of next week and with worrying about him and feeling really sick from this heavy cold, I don't feel safe to be alone. I can't sleep nights and really I am miserable and at this time I think I am not safe in being alone. Now won't you please come up and stay this week with me? I will pay your expenses very willingly. Won't you come up on the early train Tuesday?

At any rate I shall look forward to your being with me and that will help me to feel a little better. Father will be willing I know under the circumstances to let you come. I am not in

*the habit of complaining, you know, and I would not send
for you now if I could get along without you. I have taken to
my bed this afternoon—I have tried to sit up until I have lost
all backbone. I am so sorry this cold should come just now.
Now don't disappoint your daughter.*

"Why doesn't she go?!" I wailed, caught up in the drama. "It
wasn't that far, was it?"

"No," Mom answered. "Just Boston to New Hampshire,
though it took a lot longer to get around in those days." Perhaps
she noticed my distress, for she patted my hand. "I would be
there in a second."

Mary Parkhurst did make the journey, it turned out, though
she stayed for only a few days. In her final letter Josephine
again urged her mother to visit:

September 6, 1863

My dear mother,

*I wish you could be with me today I am not feeling well at
all and as Aunt Maria has not yet returned, I am a bit lonely
while Harry is at church. I have managed to take a little
more cold and I am so stiff and sore that I can hardly get up
or down. I am getting very clumsy anyway—It seems as if I
could hardly wait three weeks longer, I want you to be on
hand early, Mother.*

*My room isn't put in order yet for the reason the stove
man has been away and so I couldn't have the stove set. I
thought it best to make only one job of it.*

*Harry was in Boston last week. He was obliged to go to
his cousin Fred's funeral. He went down in the early train
Friday and back in the early train Saturday. He had no time
to go to see father. What do you think he brought me home?
A basket of delicious fruit, pears, plums, and grapes. They
were luscious.*

*It seemed like old times at Newton. When I used to be ill,
don't you know how very thoughtful he always was. If our
lives are only spared what a happy family ours will be after
the little one comes. I do pray that God may grant to us a
dear little child and good health.*

*Mrs. John Brown has been in today to see me. She seems
to take a great interest in me. I think a good deal of her
judgement—she has had experience you know.*

I will write you again next week, but am too tired to pro-

*long this epistle. Come up as soon as you can. With a great
deal of love to father and yourself.*

*I am, your daughter,
Josie Gilmore*

*There are two or three plants I want you to buy for me to
bring up with you; a mahunia, a white camilia what they
call candidissima and a plant called colisium ivy. Father can
buy these in Boston you know, and you can bring them up
with you, can't you? They will of course all be small plants.
Goodbye again. Love to the Smiths when you see them.*

On September 9, Josephine gave birth to Joseph Henry
Gilmore, Jr., and on September 11, she died.

My mother and I huddled together in the attic, two more
shadows lost in the disorder. Mom returned the letters and the
lock of hair to the heavy box. We folded the brittle wedding
dress as gently as we could, smoothing a century of wrinkles.

"Her little boy must have kept these things so he could feel
close to the mother he never knew," Mom said. "He was your
Daddy's grandfather, and Daddy worshiped him. He was gentle
and mischievous, and loved your father."

When Mom and I left the hushed attic it was as if we had returned to life, the way I have felt on emerging from church into
afternoon light. We rescued the family papers and the stories
they contained, and we still tell them to one another, though my
mother tells them best. We know what happened to "Harry" and
his son, and for us it is like looking into the future. Two years
after Josephine died, Joseph Henry Gilmore married Miss Lucy
Brown, who had been a dear friend of Josephine's, and one of
her nurses at the end. She was a good mother to Josephine's
child and gave him five siblings.

My grandmother died three months after Mom and I explored
her attic, and the house was sold. It has been twenty-two years
since the last visit.

My mother is proud of her Dakota forebears and the Sioux
Nation she comes from, but she has encouraged me to find both
sides of myself, and so, undiminished, I have become whole.

"You gave me a great gift," I should tell my mother the next
time I telephone. But it is hard for me to say these things.

My mother and I visited Josephine Parkhurst Gilmore's grave

at the start of my sophomore year in college. I remember I was bored and a little irritated as we wandered through the old section of the Newton Cemetery. I was anxious to meet a new roommate and wanted the school year to begin; I couldn't be bothered with ancestral spirits who were lonesome for company.

"She is here somewhere," my mother told me. "Concentrate."

I don't know why we didn't go through proper channels, why we didn't visit an office and ask for a map of the burial plots—there must have been records. But we conducted this search on our own, without benefit of bureaucracy, and I felt a little like a skeptic handling a dousing stick. I squinted at the worn gravestones, following a path my mother suggested, and just minutes after we stepped from the car I found Josephine settled between her parents.

"Over here," I called to my mother a little gruffly. It had all worked out just as she'd promised. I had found my relative so easily because she longed to be discovered and remembered. But I couldn't stand for my mother to be right.

"It's just a coincidence," I mumbled.

"Just think, you've found her," Mom whispered. "Josephine Parkhurst Gilmore, this is your great-great-granddaughter." My mother made the introductions and I probably squirmed a little, peeked over my shoulder to be certain we were alone, unobserved. I was poor company.

Mom cried a little. "It's the Irish in me," she teased, and she brushed a hand across the face of Josephine's marker. "Let's find a stone to remind us of this place." We uncovered a flat triangular rock and Mom wrapped it in Kleenex tissue.

I know my mother must have told Josephine that I was a sophomore at Harvard, because it wouldn't be rude to brag to another relative. Surely she mentioned we were Indian, Dakotas, and wondered what Josephine would make of that. She could have lectured the girl, telling her that on September 3, 1863—just three days before Josephine Parkhurst Gilmore penned her last letter—the peaceful village of my great-great-grandfather Chief Two Bear had been attacked by Generals Sibley and Sully, and our Yanktonnai band nearly wiped out.

My mother has described the scene so vividly I sometimes think she must have been there, urging the dogs to run swiftly from the slaughter, dragging babies strapped to miniature travois behind them. Her nostrils quiver when she tells me that the soldiers burned the camp and the winter stores of food, and

I know she can smell the fragrance of that wasted buffalo meat and taste the melting tallow.

But all my mother said to Josephine was "I hope your mother was there at the end. I know you weren't alone, but your husband or a friend wouldn't be the same comfort, would they? There are times when only a mother will do."

Yes, I can tell her now, *there are times.* I can agree because I am older. I finished college and then law school and then a writing program. I wrote a book. After all this education I have finally learned that I will never know as much as my mother. I stand happily in her shadow, no longer annoyed by her faith and imagination. I ask her to repeat the stories. I strain to hear her voice.

And the next time my mother visits me in Cambridge, Massachusetts, I will suggest we return to the Newton Cemetery. We will wander through the old section, patiently searching for the young lady we visited once before. This time I will be more polite, ready with presents I offer my great-great-grandmother, who is now twelve years my junior.

"Mom, look," I will whisper as I unwrap the papers. The wild myrtle is a brilliant blue—it should look fine twisted in the intricate crown of Josephine's brown hair; the white camellias are soft, snowy, and will cover her slight figure like a blanket of lace.

The Workroom, or, There are Other Tools Besides the Hammer

James Finn Garner

IT wasn't until I owned my own house—and spent countless hours ripping down plaster, installing conduit, painting trim, and generally correcting the insults and injuries inflicted on the building by its previous owners—that I began to realize what keen observers of the human condition the Three Stooges were. The way we hurt those we are most trying to help, the chaos and destruction that lurk beneath the surface of our interactions, the yearning for the grail in our fruitless attempts at inventing spotted paint—anything profound I might have had to say about the difficulties of striving to maintain a livable space for myself and my young family had already been expressed far more eloquently by a trio of short and extremely homely ex-vaudevillians.

Nevertheless, since, as Nietzsche said, "That which does not kill us gives us something to brag about at barbecues," I soon became pretty flip with home improvement advice for anyone unlucky enough to be around. It seemed only equitable that those wishing to be initiated into the ranks of the home owner should have to make as many mistakes and sift through as much misinformation as I did. Adding the modifiers "flange," "toggle," or "grommet" to any recognizable hardware word would quickly send inexperienced or passingly knowledgeable fixer uppers into retreat. Combining all three—thus creating the "flange toggle grommet"—was the trump, to be used only against those climbers who had purchased much bigger houses than mine.

A few months after our own purchase, my older brother Patrick and his wife bought their first home, a big lovely house of the Arts and Crafts school. Since their home still reflected a recognizable style, any work they had to do would need more care; our house was of old yet indeterminable style, so all we needed to do to receive compliments was keep the cracks in the plaster patched and refrain from painting in Day Glo colors. With thirty years of apartment living between us, Pat and I both faced the ominous revelation that we and we alone were responsible for fixing our own plumbing, and that certain now-indispensable tools were just too big to fit in the kitchen drawer. After much commiseration, my brother and I fixed on a solution independently, yet almost simultaneously: our problems would be over if we could only build a big workbench like our father's.

The irony of this panacea would be lost to everyone but my family and our old neighbors. My father was as adept at household repairs as a seagull at snooker. For Pat and me to invoke his spirit by building a workbench would be like taking singing lessons to emulate William Shatner. But we were each bound and determined to erect an elaborate workbench—complete with a vice, a pegboard wall, and little screwdriver wells—to pattern ourselves after our father, who, left on his own, would have had a devil of a time assembling a functional breadboard.

While our father was not in any way good or ambitious in the area of home improvement, he did enjoy the use of the workroom in our house as his *sanctum sanctorum*. Almost every man I've ever met has expressed the need and desire for a similar locale in his life, a place where he can work or not work at his own pace, somewhere to pursue doomed experiments and wrong ideas, someplace where his failures would not be on public display—indeed, where such efforts would not be failures at all. So utterly convinced of his ineptitude around the house, my father really didn't spend an inordinate amount of time down in the workroom. That might have led to home repair ambitions, which in turn would have led to projects, which probably would have led to some failures, which I don't think he would have allowed himself to have. He did, however, have his space.

Even with its lack of use, my memories of the workroom are as strong or stronger than for any other room in our home. A trip to the workroom was a mainly sensory experience; the sounds, the smells, and even the light seem so specific to that time and place. The activities I remember most in the room were my father soaking his paintbrushes in turpentine-filled orange-juice containers within arm's length of our old furnace, and cleaning his nails with an ivory-handled steak knife of unknown origin. And always, always with a Winston in his mouth. It would be nice if I could describe the hours of worldly wisdom that passed from father to son in patient exchanges and Platonic dialogue—what our more dithery era has christened bonding. It would have been nice, had it ever happened. My father was almost pathologically tight-lipped, and my brothers and I had to absorb what lessons we could from example and, in the home repair realm, from non-example.

My family lived in a simple brick postwar Georgian, boasting nothing elaborate or eccentric in its layout. The workroom was merely the corner of the basement taken up partially by the water heater and the massive old furnace, set apart by an L-shaped wall of then-ubiquitous knotty pine paneling, heavily lacquered to a spotty orange-chestnut hue. The room was thus consigned to the corner both physically and symbolically. Had we lived in an older house—well, that's moot. There's no chance we ever would have lived in an older house. Too many things could go wrong that would need fixing.

The door to the workroom was one of those swinging saloon-type doors, misaligned just perfectly so that its every use created a three-and-a-half-beat signature sound —*bada . . . bada . . . bada . . . ba*—that could be heard throughout the house. If you were dainty with this door, you would invariably catch your fingers in it, so the best course of action (especially for young, role-playing boys) was to burst through it like Jack Palance with a bug up his chaps. The only light fixture in the room also made a unique and definitive sound. A bulb with a metal shade suspended from the ceiling, the light had a chain pull that would recoil when yanked and elicit a skittery, sustained Oriental *dang* from the metal shade, announcing your presence in the room like a gong.

Although prone to strange and sometimes silly outbursts that were apropos of nothing ("Ya-ha, San Antone!" was not uncommon), my father was a taciturn man. One of the few aphorisms I can remember from him was "When you're talking, you ain't thinking," a not-so-subtle hint that conversation was an annoyance unless and until someone had something important to say. He could be intense at times, such as when he was problem-solving, but he worked hard at keeping a placid facade even when something was eating him up inside. His job, which he kept almost entirely apart from his home life except for the toll it took on his nerves and heart, was to borrow money on the commercial paper market, where a brief lapse in attention on competing interest rates can cost thousands. (I didn't understand this until I met the man who succeeded my father in his position. This man, who was in his thirties, told me he wouldn't be able to do the job more than four years before burning out; my father did it for sixteen.) This mental intensity did not serve Dad well in the role of Mr. Fix-it. Tiny mistakes grew and nagged at his sense of order and his need for tranquillity. If something couldn't be done perfectly, it wasn't worth doing at all.

If you side with the genetic proponents of the Nature vs. Nurture debate, you might find my father blameless in his workshop ineptitude, a victim of duff-handed determinism. According to my mother, my paternal grandfather was, if anything, worse around a tool than my father. In the late 1940s, Grandpa invested in the type of freestanding power tools that make most men salivate: a huge table saw, a jigsaw, and a lathe, each immensely heavy, in the dimpled olive green and chrome deco style of the Sears Craftsman variety. With all these impressive embodiments of American industrial might at his command, the only item Grandpa ever produced was the core of a toilet paper holder. My eldest brother, Tom, has since sold these behemoths to a tool collector, the type of man who loves to spend hours cleaning, fixing, and oiling old machines that either have been used within microns of their useful life or stand as mute testimony to unfulfilled mechanical ambition. What weird individuals these types must be.

Although I never knew him, in an abstract way Grandpa's lack of skill sometimes surprises me more than my father's. Often people from impoverished backgrounds are so frugal that throwing money away at a repairman is considered almost as bad as discarding a ham bone without first making soup. In 1910, with the proverbial dime in his pocket, my father's father arrived in Montreal with his sister and brother, hard and undersized children of a deceased greengrocer from Liverpool. Perhaps, along with his accent and any false nostalgia for Old Blighty, he chose to discard any reminders of his cruel and dirt-poor background, including working with his hands.

The tool with which my father was most proficient (if I might be so generous as to use the word) was the hammer. This might reflect his pronounced tunnel vision and his ability to cut right to the main thrust of any problem. The hammer is a quintessential and versatile tool. Maybe any job that needed an implement more complicated was best left to specialists. This attitude persisted despite the well-intentioned advice of neighbors. Shortly after we moved into our house, our neighbor Mr. Weier visited and offered in all sincerity the sage advice, "You know, there are other tools besides the hammer." If there were, my father wasn't interested.

When I was very young, Dad put together a few projects for my brothers, which consisted mainly of large sheets of uncut plywood. Nail some two-by-fours around the perimeter of a piece of plywood, add a bit of green and brown paint, and the result was a landscape for a train set. Attach three tall sheets of plywood together with hinges like a triptych, cut out a medium-sized hole in the middle sheet, add a small curtain—ta-da, a puppet theater! (As the youngest, I guess I was expected to inherit these things, because I don't remember any large-scale project intended for me. Then again, I can count on the fingers of one hand the large-scale projects ever attempted during my youth.) At some point, my father erected three stalls at the foot of the basement stairs for our coats, along with cubby holes for our Frisbees and baseball mitts; we greeted this accomplishment with loud huzzahs. This miraculous construction was on a par with the erection of a tree fort with swimming pool.

During my grade school years, my father did something that allowed him to expand his manual non-dexterity in new and untested areas: he invested in a boat, first an old, blunt-nosed Matthews cabin cruiser with much too much wood to varnish, and later a slightly bigger Egg Harbor. When these two boats had been built, fiberglass was still an exotic element. Their wooden hulls and teak decks were in need of constant work, a race against their inevitable mortality that my father could never win. At this time the smells that I will always associate with our workroom were introduced—varnish, hull paint, Mr. Thinzit, and Cuprinol. And cigarettes, always cigarettes. These ineradicable odors permeated and formed an olfactory link between the workroom, the boat, and my father's no-frills, putty-beige Ford Maverick. And also his horrifically paint-splattered Top-Siders, which my mother could never persuade him to toss out.

I don't know whether my father bought the boats to get away from the worries of work or the worries of the house, or neither. He got his main relaxation from the nautical lifestyle on Friday nights, when he would sit on the back deck with a Stroh's in his hand, staring upriver at the seven smokestacks of the Edison plant, and think grand thoughts. (At least, I thought they were grand—they were certainly elaborate and beyond my comprehension at the time. Asking an open-ended question at times like these would trigger an inundation of fact and opinion that would make me wish I'd taken his example and figured it out for myself.)

By Saturday, the aggravations of the physical world would reappear. General maintenance, such as scrubbing the teak deck, was ongoing. The big engines would regularly break down during the course of the summer, giving Dad another lesson in humility in the face of mechanical demands. Leaning into the big hatches in the deck, he would sweat and strain with the monstrous creations, using words he would never use in any other situation. His hammer had by this time been replaced by a monkey wrench. The increased variety of striking surfaces the wrench offered might have been seen as an improvement on the hammer, but the banging was as ineffectual as ever. Invariably a neighboring boat owner would come by, or a mechanic from the marina across the river would motor over, and with a few deft moves solve the insoluble and fix the unfixable. Dad would stand by, eager to learn and almost completely untrainable. After a dozen years of this, the transom of the boat was almost completely gone from dry rot, and Dad decided it was time to be rid of such "relaxation." His own health was also beginning to break down at this time.

When I was a teenager, the workroom saw even less use than it had in previous years. Still, it was the only place to finish certain messy projects with paint and putty. Whenever I was down there, in memory it seems like I could always find a Tigers game on the radio. The radio of choice in the workroom was one of those round, "mod" cheapos from Panasonic, with the dimensions of a ruby grapefruit and nearly the sound quality. (Our basement was a radio graveyard—at least half a dozen were scattered around, in various states of workability, all sounding atrocious.) Next to the white round radio on the workbench sat another essential spherical accoutrement, my father's eight-ball ashtray—nine or ten inches tall, rusty, malignant, uncaring, and immovable.

In my freshman year of high school, the workroom was witness to the most elaborate science fair experiment anyone in my family had ever attempted. I hated science fairs vehemently, both bored and intimidated by the subject matter and its challenge to my academic record. However, I managed to find an experiment in a library book that actually intrigued me. Over the strenuous objections of my mother, I bought six newly weaned white mice, paired them off in separate small glass habitats, and fed them diets of varying quality to see how it would affect their growth as they matured. Not surprisingly, the two that were fed nothing but sugar and bacon grease were small, jumpy, and inclined to bite your fingers when touched (not unlike myself in those years, I now realize). I won a ribbon in the city-wide competition that year, and sold my exhibit to a classmate's sister for her own use later. The valiant mice, their lives already dedicated to science and the education of young minds, became lunch for the boa constrictor in a local third-grade classroom. The next year, to protest mandatory participation in science fairs, I prepared an elaborate display describing in detail the scientific principles of embalming and related funerary practices. It didn't win a ribbon.

My hometown owes its current size and prosperity to that workshop putterer par excellence, Henry Ford, whose very name strikes fear and awe into the hearts of the world's mechanically disinclined. What these people may not realize is, when Ford built his first workable horseless carriage, he failed to take into account the width of his garage door. Undaunted, he took a hammer and knocked away the bricks on either side of the portal so he could drive out. Shades of Larry, Moe, and Curly.

One of Ford's many side projects was assembling an enclave of historic buildings, in which the preeminent tinkerers and mechanical whiz kids of American industrial history had clocked some hours. Over time it became a tourist destination called Greenfield Village. My mother and my brother Patrick worked there seasonally, and one year my mother convinced the head of the crafts department that I was good with my hands, her sole evidence being a precut pine bookshelf that I had pieced together and secured with a dozen finishing nails. So I was hired for the summer, and one cold rainy day in May I was assigned to work in a one-room cooper shop built in 1795. In addition to two hundred years of grime and a fireplace in which a half-dozen people could stand comfortably, it boasted three rough but phenomenally well-used workbenches.

I was cursorily educated in the art of barrel-making (or at least the remedial cooperring done by apprentices) by a patient and affable man in his seventies who could demonstrate many of the other crafts around, such as tinsmithing and leatherwork, with admirable skill. While he had the gait and demeanor of someone who'd been a handyman all his life, I found out later he had been involved in groundbreaking statistical work that was used in the creation of the UNIVAC. Carving water buckets and butter churns out of warped, grainy hemlock planks entirely by hand was not the easiest thing I had ever done. On the other hand, it was not something that the average tourist knew anything about. So with a little flair and misdirection, I could easily take attention away from my slip-ups with the draw knives (except of course when I drew blood). My numerous mistakes didn't cause anyone any grief, and were usually burnt as tinder in some other exhibit. My successes were used to decorate my work area, and were occasionally taken away for sale. The tourists rarely pointed out what I was doing wrong—they could scarcely understand what I was doing anyway, or why—and my bosses just wanted me to stay chatty and informed. Thus, flying in the face of my genetic inheritance, I finally taught myself to enjoy puttering around a workbench, experimenting and exploring for the fun of it. Suddenly my manual mistakes no longer seemed life-threatening or divinely predetermined. During the winter holidays, I was hired back, to make wooden toys and carve baby rattles on a foot-powered lathe once owned by Thomas Edison.

Many times I would drive after work, covered in sawdust and linseed oil, to pick up my father at the world headquarters of the company Ford had founded so many decades earlier. It somehow felt very grown-up to do this, a "two men on their way home after a hard day's work in the salt mines" kind of feeling. It's not like we ever talked about anything profound. I'd complain about the ridiculous questions the tourists would ask ("For years I've heard of 'the old oaken bucket'—what did they make those out of, anyway?"). Dad would just mock my exasperation and say, "You tell 'em, Jimbo, you tell 'em!" I felt like an adult because the gap between what we needed to know about each other's passions and our ability to communicate was widening. I knew it would continue to grow before it had any hope of narrowing.

Dad had already had at least one heart attack by this point, and was supposed to be easing up on his workload. He was still putting in eight-hour days, though, and more than likely was still feeling too much stress. After his second heart attack, he more or less was confined to home. At this time of life, many men take to their workrooms and begin to create furniture, fix old engines, or rehab their homes or garages. Of course, this was not an option in our home. With his time now his own, Dad channeled his energies in an entirely unexpected direction.

For years, the only attention my father had given to plant life was a few treatments of Milorganite on the lawn in the spring. After his heart had effectively retired him, he began to work earnestly to turn our small backyard into an elaborate, even overstocked garden. At the same time, his workbench was retired too, and transformed into a sort of makeshift greenhouse. Rows and rows of flower seedlings incubated there in the winter and spring under the grow lights, cozy next to the furnace in their little cups filled with peat. The smells of paint and solvent in the workroom began to fade, but never disappeared.

Dad poured himself into that garden and was, I think, very gratified with how well it did in such a short time. Phlox, impatiens, lilies, and petunias now spilled forth from among the stalwart, low-maintenance evergreens, and by summer's end the backyard was a carnival of color. A few plantings might have failed to take, but these were nothing compared with the teeming beauty he was now adept at bringing forth.

"Why are you bothering to grow these things?" I would tease him. "What good are they? You can't eat any of them."

"Add a little beauty to the world, Jimbo," he would intone in his characteristic way, as if calling to me from across a chasm, "add a little beauty to the world."

Dad used to wear a wide straw hat when he worked in the garden, to protect his Anglo-Irish skin from the sun. Whenever he wore it, I called him "Brother Orchid," after an old gangster movie in which Edward G. Robinson went on the lam and hid in a monastery, where he learned to till the most glorious gardens. Although he never said so, I think Dad liked it when I called him this—he was the kind of guy who liked to use a lot of nicknames.

My father got to enjoy his new garden for only a couple of summers before his heart rebelled one last and irrevocable time. Among so many other things he has since missed, he never got to visit the many ramshackle apartments I've lived in, and was never able to offer advice to me or my brothers when we bought our first houses. It's probably only a coincidence, but my brothers and I all have fathers-in-law who are incredibly adept around a workroom. I often wonder how my dad would get along with my wife's father, Dave, an ebullient and inquisitive man who is as given to superlatives as my father was to silence. I'm next to positive that a great deal of goodwill would ignite in the spark between these two opposites, but I know that the Saturday morning work detail (which is now compulsory around our house, ever since I married into good Calvinist stock) would be a trial. For one thing, Dave's workbench is too well organized and complete, and for another thing, it gets used.

It is now a standing family joke that my brothers and I inherited, along with his high forehead, double chin, and intractable stubbornness, my father's ten thumbs. This generalization persists despite growing evidence to the contrary. Tom has done a good job around his houses, although he seems predisposed to new construction, and Pat has practically gutted the second and third floors of his house (of course, putting it back together is another proposition entirely). I myself have torn apart about three quarters of our house in the past two years, although the help of others—including my wife's cousin, who is currently building his own house without the aid of blueprints—has been indispensable. Our current house has a small workroom—basically just the area under our back porch, walled off, uninsulated and unfinished. Only a very imaginative real estate agent would describe it as a workroom. I have yet to build the big workbench I've dreamed of.

My wife's father would object to the generalizations about my ineptitude as a handyman. He is, however, the soul of charity. When my in-laws visit on the weekends, Dave always brings along work clothes, and I prepare for my next tutorial. He and I agree that you have to be willing to make some mistakes if you want to become a good handyman. And believe me, I can make mistakes as quickly as anybody, then ponder them intensely while I wait for the proper time (and assistance) to solve them. But what the hey, it's my house. If home means anything, it's a place where you're allowed to make mistakes. I think this is the lesson that always eluded my father.

The legacies my brothers and I received are so numerous and pervasive that my inadequacies in the workroom have never bothered me. Of course, these legacies become more apparent with age, as does my acceptance of them. My niece Hannah Rose now sleeps in the crib that my father assembled for his sons. It unmistakably belongs to our family. My mother only has to point to the side of the crib and explain, "That's when your dad threw the little felt washers across the room and just tried to force the pieces to fit."

There in the blond wood, you can clearly see the crescent marks left by the impatient hammer of my father.

The Garage

Gish Jen

THAT which was our garage is now our luau room. We've taken two walls out of it. We've put in brick arches of the pizza oven type, only larger. There is also a bluestone floor; and the problem ivy that used to grow up our neighbor's wall, under our rafters, and into the garage is no longer a problem. Now it is a feature. An ivy cascade! It could be right out of Martha Stewart—a perfect backdrop for a buffet table laden with pineapple boats and cornball drinks. In short, our garage has become the kind of space in which resorts used to set up their theme cookouts, and when I think of mortality, and our short moment on earth, and what it means to seize the day, I realize that I will not die truly happy until we have had a pig roast there, with coconut bowling out on the lawn.

We are awaiting an appropriate occasion. A wedding? A baby shower? It has only been six months since the luau room came into our lives, but we are impatient. Luckily, we have other activities to pursue in the luau room. Crafts, for instance. (My husband, Dave, and I have a preschooler, Luke.) We want to do papier-mâché volcanoes, egg carton igloos. We want to picnic out there in the warm weather, and for the cold weather we have bought (for half price) a Lillian Vernon inflatable ice-skating rink; add schmaltzy music and we can have winter wonderland parties. The luau room is also a good space for other parties: for Luke's third birthday we had a Russian puppeteer perform under the ivy cascade, and while this was not the same as having a luau, it was nonetheless great fun. (We had box juice instead of tacki-tacki drinks, and a cake with an excavator on it.)

Is the luau room actually a gazebo? It depends, I suppose, on whether a gazebo can have a storage shed across the back and be partly made of cinderblock. An architect friend says it's a folly, and that seems closer to the truth, except that the essential nature of follies has always seemed to me ornamental. This seems to be a folly crossed with a multipurpose room—multipurpose room being the name of a certain (multipurpose) room in the elementary school I transferred into in fifth grade. (This was Greenacres Elementary, in Scarsdale, New York.) How up-to-date that name seemed then!—and how much it epitomized the difference between my ex-school and my new school. My ex-school was St. Eugene's in Yonkers, New York—a Catholic school in a working-class neighborhood where a small class had forty kids in it, and some classes had sixty. Every room was a classroom except the bathroom. We played out in the parking lot, and for a jungle gym we had the steps leading up to an all-weather Virgin Mary. I seem to remember some metal handrails, too, and of course there was the chain-link fence. Our new school, on the other hand, had swings! A library! Overhead projectors! And of all things, a multipurpose room. From the school's point of view, this was probably an overbooked space expected to accommodate way too many needs. But from my point of view, it was an extra room; and this was an unimaginable thing. An extra room! In a school!

I am still thinking about it, thirty years later. Thirty years later, the proud owner of a garage turned luau room, I am still thinking about extra rooms, and undesignated space. What does the presence of such space say to us? In some places, it says that there may be important human activities that do not easily fit into conventionally planned space; that the community can afford unnecessary activities; and that these activities are even to be encouraged. In other places, it says simply that there is surplus space, who knows why; in others still, that this place does not matter to society, that nobody cares enough to claim it.

Do these distinctions matter, necessarily, to the imagination? In my new fifth-grade world, there was this amazing multipurpose room, with sliders and partitions—a consciously flexible space, a legitimate space. But in my old world, we had, behind our old house, just beyond the brave row of knee-high hemlocks that formed our someday-to-be-a-hedge, a large stretch of woods. There were gargantuan rocks there, with deep holes that filled with water, and one of my earliest memories is of reaching into one of those holes and discovering that the water had mysteriously turned to ice. I can still remember the shape of the hole, how cylindrical it was; and that all around me was a brilliant fall day, nowhere near winter yet. I remember that there were two other holes, both of which merely held cold water. But in that one hole there was ice; and I remember that I poked at that ice and felt it resist me, as solid a thing as the rock around it. I remember that a patch of light fell on the hole and on the surrounding rock, and that I found that patch inexplicably satisfying. I remember that on the way home there was a big daytime moon.

Did I learn anything from that? About ice? About the rock? About the moon? As usual, I learned nothing. I am a child of immigrants, which is to say a child of busy parents. There was no one to explain things to me; no one got out the encyclopedia and looked up this or that. I am a person who learned things eventually—who, not knowing any better, quite enjoyed learning nothing in particular. About ice; about the hand- and footholds on Elephant Rock; about where mushrooms sprang up, and how it felt to sit on a rotted log. I talked to myself a lot out in the woods, and there is no question in my mind that that was the beginning of becoming a writer for me; that I began, not by having a role model, or by being encouraged to read and write, or by being given a typewriter, but by wandering around, unsupervised, to no purpose.

How to Beat The Wheel of Fortune

William J. Ryan

IT is estimated that 42 million people have watched the Wheel of Fortune during one show. People from all walks of life are fascinated by the puzzles on the board. They love to try to solve the puzzles, *before* the contestants do.

Have you ever wondered how some people can solve the puzzles early while others have difficulty solving one puzzle during a show? Some people count the letters in the words, and in the whole puzzle. Some look for certain letters to appear and try to guess what other lettters go with those, while other people look for a rhythm in the puzzle. Some people look for some kind of a pattern in the words. They count the number of letters in each word. Rather than trying to solve the word pattern, they try to get a mental picture of the solution to the puzzle. Sometimes they do, but this is rare. Of course, this is the ultimate solution, solving the puzzle with the fewest clues, or none at all. Some of these methods work, but not consistently. The only consistent method for solving the puzzles is to know the word patterns on the board. That is what this book is all about.

You can't memorize the word lists, nor the places, events, and quotations. A book of quotations would contain thousands of quotes. So, the easiest method to use if you want to solve the puzzles is to know the basic word patterns. Watch for them on the board, fill in the missing letters to the pattern you know, and you will have all the clues you need to solve the puzzle.

The patterns follow definite rules for the position of each consonant and vowel. For example, this phrase appeared on the board,

Just for
the fun
of it

There are four basic word patterns in this phrase that follow definite rules. They are the VC (of, it), CCV (The), CVC (For, fun), and CVCC (Just) word patterns.

This "thing" also appeared on the board,

Plate   glass
window

There are two basic words in this phrase that follow the rules of the five letter one syllable word pattern; the CCVCV pattern (plate) and the CCVCC pattern (glass). Along with these patterns there are five other five letter one syllable word patterns which we will examine.

Note the double consonant **ss** at the end of the pattern *glass.* With the exception of a few three letter word patterns, there are only three common double consonants that will appear at the *end* of the words on the board. They are the **SS, FF,** and **LL** double consonants. We will examine the rules for these patterns.

Note the word *window* in the puzzle. The multisyllable words are composed of syllables that basically follow the rules of the one syllable word patterns which we will examine. In the word *window,* **win** and **dow** follow the most basic pattern in our language, the CVC word pattern.

This phrase also appeared on the board,

May   I
make   a
suggestion

There are four basic word patterns in this phrase that follow definite rules. They are the CVV pattern (May), where the letter **y** is a vowel, in one of the several uses of the letter **y** as we'll see. The single letter pattern (only two, **a** and **I**) and how to tell when the pattern is **I** or **a.** The common four letter CVCV pattern (make) which always ends with the vowel **e,** and the double consonant pattern (suggestion) which must be preceded by a vowel. (There are six basic four letter one syllable word patterns which we will examine).

Have you wondered why the vowel **e** is the most common vowel (in fact, the most common letter)? Besides the patterns that have the vowel **e** at the beginning or middle of a word, there are six basic word patterns with hundreds of words, as we'll see, that end with the vowel **e.** Ironically, every vowel **e** in those patterns is not sounded. It's silent.

So, if it's a single letter word or a multisyllable word, if you look for the patterns, you can solve the puzzles.

This book will give you the rules for all of the basic word patterns in our language, board examples for the patterns, and complete common word lists so that you can solve the puzzles on The Wheel of Fortune.

Any history of the English language will trace the development of our language from the Latin and Greek languages, and modified by the Anglo-Saxons and Jutes. It went through the periods of the Old English and Middle English and finally into its present form. The roots, prefixes and suffixes had been established. The archaic words were replaced, and common spellings were stabilized. More importantly, the word patterns, the positioning of consonants and vowels, had been established. This is the key to solving the words. The positioning of the consonants and vowels tells you what the word patterns are. It is these patterns that you need to know to solve the puzzles on The Wheel of Fortune.

Of course, since our language is a living language, it is still evolving. When new words enter the language (such as hippie, lotto, yuppy) the basic word patterns do not change. The new words fit into the existing patterns.

As you know the English language contains 26 letters of which 21 are consonants and 5 are vowels. The positioning of the consonants and vowels is the key to solving the words on The Wheel of Fortune. This positioning sets up the word patterns which follow very definite rules. Instead of guessing at the words, if you follow the rules presented in this book, you will solve the word patterns and the puzzles on the board. This book will also give you actual board examples showing you step by step how to solve the patterns. The puzzles comprise these word patterns simply because that is how we communicate. We don't use the 80,000 or more words that make up our language. In our daily communication we use more like several hundreds of words. The puzzles on The Wheel of Fortune verify this. If the puzzles were made up of physics problems, only physicists would watch the show.

So watch for the clues to the patterns. This book will show you the word patterns you will need. It will show you where and how to find the clues to these patterns, which will help you solve the words and the puzzles on the board.

Remember this last paragraph when you get to the end of this book.

Science

Death of a Hornet

Robert Finch

FOR the past half hour I have been watching a remarkable encounter between a spider and a yellow hornet, in which I was an unwitting catalyst. I have found several of these hornets in my study recently, buzzing and beating themselves against the glass doors and windows, having crawled out, I presume, from the cracks between the still-unplastered sheets of rock lath on the ceiling. Usually I have managed to coax them out the door with a piece of paper or a book, but this morning my mind was abstracted with innumerable small tasks, so when another one of these large insects appeared, buzzing violently like a yellow and black column of electricity slowly sizzling up the window pane above my desk, I rather absentmindedly whacked it with a rolled-up bus schedule until it fell, maimed but still alive, onto the windowsill.

My sill is cluttered with natural objects and apparatus used for studying and keeping insects and other forms of local wildlife—various small jars, a microscope box, a dissecting kit, an ancient phoebe's nest that was once built on our front-door light, an aquarium pump, pieces of coral and seaweed, etc.—none of which has been used for several months. They now serve largely as an eclectic substrate for several large, messy spider webs.

In one corner is a rather large, irregular, three-dimensional web occupying a good quarter-cubic-foot of space. It was into this web that the stricken hornet fell, catching about halfway down into the loose mesh and drawing out from her reclusiveness in the corner a nondescript brownish house spider with a body about three-eighths of an inch long. The hornet hung, tail down, twirling tenuously from a single web-thread, while its barred yellow abdomen throbbed and jabbed repeatedly in instinctive attack. The motion could not really be called defensive, as the hornet was surely too far gone to recover, but it was as if it was determined to inflict whatever injury it could on whatever might approach it in its dying. Defense, in insects as in us, it seems, is not founded on the ability to survive but on the resolution to keep from forgiving as long as possible.

The spider rushed out along her strands to investigate the commotion and stopped about an inch short of this enormous creature, three or four times her own size, with what seemed a kind of "Oh, Lord, why me?" attitude, the stance of a fisherman who suddenly realizes he has hooked a wounded shark on his flounder line. Whether or not her momentary hesitation reflected any such human emotion, the spider immediately set out to secure her oversized prey. After making a few tentative feints toward the hornet and apparently seeing that it could do no more than ineffectually thrust its stinger back and forth, she approached more deliberately, made a complete circuit around the hanging beast, and suddenly latched onto it at its "neck."

At this point I went and got a magnifying glass and stationed myself to observe more closely. The spider did indeed seem to be fastening repeatedly onto the thin connection between the hornet's head and thorax—a spot, I theorized, that might be more easily injected with the spider's paralyzing venom.

While she remained attached, all motion in the spider's legs and body ceased, adding to the impression that some intense, concealed activity was taking place at the juncture. If so, it proved effective, for within a very few minutes almost all throbbing in the hornet's abdomen had stopped, and only the flickering of its rear legs indicated that any life remained.

During this process, the spider's movements were still very cautious, but also somehow gentle, never violent or awkward as my whacking had been, but almost as solicitous, as if ministering to the stricken hornet, as carefully and as gently as possible ending its struggles and its agony. Her graceful arched legs looked, through the glass, like miniature, transparent, bent soda straws, with dark spots of pigment at the joints.

At this point the spider seemed to have made the hornet hers—her object, her possession—and her movements became more confident, proprietary, almost perfunctory in contrast. She no longer seemed aware of the hornet as something apart from her, foreign to the web, but rather as a part of it now, ready to be assimilated. She now appeared to begin dancing around the paralyzed insect, her rear legs moving rapidly and rhythmically in a throwing motion towards the object in the center. I did not see any silk coming out of her abdomen, and her legs did not actually appear to touch the spinnerets there, but gradually a light film of webbing, like a thin, foggy sheen, became visible around the hornet's mid-section.

She would spin for several seconds, then climb an inch or two and attach a strand to a piece of webbing overhead. I thought at first that she was merely securing the hornet from its rather unstable attachment, but after she had done this a few times, I saw that, with each climb upward, the hornet itself also moved a small fraction of an inch up and to the side.

It was soon clear that the spider was maneuvering this enormous insect in a very definite and deliberate manner, using her spun cables like a system of block and tackle, hoisting and moving her prey through the seemingly random network of spun silk.

In between these bouts of spinning and hoisting, the spider occasionally stopped and again approached the hornet, now totally motionless and with one of its darkly veined wings bound to its barred side. She would place herself head down (the usual position for a spider in a web when not spinning) just above the hornet's head and, again becoming totally motionless, as if in some paralysis of ecstasy, seemed to attach her mouth parts to those of her prey's, as though engaged in some long, drawn-out death kiss. The two insects would remain attached so for ten to fifteen seconds at a time, after which the spider would again resume her hoisting and fastening. Was this some further injection of venom taking place, or was she beginning to suck the juices from the wasp's still-living body even as she was moving it somewhere? I was struck, mesmerized, by this alternation of intimate, motionless contact of prey and predator, and the businesslike, bustling manipulation of an inert object by its possessor.

All in all, the spider has moved the hornet about two inches to the side and one inch upward from the point where it landed, out of the center portion of the web and nearer the window frame, where now she crouches motionless behind it, perhaps using it to conceal herself while waiting for another prey. I pull myself away from the corner and put down the magnifying glass, feeling strangely drained from having been drawn in so strongly to watch such concentrated activity and dispassionate energy. There is something about spiders that no insect possesses, that makes it seem right that they are not true insects but belong to a more ancient order of being. I like them in my home, but they will not bear too close watching.

I look back at the window corner and see that the characters of the drama are still there, once more in miniature tableau. All is quiet again; the spider remains crouched behind its mummified prey, in that waiting game that spiders have perfected, where memory and hope play no part. There is only the stillness of an eternal present and the silent architecture of perfectly strung possibilities.

from

A Book of Bees. . . and How to Keep Them

Sue Hubbell

IN early springtime, the bees' need for pollen may be greater than what is available, and then they will compulsively gather up almost any fine granular material—sawdust, bits of plastic packing material, ashes—whether it is useful to them or not. I often see them at the bird feeder, picking through the wild bird feed. At that time of year, I often get a telephone call from a dairy farmer who lives near one of my beeyards.

"Hey, Sue," he says. "How about coming over and feeding your bees? They're in the calf feed again."

He's always a little embarrassed. The first time he called me, years ago, was on a day in autumn. There were, he insisted, bees flying all around the inside of his milking shed. He didn't want to spray them with insecticide, but he was going to have to do that unless I could lure them out.

It sounded like an odd way for bees to behave, but I drove over to his place. There they were, golden-striped fuzzy insects flying around inside his barn, darting here and there. They looked like bees, but they didn't act like bees, so I captured one in my hand. The creature did not sting me as a honeybee would have done and on close scrutiny its beelike appearance disappeared. Moreover, the insect had only a single pair of wings, not two sets, as a bee has. The two wings, a single pair, puts any insect into the zoological order Diptera (which means two-winged), the order of flies. Honeybees belong to the order Hymenoptera (or membrane-winged), which includes not only all the bees but also wasps, ants and other similar insects.

I wasn't sure which flies these were in the milk barn, because I don't know much about Diptera, but I knew that there were a number of fly species that mimic bees in appearance. I showed the farmer the single pair of wings and told him that this and the others in the air were flies, not bees. He was interested, and asked more questions than I could answer. When I got home, I photocopied as much information about bee-mimicking flies as I could find on my bookshelves and sent it to him. Now when he calls he always makes sure that the insect about which he is lodging a complaint is indeed a honeybee.

The first time he found bees in his calf feed he was worried that they were after the calves, and might sting and frighten them. I assured him that the bees were not the least concerned with the calves but were looking for the pollen they needed as food in the springtime. As soon as some pollen-bearing flower bloomed, I told him, the bees would disappear from the calf feed, but in the meantime I'd try giving them a pollen substitute that might satisfy them.

Beekeeping-supply companies sell a commercial pollen substitute made of a combination of protein-rich materials such as soy flour and brewers' yeast. This powder can be mixed with honey to make into patties, which can be squished down between the top bars on the frames of the upper hive bodies. Many beekeepers recommend the feeding of pollen substitute as a regular routine, and for a number of years I made up patties and fed them to all my hives. In some parts of the country where there is not a dependable source of pollen this may be a good practice, but I have concluded that it is not worth the expense or time here in the Ozarks. Bees prefer the real thing—fresh pollen—and although a day or two in these hills may pass when they can't find any, something usually bursts into bloom and they scorn the substitute, leaving it to molder inside the hives. So I stopped feeding pollen substitute, and find that productivity of my hives is no poorer for doing so. Indeed, the per-hive yield of honey from my bees has grown greater in what appears to be a direct relationship to the decrease in the number of times I open the hives. The less I disrupt and fiddle with the bees, the more they can concentrate on making honey.

Now when the dairy farmer calls, more as a public-relations gesture than anything else, I go to the health-food store and buy fifty-nine cents' worth of soy flour, take it over to the hives near his place, lift off the outer cover of each hive and sprinkle some of it on the inner cover. I did that a few days ago, and today I stopped by his place to give him a jar of honey as a recompense for the nuisance my bees had caused him.

I asked if the bees had stopped coming to the calf feed.

"Yep. They've left. Thank you kindly for feeding them."

"No trouble. Thank you for calling me and letting me know. I don't like the bees to be a bother to you."

Then I drove over to the hives and lifted up the telescoping covers. The soy flour stood unused on the inner covers, and I shook it off on the grass. The bees had not wanted it. Flowers have begun to bloom somewhere, and the bees, their rear legs wadded with golden pollen, are flying into the hives so heavily loaded they find it hard to stay airborne.

The farmer is happy. The calves are happy. The bees are happy.

I sit down beside the end hive and watch the bees flying in with their loads of pollen, which will assure the development of the thousands of young bees needed to gather nectar and make honey in the months to come.

The sun is shining on my back as I watch, and I can feel its warmth. The air is fragrant. There are flowers in bloom everywhere today.

And I am happy.

Trap-door Spiders

Paul Hillyard

DR. WILLIS GERTSCH of Arizona called the trap-door spiders the Houdinis of the spider world—"One moment you see it, the next it is gone." Trap-door spiders live underground in finely constructed tunnels that they excavate with their jaws. The burrows, from a few inches to more than a foot deep, are usually silklined and spacious enough to allow the spider to turn around. Many have a tight-fitting door that blends perfectly with the surface of the ground. Often all that can be seen is a hairlike crescent shape on the surface. When the spider feels the vibration of a passing insect, it lifts the door, rushes out, grabs the prey, and returns to its burrow . . . to perform its disappearing trick.

Trap-door spiders are found throughout the hotter regions of the world. Their lifetime of several years is a solitary one but the burrow is a haven protected from heat and rain. They are classified in a number of spider families, of which the best known is Ctenizidae.

The American trap-door spider, *Bothriocyrtum californicum,* builds a thick, heavy door, made up of alternating layers of soil and silk, which fits in the opening like a cork in a bottle. When disturbed, the spider tenaciously holds the door down with its claws and fangs, bracing its legs against the side of the burrow. Even with the aid of a knife, a person has great difficulty in forcing it open. The strength of the spider was measured by Walker van Riper of the Colorado Museum. He drilled two holes in the door, passed a loop of string through them and measured the pull with a spring scale. A force of 14 ounces was indicated. As the spider weighs about .1 ounce, the force is 140 times the spider's own weight. For a 150-pound man the equivalent would be over 10 tons. However, the spider can keep this up for only a short time, so to make doubly sure, during the hottest part of the year when parasitic wasps are most active, the trap-door may be fastened shut and sealed with extra silk.

Many years ago, on the French Riviera around Menton, the same habits of construction and defense were observed among the local trap-door spiders by the arachnologist J. Traherne Moggridge, who was a friend of the zoologists and arachnologists

Henry Bates, Alfred Russel Wallace, Octavius Pickard-Cambridge, and Eugène Simon. Moggridge opened our eyes to the architectural skill of these spiders in his classic work *Harvesting Ants and Trap-door Spiders* (1873). Its observations are original and its illustrations are delightful.

Moggridge distinguished two basic kinds of nests: the "cork nest," with a thick door, and the "wafer nest," with a thin, flexible door. He discovered that many nests are not just simple tunnels. Sometimes there is a second door leading to a side shaft. If an intruder enters, such as a centipede, the spider retreats to the branch tunnel and slams the door shut. In Australia, Dr. Barbara Main has discovered that the trap-door spider *Dekana diversicolor* builds an unusual escape route, a second hole on the surface loosely capped with sticks and stones through which it can easily push if threatened.

Moggridge was fascinated by the ingenuity of trap-door spiders, but he lamented the fact that field naturalists had made much less progress than "cabinet naturalists" (those working on classification). The following is an extract from his book:

When at Hyères on the 11th of May, 1873, the evening being very warm and a bright moon shining, I went with my father and sister to see what the spiders would be doing on a hedge bank where we had previously marked five cork and eight wafer nests. The moonlight did not fall upon this spot, but I was provided with a lantern, and by its light the nests at first appeared to be tightly closed, but we soon perceived first one and then another with the door slightly raised, ready to close on the smallest alarm, whether from a footfall or from the flickering of the lamp. On either side of the raised door of one of the wafer nests I could see the feet of the spider projecting, and just at that moment I caught sight of a beetle close at hand, feeding on the topmost spray of some small plant below. I contrived to gather the spray without shaking off the beetle, and gradually pushed it nearer and nearer to the nest. When it almost touched the lip of the nest the door flew open, and the spider snatched at the beetle and dragged it down below.

For a few seconds the door remained tightly closed, and then, to our great surprise, was suddenly opened again, and the distasteful beetle was cast alive and unharmed out of the nest.

Remarkable Jumpers

Paul Hillyard

JUMPING spiders (family Salticidae) are daytime hunters. Their takeoff thrust comes from the last two pairs of legs while the first two reach out ahead for the landing. Jumps are mostly over short distances but can be up to twenty times the spider's length. The so-called flying spider of Australia *(Saitis volans)* has winglike extensions along the body that enable it to glide during leaps.

Jumping spiders have sufficient visual awareness to be able to turn and look at a person who looks at them. They can also see in color—their pretty markings are displayed during courtship. Two of their eight eyes, the central front pair, are large and can recognize objects. Despite the small size of most jumping spiders, the central eyes are based on long tubes that work like miniature telephoto systems.

Having detected movement with the other eyes, a jumping spider turns to bring its central eyes to bear on the object. A jumper stalks its prey slowly, like a cat. The prey consists of insects such as flies, but also other spiders. When sufficiently close, the spider lowers its body, fastens a dragline to the surface, and then leaps onto the prey. But the spider does not necessarily approach in a straight line. It may detour and temporarily lose sight of the quarry. In fact, detouring suggests a remarkable problem-solving ability for a spider. ("Why did the fly fly?" asked the old English riddle. Perhaps it was not realized how correct the answer was: "Because the spider spied her.")

Jumping spiders also have the honor of holding the spider world altitude record. Major Hingston collected in the 1920s a number of specimens at 22,000 feet on Mount Everest. Two species were named many years later by Fred Wanless as *Euophrys everestensis* and *Euophrys omnisuperstes*. According to Hingston:

> There was no sign of any other small creature at 22,000 feet; at this altitude all kinds of plant life had been left behind thousands of feet below. Finding the spiders by turning over stones was a great labor, partly on account of the exhaustion experienced at this altitude and partly because the stones were all frozen to the ground.

Since that initial discovery, it has been found that these *Euophrys* species feed on tiny creatures that are part of a food chain based on plant material blown up from lower altitudes. Most of the 4,400 species of jumping spiders live in the tropics; the family is highly diversified. One of the most extraordinary species is *Portia fimbriata* of tropical Australia. Because of its wide repertoire of hunting tactics it seems to be the cleverest of all spiders. *Portia* hunts in many different ways, including invading the webs of other spiders—which is most unusual. Typically, hunting spiders move with great difficulty in webs, and webbuilding spiders are ill at ease in the webs of other kinds. But not *Portia*—it can move about and capture prey in all sorts of webs. It can even spin its own web, which is also irregular for a jumping spider. Sometimes *Portia* builds its web adjacent to another spider so that when the neighbor follows an insect in hot pursuit across *Portia's* web, it can be attacked.

Portia is not pretty or colorful; in its cryptic posture it has a very curious, hunched appearance that looks nothing like a normal spider. In a web it is easily mistaken for a piece of rubbish; when walking it makes slow, jerky movements. But *Portia's* jumps are quite impressive. The female measures about half an inch and can jump directly upward as much as four to six inches. Upon landing, *Portia* either freezes or runs about four inches and then freezes. When invading the webs of other spiders, *Portia* makes vibrations to deceive the occupant. If it comes out expecting an insect, *Portia* leaps onto it. When bitten, the victim usually runs some distance but becomes paralyzed after ten to thirty seconds. Sometimes, however, the host becomes alarmed by the strange vibes and hastily decamps.

When stalking normal jumping spiders, a particularly strange posture is adopted by *Portia,* one that is not used when pursuing a fly. Researchers Jackson and Hallas found that the jumping spider quarry did not recognize the slowly approaching *Portia* as another salticid, or any sort of potential predator, or even as another animal.

Predation by spiders on other species of spiders is a dangerous occupation but *Portia* has a secret weapon; its exceptional vision. It can distinguish mates and prey at distances of up to 10 inches, a 3-inch advantage over other jumpers. Not only is *Portia* the sharpest-eyed of all spiders, but also, according to M. F. Land, its optical resolution is superior to all other terrestrial invertebrates, most of which have compound eyes. *Portia's* principal eyes are of the simple type and comparable with our

own, but what is most remarkable is the tiny space they occupy. The size of the retinal receptors are close to the theoreti-
cal minimum, given the physical properties of light.

Keeping an Insect Zoo

Edwin Way Teale

ONE of the best ways of becoming acquainted with many six-legged creatures is to keep them in an insect zoo. A number, including most of the fiddlers in the night orchestra, thrive in captivity. Compared with rabbits and other animal pets, insects eat little and occupy only a small space. Several of them will live indoors far into the autumn and winter.

If you are located in a part of the country where the praying mantis is found, start your zoo with it. It does not even require a cage. Place it on a house plant or curtain and it will cling, oftentimes in one place, for hours. In a wild state, the mantis eats nothing but living prey. Indoors, I have found I could feed my captives on bits of meat, such as corned beef or hamburg steak, offered at the end of a toothpick or a pair of tweezers. The insect grasps its food in its forelegs and devours it like a boy eating an ear of corn.

If you provide a cage for your praying mantises, you can place grasshoppers, crickets and other living insects inside. In the course of time, they will be captured and eaten by the carnivorous mantises. Like the black cricket, the mantis is cannibalistic. So don't put big and small mantises in the same cage. When I did that once, I found, at the end of an hour, a little pile of wings and legs, all that remained of a medium-sized inmate of the cage. Besides its diet of meat, give a captive mantis water to drink each day. Sprinkle the wire of the cage so it is covered with "dew" morning and night and the mantis will get sufficient moisture.

In the fall, collect the female mantises and place them on twigs stuck in jars of water or in wet sand so they will keep fresh. If you have half a dozen or so of the females, you are likely to see one or more make the curious froth ball which solidifies and protects the eggs of the insect over the winter. The process takes from one to three hours and is a sight you will never forget. Once, one of my captive mantises made her egg case on a windowsill just above a radiator. The heat hastened the hatching so the young insects appeared exactly on the first day of winter, December 21st.

Another curious insect that eats nothing but living prey when it is in its wild state is the ant lion, or doodlebug. Also, like the mantis, it can be kept without any special cage. All that is needed is a box or pan of fine sand. The ant lions will dig tiny round depressions in the sand, tossing the material out with explosive jerks of their heads. Then, hidden at the bottom, they wait for some ant to slide down into the pit they have dug. With long pincer-jaws, they grab the luckless insect and begin at once to devour it. By placing a few ants in the dirt-box, you can feed your doodlebug captives. Almost any sandy stretch will provide you with ant lions for your zoo. With a scoop of your hand, dig under one of their depressions and you will bring the doodlebug to the surface. Once, I saw one of these gray, flat, little creatures almost fall prey to another of its kind. In sidling over the sand in search of a place to dig its pit, it fell into the depression of another ant lion which promptly tried to eat it.

For your katydids, walking sticks, grasshoppers and other large insects, you can construct a satisfactory cage by tacking wire screen to a simple framework, about two feet wide, three feet long and two feet high. This will give you room for a number of insects that feed on leaves and not on each other. The top should be hinged or removable. Inside, you can have leafy twigs stuck in sand which is kept damp, or in jars containing water. Be sure to get the same kind of twigs as those on which you found the inmates of the cage. Katydids seem to favor the leaves of cherry, oak, maple and apple trees. But they can be kept happy on a diet of lettuce and fruit. Grasshoppers like fresh grass, clover and almost any kind of fruit. Most grasshoppers are particularly fond of fresh corn silk. Walking sticks, like katydids, should be given the leaves of the trees or bushes on which they are found. Leaves and more leaves form their diet.

Crickets are easy to keep if a few simple rules are observed. The big black cricket you catch in the fields will eat both meat and vegetables. It is always well to add a bit of meat or bone meal from time to time to the regular rations of lettuce, fruit, moistened bread, and, what they enjoy especially, bits of melon. If you do not feed your crickets meat occasionally, they will take matters into their own hands and begin devouring each other.

A simple cricket cage which will enable you to see everything that takes place inside can be made by combining a lantern chimney and a flowerpot. Fill the pot with dirt and place a twig in a jar of water which is embedded in the center. Then put the lantern globe in place, pushing it down into the dirt. Place your captives inside and cover the top of the chimney with a bit of mosquito netting, held in place by means of a rubber band. The netting can be removed when food and water are given the crickets and the chimney can be pulled out of the dirt when twigs are changed.

Among the beetles, there are many which you can keep in your zoo. Some will thrive in a lantern-chimney cage such as has been described. An even better home for captive beetles consists of a flat block of plaster of Paris containing two hollowed-out depressions, a large one and a small one. The small one is filled with water which gradually seeps through to the large one in which the beetles live, thus keeping it in a moist condition. A pane of glass placed over the top of the plaster block will keep the beetles from escaping and will permit you to see all that takes place inside.

One of the most interesting corners of your insect zoo probably will be made up not of insects but of "worms." The caterpillars of various moths and butterflies are easy to keep and they provide an exciting show in several acts. You will see them grow and shed their skins; you will see them make their amazing change into cocoons and chrysalises; and finally, you will see them appear transformed into beautiful creatures of the air.

The larva should get sunlight and plenty of fresh leaves of its favorite tree or plant. Note where you find each caterpillar and supply it with the same sort of leaves. In looking for butterfly caterpillars, the following tips may help you. Look for Tiger Swallowtail caterpillars on wild cherry; Cabbage butterfly caterpillars on cabbage; Black Swallowtail caterpillars on carrots, parsley and wild ginger; Thistle butterfly caterpillars on burdock; Monarch caterpillars on milkweed; Viceroy caterpillars on poplar and willow; Buckeye caterpillars on plantain and snapdragon; Clouded Sulphur caterpillars on clover; Red Admiral caterpillars on hops and nettles; and the little American Copper caterpillars on sorrel.

Among the moth larvae, some of the favored foods are: Luna: walnut, hickory, sweet gum and persimmon. Cecropia: willow, maple, lilac. Polyphemus: oak and birch. Ailanthus: wild cherry, lilac, ailanthus, linden. Promethea: wild cherry. Darling Underwing: willow, poplar.

You can use lantern-globe cages for your caterpillars or you can make a larger cage by pasting mosquito netting across the top of a shoe box. Or you can produce a cheap "community wormery" by tacking wire screen over a soapbox. Without any indoor cage at all, you can raise caterpillars on the trees where they are naturally found by doing what is known as "sleeving" a branch. Slip a cylinder of mosquito netting over the branch and tie it tight at both ends. Within this net, the caterpillar lives a natural life with abundant fresh food. If the larva is one that pupates in the ground, you will have to extend the sleeve to a flowerpot filled with earth in which the larva can make its chrysalis. Incidentally, it is a good idea to have some pots or boxes of dirt in your caterpillar cages. Some of the captives may be larvae that descend into the ground for their change into chrysalises, instead of making their cocoons on twigs or forming the chrysalises on the tree or plant on which they feed.

When you place twigs in jars of water within cages for caterpillars to feed on, be sure to stuff cotton batting or rags around the top of the container holding the water. Otherwise, the caterpillars may crawl down and get drowned. Instead of water or wet sand, you can sometimes use potatoes to keep twigs fresh for a considerable time. Stick the end of the twig into the potato. It provides moisture and a base for the twig at the same time. Because larvae use only very small amounts of air, you can sometimes keep their food fresh by enclosing both leaves and larva in a Mason jar with the lid tightly screwed in place. This prevents evaporation and so keeps the leaves juicy and green.

Most caterpillars are like kittens. They do not thrive if handled too much. Also, many have sharp spines which discourage people from handling them. The best way of transferring a caterpillar, both for you and the larva, is to carry it on a twig or by means of an old discarded tablespoon. When several of your "worms" have changed into chrysalises, it is a good idea to remove the remaining caterpillars to another cage. Sometimes, when food runs low, caterpillars will begin gnawing on the chrysalises if they are left in the same place.

If you keep a "logbook" of the occurrences in your insect zoo, it will increase your sport greatly. Put down the date and the hour when you see, for example, eggs being laid, when they hatch out, when the molting, pupation and emergence of the adult occur. The more notes you have, the more interesting things you will learn. Just as it has been discovered that butterflies emerge frequently before a thunderstorm; that mantis egg cases hatch out most often between eight and nine in the morning; that the speed of ants is governed by the heat of the day; so you may discover interesting facts by watching the inmates of your insect zoo and keeping a "log" of the things you see.

Silver Ants Sup When the Temperature's Up

Whit Gibbons and Anne R. Gibbons

WHEN the sun rises above the Sahara, most animals head for shelter, usually underground. Each day, however, a few insects and other invertebrates die because they fail to escape the rays of the rising sun. This is not an unusual phenomenon in nature; animals die all the time, and other animals eat them. Enter the silver ant. Like many other ants, these are scavengers that feed on the carcasses of invertebrates. But a big difference between silver ants and other ants is their sense of timing. Silver ants forage during a hot part of the day. In fact, whereas other ants disappear from the surface before temperatures in the summer reach 113°F, silver ants do not even leave their burrows until surface temperatures are above 115°F. Such extreme temperatures would be lethal for most animals.

One ecological question is, why do silver ants feed only at such blisteringly high temperatures? Why not *start* foraging when temperatures are a little cooler? An earlier start would allow more time to find food. Ridiger Wehner and Sibylle Wehner of the University of Zurich and A. C. Marsh of the University of Namibia investigated factors that restrict the foraging activities of the silver ants.

The highest temperature that individuals can withstand and still recover from behaviorally and physiologically is called the critical thermal maximum of a species. Silver ants hold the record, enduring temperatures on the floor of the Sahara that are above those recorded for any other terrestrial animal. Few land dwellers, which can ordinarily escape thermal extremes by retreating beneath the surface, can survive when body temperatures rise much above 100°F. But silver ants discontinue foraging when their body temperature approaches 128°F!

Because silver ants get a late start in the morning, waiting until surface temperatures are already too hot for most animals, their foraging time is limited to only a short period each day. By observing the daily life of ants and other organisms on the desert floor, the investigators discovered the answer to why silver ants restrict their foraging time. Silver ants begin their search for food at a time of day when another animal stops. By being on the surface only at midday, silver ants avoid predation by a particular species of desert lizard. Although the lizard can withstand fairly high temperatures itself, it retreats from the surface when the surface temperature reaches about 115°F—the temperature at which silver ants become active. The behavior of the ant-eating lizard has apparently shaped the ant's behavior by defining the lower limit of a thermal window within which the ant can safely forage. The upper thermal limits of silver ant activity are set by potential heat stress. The sands heat fast in the Sahara, and even a silver ant can get too hot.

How do ants in the colony know when it is hot enough for the lizards to be gone and, therefore, safe for them to leave the burrow? The researchers observed that each day a few ants were active on the surface around the entrance of the colony, apparently monitoring the temperature. When a suitable surface temperature was reached, those on the surface signaled those in the burrow, triggering the emergence of the silver ants. As is commonly known, social insects such as ants and bees have remarkable abilities to communicate. Silver ants may use secretions from glands in the head to deliver the message. Silver ants stake their lives on attaining the critical temperature that signals the disappearance of the lizards. Once the message to emerge is received, all the ants surface at once and swarm over the desert floor in the vicinity of their nest in a speedy effort to find food. Their foraging time is short, they return to the burrow within minutes to avoid the fast-rising desert temperatures. Although the threat of the lizard predator diminishes with a rise in temperature, the threat of heat stress in the Sahara increases.

Swims With Frogs

Roger B. Swain

THE best approach to frogs is on their own level. Leave the meadow its milkweed and August asters, and instead belly up to the pond's bank in an inner tube. Half submerged, legs spread, arms dangling, you can scan the shore—the sedges, the ferns, the colonizing alders—and count each pair of bulging eyes. Where the sphagnum moss curls down over the pond's lip is where the bullfrogs crouch, looking like fat, clenched fists.

It is futile to stalk them on foot; they'll jump at your approach. But drift up to them slowly, staying low in the water yourself, and you can get close enough to look into their eyes, the black horizontal pupils with their encircling rings of gold. And if you hold your arm so that it's underwater, you may even be able to reach out and briefly finger a soft mottled-white chin. Then, with the suddenness of a kingfisher's cry, the frog will shriek and leap out over your head, sometimes slapping two or three times across the water like a skipped stone before diving and burying itself in the mud at the bottom. Scull to where it disappeared and cup your eyes against the surface glare, and you can see where it is hiding, down past the long amber-flecked cords of pondweed, down where the shafts of sunlight converge.

This tiny blue chip on the United States Geological Survey map is our investment in frogs, though we didn't know that twenty years ago when we built the pond. At the time, we were simply taking the Soil Conservation Service up on its offer to help landowners construct farm ponds. The Soil Conservation Service was intent on the advantages of such ponds for flood control, for watering crops and livestock, for fighting fires. We, on the other hand, were thinking of swimming. Nobody was planning for frogs.

Two hired bulldozers did the excavating, uprooting the stumps of the trees we had felled, pushing the topsoil and rocks aside, and scraping the underlying material into a two-hundred-foot-long crescent-shaped earthen dam. The engineers had designed the dam to raise the water to a depth of only four feet, so, in the interests of swimming, we sent the machines deeper still, until we were looking down on the tops of the twin earthmovers, their bright yellow flanks caked with the gray mud of freshly exposed glacial till.

It took a week before operators were finished digging and shaping the pond's contours. Their last act was to breach a temporary dike they had constructed to divert water coming from the spring that bubbles out of the ground among witch hazels and royal ferns a short way above the pond. But other springs within the pond were already filling it. So were the frogs. Scarcely had the last bulldozer rumbled back up the hill toward the road than the first frogs appeared, staking their claims at the edges of the muddy, oil-speckled pools.

By the time the water reached the level of the overflow, the pond was fourteen feet deep and a third of an acre across. It took a winter for the water to clear. And it took a few years more for vegetation to cover up the last of the machinery scars. Today, though, a meadow of wildflowers covers the dam. Daisies, orange hawkweed, black-eyed Susans, goldenrod, pearly everlasting, and vetch have taken the high ground. Closer to the water are clumps of turtlehead, gentians, and the roundleaved sundews, whose sticky red hairs slowly digest passing ants. Were we to stop our annual mowings, the surrounding white pines, gray birches, and red maples that are mirrored in the water's surface would soon press their offspring right up to the shore.

We like to boast that we swim here nine months of the year, and we have pictures to prove it—one of us grinning manically at the camera after going in on a dare on the tenth of March, posing barefoot on a sheet of ice. But most years it's not human swimmers but frogs that take the first plunge. The seven species of frogs and two species of toads that occur in this part of New Hampshire all lay their eggs in freshwater. To them the fact that this pool is unchlorinated is even more attractive than it is to us.

The wood frogs—diminutive frogs with dark-brown raccoon-like masks—hibernate under forest debris and swarm to the shore when there is still some ice on the pond. After a few days of frenzied mating and egg laying, they disappear again, back to the privacy of the woods. It is easy to miss the emergence of the wood frogs, but there is no mistaking the spring peepers. You may not see the tiny frogs themselves, but their high-pitched clear calls, massed like the incessant jingle of tiny bells, can be heard a quarter of a mile away. Their nightly nuptial chorus goes on for weeks, the males calling from wet hillocks of grass or the stems of shrubs at the water's edge. It is as much the signature of spring as the cicadas' song is of summer.

We are not privy to all the amphibian mating that goes on along our pond's banks, but we can certainly spy the consequences. On the mornings after, we find the shallows littered with eggs, some in gelatinous clusters, some loose on the bottom, others attached to submerged stems or bound in long jellied ropes. They aren't all frogs' eggs, or even toads', for we also have salamanders, the blue-spotted and yellow-spotted ones, and the red-spotted newt.

The mating and egg laying pass quickly. By the time we have finished planting the garden, it's not eggs we see but tadpoles—or, rather, pollywogs, as we say in New England. Their appearance coincides with our own annual return to the water.

There are many attractions to a farm pond. It's not the exercise, for there is enough of that on the land. But a swim is a chance to soak one's black fly bites, a way of washing up without the inconvenience of a formal bath, a break from the endless cycle of work. But in a pond like this what is even more alluring are the tadpoles. They are the reason we linger, after the requisite swim to the other side and back, after the lathering up with the bar of soap and the one last plunge. There is something endlessly fascinating about frogs-in-the-making, and kitchen strainers were made for scooping up tadpoles. There in the bottom of the mesh basket, you can check each fat, shiny wriggler for signs of legs. Our own prenatal growth is visible only through fiber-optic lenses and ultrasound, whereas the metamorphosis of frogs takes place in full view. So we begin every summer by scouting the shallows, scooping up tadpoles ahead of the spreading cloud of silt, performing our well-baby-frog checks.

By August, however, the nursery has largely emptied out. The frogs we spy as we drift in our inner tubes are chiefly bullfrogs and green frogs. There's no mistaking the bullfrog's call, its distinctive "jug o' rum, more rum," which it continued to repeat all the way through Prohibition. The green frogs don't grow to be as large, but you can't tell the two species apart by size alone. You have to get close enough to look for the lengthwise fold of skin that runs along each side of the green frog's back. The leopard and pickerel frogs at this time of year have gone farther inland to forage. We regularly surprise them as we pick beans in the garden—athletic-looking frogs with lines of dark spots or squarish blotches down their backs, jumping across the rows of peppers, taking refuge beneath the potato vines. But like the warty toads that patiently share the garden, they too, have come from the water and to it they will eventually return.

Some of our summer visitors, joining us for a swim, are less appreciative of our pond's wildlife, and a few are downright hostile. Other newcomers take the opposite tack and ask whether we have stocked this pond with fish. Or they tell us that they have just seen a fish break the surface out in the middle. We say it was probably a turtle surfacing or a dragonfly laying eggs. When they insist on showing us the fish, we take a look ourselves and patiently explain that it's a newt or one of the slow-maturing bullfrog tadpoles, which take two or three winters to become frogs.

Our certainty that our pond has no fish in it comes not from any fisherman's frustration, nor from the fact that we have swum here so many times that we know the pond's waters cold. Rather, it comes from the way that the pond is constructed. A vertical pipe, two feet in diameter (big enough, the engineers say, to handle all but the hundred-year flood) rises to the surface under the dock. Water flowing over its lip drops three feet to a concrete pad before exiting sideways through a pipe that runs through the heart of the dam. Over the years I have on more than one occasion cursed this design; for example, when beavers exploring upstream neatly packed it full of branches, mud, and moss. Since then, we have enclosed the pipe's mouth with a chain-link fence, and covered it with the dock.

There are those who say that piped spillways are inherently bad designs—that sooner or later they always get plugged up or leak. But at the moment we have come to see this spillway as something special. Yes, its maintenance is an added chore. But it serves to keep fish out of the pond. Even the most gung-ho trout will not be able to fling itself up the vertical section of the overflow. And this very fishlessness of our pond, far from being a disadvantage, is what has given us our abundance of frogs.

On the face of it, you might think that any pond big enough to support fish ought to have them—that they would complete the diversity of pond life. But, in fact, fish are such extraordinarily efficient predators of amphibians that their presence actually decreases diversity. They snap up tadpoles with enough thoroughness to extirpate entire species.

We didn't discover this for ourselves, because, despite the repeated encouragement of friends, we've never set about to stock this pond. Instead, the insight comes from Owen Sexton, a professor of biology at Washington University in St. Louis. *Signals*

from the Heartland, a recent book by Tony Fitzpatrick that profiles the ecology of Illinois and Missouri, contains a chapter describing Sexton and the remarkable story of his inadvertent experiment with frogs and fish. The bare facts are contained in a
1986 paper in the *Transactions, Missouri Academy of Sciences,*
titled "A Qualitative Study of Fish-Amphibian Interactions in 3
Missouri Ponds," but that makes it sound like a dry tale.

In layman's terms, what occurred was that a series of three
artificial ponds were constructed at Washington University's
Tyson Research Center, located in western St. Louis County.
The largest of these ponds, the so-called Railroad Pond, is, like
the others, filled only by runoff water. It is situated some two
hundred yards from an intermittent creek that runs to the Meramec River. Repeated sampling of the pond by Sexton and his
students in the years after its excavation in 1970 found eleven
species of amphibians using it for some stage of their life cycle.

On April 11, 1979, nearly five inches of rain fell in one hour,
and the overflow from Railroad Pond created a short-term connection between it and the stream, and on December 8, 1982,
heavy flooding of the Meramec River sent it high enough to flood
the pond's outlet directly. Both events introduced fish. Fathead
minnows, green sunfish, and golden shiners were the first
species found; later they were joined by black bullheads,
bluegills, and largemouth bass. In the years since these two in-
vasions, amphibians have continued to be abundant in the
vicinity of Railroad Pond. And in fact, their abundance hasn't
changed in the one pond that wasn't flooded. But the number of
amphibian species found in Railroad Pond itself has plum-
meted. From a preinvasion species count of eleven, censuses in
the years since—with seines, dip nets, drift fences, and pit
traps—have never yielded more than two. The only consistent
species has been the bullfrog, whose tadpoles are not only the
largest, and thus the hardest to swallow, but also have distasteful skin. For all the others, however, Railroad Pond has become
a lethal nursery.

You don't have to be a herpetologist to be aware that frogs
and other amphibians are facing hard times—not just in ponds
that have been intentionally or unintentionally stocked with
fish, but all over the world. Since the 1970s, and especially in
the last decade, researchers have noticed dramatic drops in amphibian populations in a wide variety of habitats in Europe,
Asia, Africa, and Australia, as well as in North and South America. And what is most disturbing is that some of these declines,

87

like that of the golden toad in Monteverde, Costa Rica, have occurred in seemingly pristine locations.

The dependence of most amphibians on freshwater for reproduction has, of course, made them especially vulnerable to urbanization and its accompanying draining or filling of wetlands. Water pollution from chemicals, pesticides, and acid rain have all been implicated in the decline. Even the increase in ultraviolet radiation as a result of ozone depletion may be part of the problem. And frogs under stress may have become vulnerable to epidemics, such as the red-leg disease that has recently been suggested as a proximate cause in *Froglog,* the publication of the Declining Amphibian Populations Task Force.

In the wake of his paper's publication, Owen Sexton says that he has received a number of letters from pond owners around the country not only reporting similar results when they introduced fish but also saying that now they were sorry they had done it. I, for one, am cheered by the news, the word that our investment in frogs has proved to be the right one. In a world that is already well stocked with anglers and fish hatcheries, what we need are more frog hatcheries—places where the water is fresh and clean and fish-free. Some will be temporary pools—seasonal accumulations of runoff, whose short duration precludes any possibility of fish. But others will be permanent bodies of water, like this pond, that by design or historical accident have never been colonized by fish. Whether created by glacier or bulldozer, these are special waters, attracting many voices. We who swim with frogs need to add our own.

In a Country of Light, Among Animals

Barry Lopez

I DON'T know, of course, whether you've ever been in the high Arctic in the summer, but I would begin by telling you how striking the light is. For two months or more the sun doesn't dip below the horizon. In a treeless, winter-hammered landscape like Alaska's north slope, the light creates a feeling of compassion that is almost palpable. Each minute of light experienced feels like one stolen from a crushing winter. You walk gently about, respectful of flowering plants, with a sense of how your body breaks the sunshine, creating shadow. You converse in soft tones. The light is—perhaps there is no other word—precious. You are careful around it.

The wind always feels close here, a gentle breeze, a heavy blow, the breathing of an unfathomable welter of clouds which passes continually overhead, an ocean in which weather is being conceived. It's figuring out what it wants to do before moving south and east across North America: now altostratus, now cirrus, now cumulonimbus, like exercises. After lunch a mare's tail sky; at one in the morning a rainbow appears to the south, half as broad as my fist, driven into the tundra like a sheet of iridescent steel.

But for the wind against your ear and the keening of fifty species of birds, it is as quiet as the moon. The wind surrounds the bark of a fox and it evaporates. In sun-warmed, goose-down clothing, you turn your cheek to the source of light and feel sheltered; you see amid the dwarf birch and dwarf willow at your feet speckled eggs cradled in birds' nests. The grace so apparent in first life seems nowhere else so tender, because night never comes here.

From the slope of a hill above this river, you can look out across two hundred square miles of tundra through air transparent as a polished windowpane. If the Earth were flat you could see all the way to Iowa. It was into this expansive country, this place of interminable light and clear, rolling air, that Bob and I had come. In it we would watch wolves.

Bob spent our first morning in base camp transferring data from his field notebooks to a pile of topographic maps. I heated three gallons of river water and bathed. We were sharing this wall-tent camp with other biologists from Alaska and Montana living in varying degrees of general excitement and anxiety about, respectively, the calving close by of a herd of thirty thousand caribou and the proximity of tundra grizzlies.

Fourteen miles to the west of us was an active wolf den, set just below the rim of a high cutbank above a twenty-foot-wide stream called Iligluruk Creek. Two miles south of the den, across an open valley, was an elongated barren rise where Bob and I planned to camp. From this ridge, running roughly parallel to the cutbank, Bob and I could watch the seven Iligluruk adult wolves in this pack and the four pups born to them earlier that June.

One evening Craig Lofstedt, a pilot Bob and I had flown with on other wolf research trips in Nelchina Basin in the Alaska Range, six hundred miles to the southeast, helicoptered us out to our campsite on Ilingnorak Ridge. On the way we landed to inspect a caribou kill made just the day before by a yearling Iligluruk wolf. Bob retrieved the lower jaw, from which the caribou's age could be determined, and a femur. From its bone marrow the animal's general state of health could be deduced. The carcass had been picked clean. One kill had fed many of *amaguk*'s neighbors, likely *tulugak,* raven, and *kaiyukuk,* red fox.

As Craig flew us in a wide arc high above the den, we watched a light-colored yearling female stand up and stretch—she was "baby-sitting" while the other wolves were off to the west, hunting into a good wind.

Craig put us and our gear down on the ridge. We agreed on a rendezvous hour three days hence and he slipped away, lifting the Bell 206 off quietly to the south before heading back east, a courtesy to the wolf at the den.

Bob and I set up our spotting scopes immediately. Straight across the tundra plain in front of us the light-colored female had lain back down. To the east and west were a scatter of caribou, sixty or seventy of them. The wind was strong from the northwest, gusting to twenty-five miles per hour, and the air was chilly. An hour after we began our watch, two adult wolves loped into view from the west, headed for home. We studied them while they followed the cutbank above Iligluruk Creek for three miles. When they arrived the pups bounded up out of the den. Amid much tail wagging and face licking, the returning adults regurgitated meat for the pups, which they ravenously consumed. A few minutes later the scene was still. All seven animals were resting on the shallow slope above the den entrance.

Bob and I felt initiated into the country.

Because of the perpetual light and our unobstructed view, we were able to observe animals at any hour over almost forty square miles of tundra. During the odd hours we chose to sleep, we set up a spotting scope in the tent entrance. If you woke up, you'd take a quick look around. Something new—a ground squirrel hiding behind a rock from something, a wolverine preparing to lie down—was always going on.

The suffusion of sunlight, seeming to empty the landscape of any threat, could make you forget how very remote the country was. When I lay down to sleep I was aware the soil only a few feet below my head was frozen solid, that in the hills around us grizzly bears were tearing up the earth in pursuit of ground squirrels, that somewhere a willow ptarmigan had become an explosion of feathers in a gyrfalcon's fists.

*   *   *

One evening I sat on the tundra near the tent watching *nagrulik*, horned lark, on her nest. It was cold. The lark, her feathers ruffled to insulate herself, sat resolutely on four eggs, staring back at me. I recalled a story. Bob and several Nunamiut were out looking for animals one summer night when a chilling fog settled over them. The men began gathering willows for a fire to heat tea. Suddenly one man made a beckoning gesture with a willow stick. At first no one could see what was up—he was waving at a porcupine, telling him to come over and join them.

When I looked up (it was as though I had been telling *nagrulik* this story), a caribou cow was looking at me, a hundred feet away. When finally she caught my scent she snorted violently and trotted off. Whatever I was to her, she'd grasped it and dispensed with me. A good feeling, I thought, for an interloper like myself to imagine here.

At midnight each night, when the sun was low in the northern sky, the clouds seemed to glow in greatest spectacle. We'd fix dinner and sit with our tin cups of tea, bundled in parkas and wind pants, and watch solar iridescence, a faint, translucent lime green and soft pink marbling in the clouds. Our rudimentary meals, under such auspices, seemed exquisite. We would glance at each other and cock our heads, speechless before the expanse of pleasure.

At 3:30 one morning a light-gray female wolf appeared at our camp. She came up over a rise, watched us for fifteen or twenty seconds, then moved away obliquely downhill. Every hundred yards or so she stopped and looked back at us, until she was about six hundred yards away. We watched her for a half hour as she continued north toward the den, investigating a clump of dwarf birch, flushing a ptarmigan, rolling on her back in the lichens, leaping in the air repeatedly to snap at long-tailed jaegers dive-bombing her.

She might have stumbled onto us while returning from a hunt, or come over on purpose to see who we were, in her country.

Late one afternoon we started out across the stretch of tundra that separated us from the den, to see if we could get any closer to the wolves. There is no walking on level, open ground as arduous as walking across wet tundra in summer. It's like walking across a field of bedsprings covered with a layer of basketballs. In an hour we'd gotten no more than three quarters of a mile. By then we'd lost sight of the den behind a rise of land and a storm had begun piling up clouds in the west. We turned back. *Nipailuktak,* short-eared owl, watched us from his hunting perch on a tussock. We passed *avinnak*'s house. *Avinnak,* tundra vole, was poised right there in his entrance. Hey, *nipailuktak!* Look at this! On the vast plain, Bob and I were like two small birds, sparrows or warblers, against the sky.

The wind changed around to the east that evening. When the wolves left to hunt they headed east for the first time since we'd arrived. We followed a single wolf with our scopes. He was sneaking up a willow-lined ravine, drawing close to several grazing caribou. The caribou got wind of him and exploded away. A second wolf appeared and both wolves gave chase. The gap between the caribou and the first wolf remained at two hundred yards or so for four or five hundred yards before the second wolf broke away to disappear over a rise, followed soon by the first wolf. A mile later the caribou slowed back to a walk.

The storm came up while we slept, holding us tent-bound for twelve hours. When I stepped outside once to re-anchor the tent against the savage punch of the wind, I suddenly saw golden plover in my mind and horned lark, the birds I'd been visiting, sitting there on their nests in the wind and rain.

After the storm passed, the evening warmed and a few mosquitoes came out, the first we'd seen. Nunamiut distinguish between juvenile mosquitoes, *migulaitchiak* (literally, "white socks"), and larger mosquitoes, *kiktugiak*. These were *kiktugiak*, big as horseflies. But the wind picked up and they were swept away.

About eight that night Bob stood away from his scope, stretched, and wandered off. I continued to study the country in slow, methodical sweeps, along Iligluruk Creek, along the ridges, down each crease in the land, the likeliest places to pick up something. Caribou were moving west, several hundred of them in enclaves small and large, drifting over some twenty square miles. One group of fourteen would pass, I saw, within three or four hundred yards of the den if they grazed on in a straight line. Four of the adult wolves were off hunting and two more were asleep in willows at the foot of the cutbank, where they wouldn't see the caribou. The seventh adult was sleeping at the crest of the bank. If for some reason she woke and stood up, she might see them.

The caribou came on unawares. I called to Bob to return to his scope, though it seemed unlikely anything dramatic would happen. The caribou were now almost in line with the den, just to the north of it. The three wolves remained asleep. Then the one at the crest rose to stretch. She saw the caribou and took off quickly to the east, downwind of them. One of the two wolves at the foot of the cutbank, responding to some signal, bounded out of the willows and ran up the cutbank. He, too, looked at the caribou before taking off after the first wolf.

Several minutes later, fourteen placidly grazing caribou jerked their heads upright and bolted west in a stiff-legged trot. The wolves might have let themselves be seen, to set up an ambush by the third wolf, or the caribou might have caught the scent of the den. We didn't see them following in the caribou's wake. Like most caribou-wolf encounters, this one came to nothing.

While we were watching this event unfold, Craig Lofstedt flew up and landed on Ilingnorak Ridge. He shut down the helicopter's turbine. The ridge fell back into its deep quiet. The three of us stood there with our hands in our parkas. I wondered if I would be able to remember the *skree* of the plovers, if I could make that sound in my head again; or remember the resistance to my arms and shoulders of rocks the size of oil barrels a grizzly bear had shoved aside in its search for a ground squirrel; or recall an image of caribou crossing the gray-green Utukok late at night, shaking off water in twos and threes against the sun, the explosion of diamond fragments.

After we loaded the helicopter I walked away in a wide circle to say good-bye to the birds.

from
Birds, Beasts, and Relatives
Gerald Durrell

EACH morning when I awoke the bedroom would be tiger-striped by the sun peering through the shutters. As usual, I would find that the dogs had managed to crawl onto the bed without my realizing it and would now be occupying more than their fair share, sleeping deeply and peacefully. Ulysses would be sitting by the window staring at the bars of golden sunlight, his eyes slit into malevolent disapproval. Outside, one could hear the hoarse, jeering crow of a cockerel and the soft murmuring of the hens (a sound soothing as bubbling porridge) as they fed under the orange and lemon trees, the distant clonk of goat bells, sharp chittering of sparrows in the eaves, and the sudden outburst of wheezing, imploring cries that denoted one of the parent swallows had brought a mouthful of food to their brood in the nest beneath my window. I would throw back the sheet and turf the dogs out onto the floor, where they would shake and stretch and yawn, their pink tongues curled like exotic leaves, and then I would go over to the window and throw back the shutters. Leaning out over the sill, the morning sun warm on my body, I would scratch thoughtfully at the little pink seals the dogs' fleas had left on my skin, while I got my eyes adjusted to the light. Then I would peer down over the silver olive tops to the beach and the blue sea which lay half a mile away. It was on this beach that, periodically, the fishermen would pull in their nets, and when they did so this was always a special occasion for me, since the net dragged to shore from the depths of the blue bay would contain a host of fascinating sea life which was otherwise beyond my reach.

If I saw the little fishing boats bobbing on the water I would get dressed hurriedly, and taking my collecting gear I would run through the olive trees down to the road and along it until I reached the beach. I knew most of the fishermen by name, but there was one who was my special friend, a tall, powerful young man with a mop of auburn hair. Inevitably, he was called Spiro after Spiridion, so in order to distinguish him from all the other

Spiros I knew, I called him Kokino, or red. Kokino took a great delight in obtaining specimens for me, and although he was not a bit interested in the creatures himself, he got considerable pleasure from my obvious happiness.

One day I went down to the beach and the net was halfway in. The fishermen, brown as walnuts, were hauling on the dripping lines, their toes spreading wide in the sand as they pulled the massive bag of the net nearer and nearer to the shore.

"Your health, *kyrié* Gerry," Kokino cried to me, waving a large freckled hand in greeting, his mop of hair glinting in the sun like a bonfire. "Today we should get some fine animals for you, for we put the net down in a new place."

I squatted on the sand and waited patiently while the fishermen, chattering and joking, hauled away steadily. Presently the top of the net was visible in the shallow waters, and as it broke surface you could see the glitter and wink of the trapped fish inside it. Hauled out onto the sand, it seemed as though the net were alive, pulsating with the fish inside it, and there was the steady, staccato purring noise of their tails, flapping futilely against each other. The baskets were fetched and the fish were picked out of the net and cast into them. Red fish, white fish, fish with wine-colored stripes, scorpion fish like flamboyant tapestries. Sometimes there would be an octopus or a cuttlefish leering up from inside the net with a look of alarm in its human-looking eyes. Once all the edible contents of the net had been safely stowed away in the baskets, it was my turn.

In the bottom of the net would be a great heap of stones and seaweed and it was among these that I found my trophies: once a round flat stone from which grew a perfect coraline tree, pure white. It looked like a young beech tree in winter, its branches bare of leaves and covered with a layer of snow. Sometimes there would be cushion starfish, almost as thick as a sponge-cake and almost as large, the edges not forming pointed arms as with normal starfish, but rounded scallops. These starfish would be of a pale fawn color, with a bright pattern of scarlet blotches. Once I got two incredible crabs, whose pincers and legs when pulled in tight fitted with immaculate precision the sides of their oval shells. These crabs were white with a rusty-red pattern on the back that looked not unlike an Oriental face. It was hardly what I would call protective coloration, and I imagine they must have had few enemies to be able to move about the sea-bed wearing such a conspicuous livery.

On this particular morning I was picking over a great pile of weed, and Kokino, having stowed away the last of the fish in the baskets, came over to help me. There was the usual assortment of tiny squids, the size of a match-box, pipe-fish, spider-crabs, and a variety of tiny fish which, in spite of their small size, had been unable to escape through the mesh of the net. Suddenly Kokino gave a little grunt, half surprise and half amusement, and picked something out of a tangled skein of seaweed and held it out to me on the calloused palm of his hand. I could hardly believe my eyes, for it was a seahorse. Browny-green, carefully jointed, looking like some weird chess-man, it lay on Kokino's hand, its strange protruded mouth gasping and its tail coiling and uncoiling frantically. Hurriedly I snatched it from him and plunged it into a jar full of sea-water, uttering a mental prayer to St. Spiridion that I was in time to save it. To my delight it righted itself, then hung suspended in the jar, the tiny fins on each side of its horse's head fluttering themselves into a blur. Pausing only to make sure that it really was all right, I scrabbled through the rest of the weed with the fervor of a gold prospector panning a river-bed where he had found a nugget. My diligence was rewarded, for in a few minutes I had six seahorses of various sizes hanging suspended in the jar. Enraptured by my good luck, I bid Kokino and the other fishermen a hasty farewell and raced back to the villa.

Here I unceremoniously foreclosed on fourteen slow-worms and usurped their aquarium to house my new catches. I knew that the oxygen in the jar in which the sea-horses were imprisoned would not last for long and if I wanted to keep them alive I would have to move quickly. Carrying the aquarium, I raced down to the sea again, washed it out carefully, filled the bottom with sand and dashed back to the villa with it; then I had to run down to the sea again three times with buckets to fill it up with the required amount of water. By the time I had poured the last bucket into it, I was so hot and sweaty I began to wonder whether the sea-horses were worth it. But as soon as I tipped them into the aquarium I knew that they were. I had placed a small, twiggy, dead olive branch in the aquarium, which I had anchored to the sand, and as the sea-horses plopped out of the jar they righted themselves and then, like ponies freshly released in a field, they sped round and round the aquarium, their fins moving so fast that you could not see them and each one gave the appearance of being driven by some small internal motor. Having, as it were, galloped round their new territory, they all made for the olive branch, entwined their tails round it lovingly, and stood there gravely at attention.

The seahorses were an instant success. They were about the only animal that I had introduced to the villa that earned the family's unanimous approval. Even Larry used to pay furtive visits to my study in order to watch them zooming and bobbing to and fro in their tank. They took up a considerable amount of my time, for I found that the sea-water soon grew rancid, and in order to keep it clear and fresh I had to go down to the sea with buckets four or five times a day. This was an exhausting process, but I was glad that I kept it up, for otherwise I would not have witnessed a very extraordinary sight.

One of the seahorses, obviously an old specimen since he was nearly black, had a very well-developed paunch. This I merely attributed to age; then I noticed one morning there was a line along the paunch, almost as though it had been slit with a razor blade. I was watching this and wondering whether the sea-horses had been fighting and if so what they used as a weapon (for they seemed so defenseless), when to my complete and utter astonishment the slit opened a little wider and out swam a minute and fragile replica of the seahorse. I could hardly believe my eyes, but as soon as the first baby was clear of the pouch and hanging in the clear water, another one joined it and then another and another until there were twenty microscopic sea-horses floating round their giant parent like a little cloud of smoke. Terrified lest the other adult seahorses eat the babies, I hurriedly set up another aquarium and placed what I fondly imagined to be the mother and her offspring in it. Keeping two aquariums going with fresh water was an even more Herculean task and I began to feel like a pit-pony; but I was determined to continue until Thursday, when Theodore came to tea, so that I could show him my acquisitions.

"Aha," he said, peering into the tanks with professional zeal, "these are really most interesting. Seahorses are, of course, ac-cording to the books, supposed to be found here, but I myself have er . . . you know . . . never seen them previously."

I showed Theodore the mother with her swarm of tiny babies.

"No, no," said Theodore. "That's not the mother, that's the father."

At first I thought that Theodore was pulling my leg, but he went on to explain that when the female laid the eggs and they had been fertilized by the male, they were taken into this special brood-pouch by the male and there they matured and hatched, so what I had thought was a proud mother was in reality a proud father.

Soon the strain of keeping my stable of seahorses with a supply of microscopic sea-food and fresh water became too great, and so with the utmost reluctance I had to take them down to the sea and release them.

from
Stalking the Wild Amaranth

Janet Marinelli

MY legs were killing me; I was ready to collapse in the sand and take a nap. Only sheer vanity kept me going: no way was I going to wimp out now and make Brooklyn Botanic Garden botanist Steve Clemants rue the day he agreed to let me accompany him on his five-day pursuit of the elusive seabeach amaranth. Feeling the weight of every Milky Way bar I'd devoured over the past twelve months, I plodded on.

It was late September, my second day of combing the ocean beaches of eastern Long Island for this rare wild relative of the showy celosias, amaranths, and gomphrenas that so many gardeners lust after. The day before, Steve and I had trudged thirteen miles through the sand, searching between tide line and dune for the plant, which had for forty years been thought extinct in New York State. Not a trace.

For years I've thought nothing about driving clear across the state in quest of the perfect delphinium for my flower border. But this was the first time I'd ever headed out to hunt for plants of the nongarden persuasion. As the sun arced across the sky and the wind continued to whip my face, I felt a new respect for professional plantwatchers such as Steve.

"Tough life," I'd replied, green with envy, when he first mentioned that he was going to the Hamptons to look for some endangered whatchamacallit. I'd trade my computer for a field guide any day.

Steve and his fellow classical botanists, called taxonomists, see life in terms of genus and species. They're interested in which plants grow where. They wield microscopes and work in laboratories but also get out into the bush. They are the front line in the worldwide effort to save species, sounding the alarm on those that are on the verge of extinction. Some write so-called monographs on particular groups of plants, while others spend lifetimes working on "floras"—basically, catalogs of the vegetation of certain geographic regions.

Taxonomists are as rare as an increasing number of the plants they study. Most young biologists these days are instead attracted to the Nobel-spangled fields of microbiology. If those who investigate the subatomic universe of plant DNA are the celebrities of contemporary botany, then taxonomists must be the grunts—or so I concluded as I nursed a blister on my big toe during one of our all-too-infrequent rest stops.

"What ever made you decide to become a botanist?" I asked dubiously.

"It happened the spring semester of my freshman year," said Steve, an understated Minnesotan with a bushy red beard and the patience of a saint. "I started out as a computer-science major. But I was spending all my days waiting for computer cards to run, playing blackjack in student lounges. One beautiful spring day I decided I'd rather be outdoors."

Thus are great careers born.

"But why *plants?*" I persisted.

"I had a garden. I like plants. And taxonomy is a little like solving puzzles."

"Right: intrepid botanists probing the conundrum of evolution," I groused, gingerly removing clumps of sand from my tattered toe.

"Besides, plants don't bleed. I'd feel guilty if I were going around collecting birds or mammals."

Whereas most American botanists track the devastation of biodiversity in the tropics, Steve is surveying the plant life of one of the largest, densest metropolitan areas on Earth: the five boroughs of New York, plus all counties within fifty miles of the city line. Big cities are the stepchildren of the botanical world. Not surprisingly, most botanists prefer exploring an unspoiled rain forest to mucking around in the Fresh Kills landfill, the Big Apple's premier garbage dump, or diving to the ground at the sound of gunfire, as Steve did one day when he was plant collecting at an abandoned warehouse on the Brooklyn side of the East River. He was convinced he was a goner until he realized that what he was hearing was a tape recording intended to keep pigeons from roosting on the dilapidated structure.

When Henry Hudson landed in Brooklyn, in 1609, he sang the praises of its white ocean strands blanketed with beach plum and prickly pear. Before the hot dogs and the hurly-burly, Coney Island's world-famous beach was backed by wind-blown dunes. Before there was an Ebbet's Field and crowds roared for Jackie Robinson, there was an ancient oak forest here. Before jets roared in and out of Kennedy Airport, southern Brooklyn was one big salt marsh, where herons and egrets flapped over vast expanses of marsh grass and glasswort punctuated by the huge, saucerlike white and rose-colored blooms of the marsh mallow.

Brooklyn lies at the western end of Long Island, a huge heap of rocks and sand deposited by the glaciers that has long loomed large in the imaginations of American poets and writers. "Fishshape Paumanok," the island's Indian name, appears often in the poems of Walt Whitman, who was born here on May 31, 1819. By Whitman's day, most of the majestic forest of oak and chestnut that once blanketed the island's spine—the great moraine left by the last ice sheet—had already been destroyed. South of the moraine, however, the immense outwash plain of sand and gravel was still largely covered with pitch pine, a continuation of the pine barrens of neighboring New Jersey. Here and there the barrens were interrupted by impenetrable thickets of dwarf oak, scarcely more than a foot high.

At the very eastern extremity of the island, a little more than a hundred miles from the first Dutch settlements in Brooklyn, the isolated promontory jutting out into the Atlantic remained essentially wilderness as late as the 1920s, when Norman Taylor observed in *Brooklyn Botanic Garden Memoirs* that "casual visitors to Montauk"—as the promontory has been known since earliest times—"are charmed by the place, the desolate moor-like downs, the depths of the kettleholes, some destitute of woody vegetation, others dark and even mysterious in their wooded interior."

Long Island has certainly loomed large in my own mind. I was born here, and over the past few decades I've watched New York City sprawl relentlessly eastward, all the way to Montauk, where Steve and I now trekked by some of the world's most spectacular beach houses in search of one of the world's rarest plants.

Long Island's mosaic of native plant communities has also been transformed by several centuries of plant immigrants brought here by human settlers from their former homelands. Some of these plants arrived as stowaway seed, hiding in ship ballast dumped along the Brooklyn waterfront, or clinging to the bottoms of people's shoes; others were brought on purpose. *Ailanthus altissima,* for example—the tree-of-heaven immortalized in the book *A Tree Grows in Brooklyn*—was introduced as a garden plant in 1784; today, ecologists might call it the tree-from-hell. Able to sprout even from cracks in pavement, it has become a noxious weed from coast to coast.

Scientists who study the flora of metropolitan areas are engaged in a kind of detective work, surveying species that have naturalized in parks and on roadsides, scrutinizing old herbarium specimens, and scouring historical documents, old photos, and period paintings for evidence of the area's former plant life. With each additional clue, they are better able to determine what has become of the oldtimers, and what the newcomers have wrought. Ultimately, this will tell us a good deal about the future of life on this rapidly urbanizing planet.

The Sugar Bush

Jim Northrup

IT is always a family affair to go to the sugar bush. Anishi-naabeg have been making syrup for hundreds of generations. We know who we were, who we are, and what to do each season. When the sun says it is sugar bush time, we gladly make syrup.

Ezigaa's first year actually started when he saw me making taps for the trees. Instead of looking at TV's Barney and Big Bird, my grandson's eyes followed the maple sticks that were drilled and carved into taps. He practiced counting them as he put the completed taps into a coffee can. The numbers he used didn't match the taps he was counting but that didn't matter because he was new at sugar bush and math. When Ezigaa went to the sugar bush for the first time, I saw the world anew again as I always do when I am watching two generations after me, my sons and grandsons, carry on our traditions.

We three left the house early. Patricia told Ezigaa that we were going to the deer's house and must be quiet when we are there.

When spending all day outside, it is easy to see winter turn into spring. At first, it is long-underwear cool in the mornings. The sun is bright on the hardly used snow. The snow is almost knee deep when we begin. It is crusty in the mornings, strong enough to support the weight of sap-gathering Shinnobs.

The cool wind wrapped around us as we showed Ezigaa how to find trees to tap. We found a good spot and started tapping. The trees were the right size and close together. There were no hills to climb. The sun had melted the snow at the bottom of the trees. The maples had a little brown collar of last fall's leaves, the emblems from the Canadian flag.

I was proud that Ezigaa knew to pause and leave an offering of tobacco at the base of each tree. From watching us, he knew how to thank the Creator for the gift of maple trees.

Using a hand drill, I drilled the holes at just the right height for a first-year tapper to get a good look. Ezigaa watched for a while, then handed me a twig to clean out the shavings. I put the tap in and the boy put a milk jug on the tap. After a few trees, he would tell me to hurry because he had a jug ready.

Standing back to survey our work, we watched the sap drip from the taps. Ezigaa looked at a couple of trees before he tried tasting it. He caught a few drops on his tongue and his smile was like warm sunshine to his gramma and grampa. As we trudged from tree to tree, Ezigaa danced along beside us on top of the snow. He was still looking for trees to tap as we followed the deer trail out of the woods.

The next morning we went back to see how much sap we had collected. On the way to the woods, I pointed out a bald eagle to Ezigaa. He didn't say a word, as if just seeing the brown and white bird was enough.

We were breaking through the crust of snow but Ezigaa was able to stay on top. He emptied the milk jugs into the buckets we carried. He was running from tree to tree.

Sometimes we boil the sap in the woods near the trees we tap. Other years we bring it home to boil. Our black cast iron kettle that takes us from ricing to sugar bush comes out again.

The fire we build invites participation. It begs to be poked and prodded so it burns better. Moving a piece of burning maple a quarter inch is sometimes necessary when tending a fire. Maybe it's just playing with fire, I don't know.

The steam coming off the sap suddenly appears for a few seconds, a sort of tentative start. Finally the steam is coming off steadily. It's like the sap finds the right amount of heat. The steam seems eager to be free. It billows out of the kettle, mingles with the wood smoke for a while, then disappears.

Brownish-colored foam begins to collect on top of the hot sap. It is skimmed off using an always handy balsam branch. The bubbling, boiling sap chuckles to itself once in a while as it cooks down.

As the sap boils down, more is added. The sap, almost syrup, roils in the kettle. The fire burns on all day until we have no more sap to add. We know that sitting around a fire is a good place to tell stories and hold your grandson on your lap.

Ezigaa tasted it as it got sweeter and sweeter. After about the 134th time, we decided we were done for the day. He stood back as we lifted the kettle from the fire. We took the syrup inside where we filtered it. The golden brown syrup was warm when we poured it over the pancakes. The best part of spring is teaching Ezigaa something he can pass on to his own grandchildren when the time comes. For now, Ezigaa takes sugar bush taps to school for Show and Tell.

Jake Bair: Protector of Chesapeake Bay

Linda Leuzzi

"TAKE Route 301 when you come down," said Jake Bair. "It takes you right across the Bay Bridge. When you cross it, you'll get a sense of the size and scope of the Chesapeake. The bridge is 5 miles [8 km] long and 380 feet [115 m] high."

The Bay Bridge ride *was* impressive. The Chesapeake shimmered, while sailboats and other pleasure vessels dotted the water. No land could be seen to the north or south.

"The Chesapeake," is the Chesapeake Bay, the largest *estuary* in North America. Its beginning flow, or headwaters, start in Cooperstown, New York. Then the mighty river rambles south 195 miles (315 km), with a width that varies from 4 to 30 miles (6 to 48 km), before it empties into the Atlantic Ocean in Virginia. A huge fishing industry thrives here; the Chesapeake is third in the nation in fishery catch, just behind the Atlantic and Pacific Oceans. More than 2,700 plant and animal species, including bald eagles, live along its shores and inlets and within its depths.

Eighteen trillion gallons (68 trillion l) of water churn and flow in the currents of the Chesapeake. Jake Bair's mission is to keep some of that water clean.

Bair, a biologist, is director and founder of the Maryland Center for Environmental Training (MCET) at Charles County Community College in La Plata. Since 1983, Bair and his staff have been training wastewater-treatment supervisors and operators in environmental techniques. Their goal: to help wastewater plants produce clean, safe, treated wastewater before it's released into the Chesapeake. "Ninety-six percent of Maryland's community waste flows into the Chesapeake, 40 percent of Pennsylvania's waste flows toward the Susquehanna drainage, [the Susquehanna River flows into the Chesapeake]."

Bair will be the first to admit his job isn't glamorous. Just how do you treat smelly waste products from homes, greasy food waste from restaurants and the poultry business, and toxic chemicals from other industries, so that they're transformed into environmentally friendly water? Bair answered this big question in simple language. "We can find forms of bacterial life to treat almost anything," he said. "And by using the principles of molecular biology, we can genetically engineer bacteria to literally eat any pollutants. We work with a number of treatment plants and try to tailor-make their *biomass*." To show how the process works, Bair drove me from Solomons Island to the Chesapeake Beach facility in Calvert County in his pickup truck.

A big, vital, kind man, Bair is clearly enthusiastic about his work. "Chesapeake Beach was the Coney Island of its time around the turn of the century," explained Bair en route, referring to the Brooklyn, New York, seaside attraction that was famous for decades. "It went into decline and now it's coming back again." The neat, modest, wood-frame homes that line the main street coexist with brand new townhouses. The year-round population of about 1,000 mushrooms to a summer population of 20,000, he explained.

As we swung down a narrow road to the wastewater facility, Bair pointed to the beach on the right. "This is the discharge point, right into shellfish beds," he said. The plant's discharge pipe runs underground—600 feet [180 m] out into the Bay. The plant pumps about 175 gallons [660 l] of treated wastewater every minute—all day, all night. A sobering fact to think about, especially when big facilities like Baltimore's disperse up to 200 million gallons [760 million l] of treated wastewater over the same time period into the Chesapeake.

"I want to show you what the final product looks like," he said as he sprang from the truck and dashed over to a 12-foot (3.5-m)-deep rectangular cement tank. It was a warm, summer day and the light-green water, which was being frothed by an *aerating* device, smelled fresh. "It has a high oxygen content, which is good for the life that the water comes in contact with," said Bair as he leaned over the tank. [The Bay's fish and shellfish must have dissolved oxygen to survive.] "The last thing we do before we discharge it is chlorinate it for a maximum of 20 minutes." Bair explained that a liquid form of chloride, which acts as a disinfectant, is injected into the water. Sulfur dioxide and gas are then applied to completely neutralize the chlorine. Chlorine neutralization is important, because wildlife is sensitive to it. "Biologists found that rock fish won't lay their eggs if even 0.03 percent of free chlorine residual is in the aquatic environment."

Bair entered the Chesapeake Beach wastewater facility and shook hands with its superintendent, Jon Castro, who had

107

taken Bair's training classes. Bair explained that most of the people who take his courses are Maryland county or state employees. (Traditionally, the work has attracted men, but Bair said that in the last few years, about 10 percent of these employees are women.)

Castro, a certified superintendent for 6 years, had just set up one of many tests he does throughout the day. A 2-liter *settlometer*, which looks like a measuring cup, containing brown sludge water was on a counter. "This will give you some idea of how the process works," said Bair. After 10 minutes, half the sludge had settled to the bottom of the cup. The water at the top of the cup was fairly clear. "The [bacteria are] metabolizing the waste product," he said pointing to the dark mass at the bottom. "It settles quickly because it becomes heavier than water."

There were two main waste pollutants in this sample, he explained. Carbonaceous pollutants—or human waste—and nutrients, which include laundry and fertilizer waste. Bacteria reproduce on carbonaceous waste. Protozoans—tiny, mobile multi-celled animals—graze on the bacteria. People like Castro monitor the distribution of the protozoans to evaluate the total biomass in a particular area. Bair is quick to point out that Castro, who constantly tests, monitors, and observes the water throughout the day is one of many unsung heroes. "I've seen a 75-year-old operator go down into a lift station in the middle of the night to fix a problem," he said.

What do the bacteria that chomp on sludge look like? Under a microscope, a teeming world of microlife suddenly becomes visible. Each of the pale-gray, Pac-Man-like cells has its own shape and personality. Some of the quickly darting round ones are known as "free swimmers." Long, threadlike filaments or filament bacteria spiral back and forth more slowly. The trick, Bair explained, is to get the right combination of organisms. "The filament bacteria tend to sew the flock together," he said. "They are also very light. If they [are dominant], they pick up the sludge and lift it out."

He went over to a "Biomonitor." It was, actually, a fish tank filled with processed water and about half a dozen fish that acted as live testers. "This is what we're putting out in the Chesapeake Bay," he said. The water was clean, and the fish were active.

Most of the processing takes place outdoors in large holding tanks where hundreds of billions of microorganisms per cubic foot do their work. In the last stages of the treatment, traps skim off floating matter, such as grease from restaurant disposals or stray grass. The brown sludge is eventually run through a mechanical device that separates solids from water. The solids are then compressed into dry matter—a cakelike substance— that is analyzed in a lab for harmful metals. Some is sent to farms to be used as fertilizer. If it contains heavy concentrations of metals, such as cadmium, mercury, lead, or zinc, the solid is sent to a landfill.

Sally J. Cole: Preserving the Past, Looking to the Future

Linda Leuzzi

SOMETIMES Sally Cole feels as if she's living as basketmakers and ancient Pueblos did centuries ago. It's usually in the morning when the first grayish-pink streaks of light awaken her. Camped out in her tent and sleeping bag on top of a canyon, she watches as the sky becomes vivid blue, then glances at the dull-green pinon and juniper forest anchored to the red earth.

Cole savors the moment—the sense of endless horizon, the soft breezes, the rustling leaves, the chatter and movement of nearby wildlife.

Cole is an *archaeologist* who is documenting some of the last Anasazi artifacts before they're destroyed forever by weather or vandalism. The Anasazi, ancestors of modern Pueblo peoples of Arizona and New Mexico, settled in the southwestern United States around 500 B.C. They lived in pit houses and multi-room masonry dwellings built into canyons and on mesa tops. They spent their days hunting, farming maize, weaving baskets, and crafting fine pottery. They also created rock art—paintings, carvings, and engravings, in which they recorded stories and important events. Rock art, also known as *petroglyphs,* is Cole's specialty. While her work involves preservation of the past, she also instills environmental practices among her crew and teaches camp ethics so that the Anasazi sites will be left the same way they were found.

Much of Cole's work takes place in southeastern Utah on Cedar Mesa, within the northern Colorado Plateau, in the Grand Gulch Primitive Area. The mesa reaches heights of 6,800 feet (2,070 m) and spans 450,000 acres of canyons. The Grand Gulch, a 53-mile (85-km)-long canyon, snakes through the mesa formation. It's hot and dry here, but pinyon and juniper trees, flowering plants, and ferns are part of the landscape. Natural springs and pools are found here and there.

Cole talked about the remoteness of the sites and how the environment affects her work.

We'll drive out to the edge of a paved state highway, then drive on an unpaved road anywhere from 3 to 10 miles [5 to 16 km]. We'll park the van there then hike to where we'll make our base camp.

This particular project has been going on for 4 years. The first year, we had pack horses that carried our equipment for our kitchen and lab facilities into the canyon. The second year we used vehicles to do it. This year we used llamas.

When you take away wheeled vehicles, your sense of time [changes]. We wake at first light, move [according to] the heat of the day, and are dependent on natural water sources. Here, we begin work when we start walking to a site. [Sometimes the site is] 15 minutes away, sometimes [it's] an hour and a half away. We react to the weather— drought, lightning, floods—and have to adapt to these conditions. The work is very in tune to the natural world.

Attracted by its beauty and history, a lot of people come to this region to hike the canyons and look at what the Anasazis left behind, Cole explained. But it's their very curiosity that makes these sites endangered.

Before we start out we have a research design. We look at the areas heavily used by tourists. Those are the most endangered because of the threats of vandalism, casual destruction, and increased erosion. You get people walking through middens—which are bits of pottery, charcoal, and other things the Anasazi left behind. Or hikers will walk near or touch the rock art. So we try to concentrate on areas of heavy visitation within the canyons.

I sit down with an archeologist with the Bureau of Land Management [an agency with the U.S. Department of the Interior that manages large parcels of land, especially in the West] and we discuss the drainage, which areas get the most impact from tourists, and where there are the biggest concentrations of Anasazi sites. So far we've sampled four major areas of the Grand Gulch canyon system.

When we do the actual research, we're doing inventory. There are no unnecessary disturbances of the sites. We locate, look at, and describe sites. There may be cliff dwellings in a rock shelter. We want to know what kind of deposits these ancient people left, for example, whether there are room blocks made of masonry, shelter walls with rock art, and milling stones lying around. People in my group draw, map, and measure [the sites] and photographers take pictures of the sites and various features.

The Anasazi occupied the area until about A.D. 1300, so what Cole finds are ancient, mind-boggling pieces of a puzzle that tell the story of another way of life. Drawings and photos of the paintings and petroglyphs are logged and tagged and Cole reports her interpretation of what they mean. Because the project takes place on public land, all this information is turned over to a place where the public can come and do research—in this case, the Edge of the Cedars State Park and Museum in Blanding, Utah. This museum is close to the research site.

It's Cole's job to figure out which features of the site and the rock art imagery are most important. The wall images include large humanlike figures with rectangular or triangular-shaped bodies. Many are wearing earrings, armbands, and sashes. Birds, snakes, flute players, and a recurring lizard man are also part of the art landscape. She's discovered painted figures on walls in the rock shelters that are an impressive 5 to 6 feet (1.5 to 2 m) high.

Cole explained that patience and persistence are what is needed for the discoveries that provide a bigger picture of this culture.

It's through dogged persistence that you really learn. It makes us see the complexity of past cultures, and that they didn't just live one way or make one kind of image. There are many questions to answer . . .

You may see a wall with life-sized polychrome [multicolored] figures, but then you'll see hundreds of tiny scratches, or some figures that are faded and can only be seen when the light hits it a certain way, and when it does you say, "Look, there's a whole wall of big-horned sheep!"

[You have to wait for just the right moment] to take a photograph or make a drawing. But [if] you're willing to spend the time watching the light change over a week and a half, a wall of art that [didn't seem] very significant [may have some surprises for you. You may even make some] really interesting discoveries.

Because Cole isn't affiliated with a museum or university, the funding for her projects has to come from a variety of sources.

She must also apply for a research permit because her work is on public land and the research must benefit the public.

Her research on the Cedar Mesa is sponsored by the Bureau of Land Management. This organization lends her logistical and technical support (like supplying water tanks and providing park rangers who know where specific Anasazi sites are). For the last 4 years, Cole's funding has come from Earthwatch, an international organization whose volunteers pay to work side-by-side with scientists on environmental, wildlife, and cultural projects around the world.

Cole plans the projects and is in charge of executing them. She has a core staff of six, including three archaeologists and a former teacher who speaks three languages and has a good background in anthropology and archaeology. Each summer, twelve to fifteen Earthwatch volunteers sign up to help document the artifacts. Cole is passionate about emphasizing the sacredness of the environment to her volunteers.

When we come to a site, we're all environmentalists in theory. We all recognize that you have to preserve more than [what you see] on the wall. You have to preserve the whole system in which the [rock art] occurs to understand the past and be in harmony with the present situation.

We talk about the complexity of the semi-desert soils at the base camp. I teach that every time you walk from kitchen to camp you walk the same path to avoid causing further erosion.

We also talk about the trees and the vegetation. We discuss why in 110°F [43°C] temperature, you don't jump in spring water. It's a source for wildlife and for us. If you're out and you see a nice pothole of water, remember it's the only water [available] for amphibians. The backpackers who come here to recreate sometimes forget what a delicate environment this is and they'll jump into potholes of water.

We make a point to take the most environmentally friendly route, like walking on rock instead of soil when we can. When we leave a site, we brush over our trails, because that worn path of sandy soil will attract others to use it. Many people come to see the archeological sites as well as the canyons and that's fine. But we don't want to have a site become Grand Central Station and set a precedent for heavy visitation. Things grow slowly here, and you can do a lot of damage [if you're not careful].

113

Last summer there was a major drought here and we pumped water out of one particular spring. There's a fortified masonry dwelling in the cliff above it, and while we were gathered around the spring we discussed [what it would have been like to live here] 1,000 to 700 years ago, how stressful it would have been to know that we had to depend on this one spring for our livelihood.

We knew we could have hiked out to get water because there was a 500-gallon [1,890-l] tank of water sitting up at a side canyon, but to the Anasazi, this water source was so important to them that they fortified the area around it. They had much more invested than we do—their homes, their tools, their agriculture were all here.

If the water dropped very low . . . they might not have lived. If they had to leave, [where would they go?] Where was the next spring? How far would they have had to walk? [Should they] leave behind most of [their] stored food and belongings? Can everyone go? What about [their] sense of history? The family cemetery? [Their] ceremonial rooms and paraphernalia?

That's something to think about.

Edward Toth: Saving Brooklyn's Last Forest

Linda Leuzzi

A JOGGER ran along a path where the Long Meadow slopes up to the old, low-branched white oaks. A woman strolled with her dog nearby, where tall meadow grasses and lush wildflowers gently sway in the breeze. A man spread a checkered tablecloth on the soft, green grass.

The Long Meadow in Prospect Park, with its broad stretch of softly curving green grasses and trees that outline its perimeter, brings out the best in people. More than 100 years after Frederic Law Olmsted and Calvert Vaux designed the park, its landscape still invites people to play.

Every year, more than 6 million people visit Prospect Park, which is on the National Register of Historic Places in Brooklyn—a bustling New York City borough. The grounds are a welcome relief for city people who need to connect with nature. Unfortunately, some of those people are killing the park they love. Edward Toth's job is to make sure that the park remains vital as well as accessible to visitors. He's in charge of saving Brooklyn's last forest.

Toth's office is in the basement of the red-brick Picnic House. His windows look out on the north-central end of the Long Meadow and his current project—reforesting 250 acres of the park—is among the largest natural restorations in the northeastern United States. Funds, a substantial multimillion dollars in support, will come from the Prospect Park Alliance—a group of private supporters, the Lila Wallace-Reader's Digest Foundation, and the City of New York. Making a reforestation project like this work in an area surrounded by brownstones and concrete buildings is pretty overwhelming when you think about it. So how is he doing it?

"We've identified about six major problems that absolutely must be addressed. Some of the worst problems have to do with soil compaction and down-slope erosion," Toth explained, quickly getting to the heart of the matter on a quiet weekday morning. "These are ecosystems driven by human impact," he went on. "We have to learn to live with them and manage them. Six million people come to this park each year and there are only 500 acres. Sometimes we have to remind ourselves what goes on here on the weekend with the wall-to-wall people."

Toth is referring to the visitors who aim for their favorite paths. The constant walking has worn the soil down to the point where it's positively lifeless. Then there are the bikers and trampling visitors who go off designated trails and unknowingly kill young seedlings just pushing up through the top soil, not to mention smaller plants that act as little soil anchors. Constant human use has created huge gullies on the eroded hillsides. When it rains, soil runs down these gullies into the park's lakes and ponds, forming a mineral deposit known as silt. When sludge accumulates, it may strangle aquatic plants and cause algae buildup, which kills fish. The repercussions are felt all the way up the food chain.

Getting the visitors to cooperate is one of the major keys to the program's success. Toth and his staff are constantly thinking of ways to discourage the city's wanderers who plunge into the woods looking for peace and quiet. "We mapped out all the 'desire paths,'" said Toth. ("Desire path" is a park term. It's a path or walkway visitors desire to use.) Toth was leaning over a park map with the problem areas marked. The darkened areas represent down-slope erosion, cross-hatched lines mean bare soil, and flat lines highlight the desire paths.

We had to figure out which [paths] could be closed off easily. We thought about the people who wanted to get off the regular walkways and explore . . . the woods and said: "OK, we'll establish some secondary paths with wood chips so that there is some percolation in the soil." Short of breaking the soil up, if you add organic matter like wood chips, it builds new soil as people break the wood chips down.

We've eliminated some of the desire paths by slowly introducing plants and some of the major paths were narrowed this way. Some trails are lined with low wooden railings because people don't always know where a path is. We devised a railing that was low to the ground. We didn't want to put up a major barrier because, if we did that, people would vandalize it.

The crew learned to be their own worst enemy. We'd put up a fence four or five times to keep people out of an area and they would [keep knocking] it down. So now we've narrowed [the fence] up.

A lot of times the new plants get heavily abused, and some even get pulled out. It's really odd. People don't seem to like something new. Then at some point, it's accepted as background and left alone.

Other efforts to improve the park's fertility, besides the desire path plan, include loosening the compacted soil with shovels in some areas—some as small as 100 square feet (9 sq m). In other areas, topsoil and compost were added. The project also involves erecting 40 miles (65 km) of snow fencing to protect young plants and help them take hold of the soil, and nailing 90,000 feet (27,000 m) of logs to the ground to stop erosion on hillsides and to hold new plantings. This will take place over the next 25 years.

Back in the late 1800s, Olmsted, who created the country's major city parks, had a staff of 600 to weed and work the grounds of Prospect Park. But times have changed. Toth has a staff of ten. Luckily, he also has a dedicated team of about thirty weekend woodland volunteers. They include local residents, one of whom is a high-school student who is doing his own park study on soil properties as a science-fair project. Some volunteers come weekly, but most show up about sixteen times a year. Hundreds of schoolchildren as well as very young and handicapped kids participate in a separate volunteer program.

Because his regular staff is so small, Toth has had to plan a park that can virtually take care of itself. Besides helping the soil regenerate, his design includes reintroducing native species like tulips and sweet gum trees as well as plants and shrubs like blueberries, and reducing the need for chemical fertilizers that tend to leach into the park's lakes.

In all, the park revitalization project calls for the planting of 240,000 wildflowers and 134,337 native trees. Toth emphasizes planting native trees because they are best suited for the area's soil, weather, and geological conditions. As a result, they tend to be hardier and require little or no care.

The 150-acre forest core, which is basically in the center of the park, is where Toth has his highest hopes of revitalization. Many of the old, established trees are in jeopardy because their roots are exposed as the soil is worn down by erosion. Also, because the soil was compacted, there are not enough air spaces to hold water for the trees. As a result, most of the trees have begun to wither. Many of the trees have already died and fallen over, leaving large lightgap areas in the forest.

How does Toth plan to save the forest? "We now have a low-mow policy. If we simply stop mowing certain areas, in 15 years, we'll have a young forest of wild cherry trees. You don't keep a soil healthy by constantly disturbing it." The result will be a less manicured look; while places like the Long Meadow will continue to be mowed every 2 weeks, areas near the edge of the woods are now mowed just three or four times a year. In some places, wildflowers wave cheerily where grass once grew and there are signs informing visitors that this less manicured look is intentional.

Forest growth and diversity attract more animals, especially birds. Toth has hired a wildlife manager, a first for the park, in anticipation of a healthy forest ecosystem. "When the park was first designed, Olmsted wasn't thinking [of it as] a preserve with endangered species. . . . We think we can support more wildlife. For one thing, [the park is] very important to migratory birds. This is the eastern flyway and they stop here for shelter, rest, and food."

The park first came under scrutiny in 1980, explained Toth. At that time, it was in bad shape. The grounds were a mess and park buildings were neglected. A series of reports were commissioned to study how the park could be improved. Prospect Park had been declared a landmark and a lot of people were interested in saving it.

When Toth joined the park's staff in the mid-1980s as a natural resource manager, he was involved with day-to-day fieldwork, which meant planting and digging up trees. Toth said he began thinking about how the forest could be saved on the very first day of his job.

> The park was in the middle of its ravine restoration. The basic horticultural planting consisted of groundcover and horticultural plants not native to the area. There were many things I saw being done that were counterproductive. An ongoing problem [was] non-native trees introduced by Olmsted. They formed large stands [groups of trees] and very aggressively crowded out other species. Olmsted didn't know about ecology. . . . What he was interested in was presenting natural settings to the public. He didn't know that some plants could be invasive.

As these non-native plants grew, they formed tree groups dominated by one species, Toth explained. This was bad news because too many plants of any one species are an easy target for disease and insect ravage. Simply put, different plants have different natural defenses for fighting invaders. But trees of the same type can be wiped out in a very short time.

What I studied in school was plant and insect taxonomy. I had worked as a field biologist doing various things, so my interest [in the park] was from an ecological [point of] view.

[When I first arrived,] we would go into large lightgap areas and cut down small, native wild cherry trees. [By doing this,] we were constantly interrupting and preventing *succession*. In these woods there was no understory, that is, young plants and trees, as well as trees that grow slowly.

If an acorn dropped it wasn't germinating. [Most of the time, it couldn't push up through the compacted soil.] In those cases where it would make it to a seedling, people who left the paths would trample it. What people saw was an oak canopy and grassy areas and nothing in between except a nice, wide-open view. To me, it was a landscape in collapse. Clearly there was no understory because the soil was nonconducive [to life].

At one point I got away from the fieldwork and began working on the ecological problems. My administrator, Tupper Thomas, said I badgered her about the changes I thought were needed. But the seminal moment was when I took her to see the regenerating process at Young Woods in Staten Island and how it worked. Tupper is a strong woman, but she has an open mind and once she was convinced, she never looked back.

Toth added that the absence of understory growth was also a result of a park policy in the 1960s. At that time, workers were expected to clear underlying brush for the public's safety; that is, to remove potential hiding places for muggers who might pounce on visitors.

Toth became the park's landscape director in 1990. Through recommendations from a series of meetings, and grant funding from the National Endowment for the Arts, he compiled a 205-page study that pointed out the park's problems and suggested specific methods of saving the woodlands. The study meant reviewing Olmsted's original plans. It also meant working with scientists in the Interior Department who advised Toth which plants the soil could support. Summer interns pitched in too. One even researched all the native flora on western Long Island. The study was completed in 1994.

Bur Oak

Aldo Leopold

WHEN schoolchildren vote on a state bird, flower, or tree, they are not making a decision; they are merely ratifying history. Thus history made bur oak the characteristic tree of southern Wisconsin when the prairie grasses first gained possession of the region. Bur oak is the only tree that can stand up to a prairie fire and live.

Have you ever wondered why a thick crust of corky bark covers the whole tree, even to the smallest twigs? This cork is armor. Bur oaks were the shock troops sent by the invading forest to storm the prairie; fire is what they had to fight. Each April, before the new grasses had covered the prairie with unburnable greenery, fires ran at will over the land, sparing only such old oaks as had grown bark too thick to scorch. Most of these groves of scattered veterans, known to the pioneers as "oak openings," consisted of bur oaks.

Engineers did not discover insulation; they copied it from these old soldiers of the prairie war. Botanists can read the story of that war for twenty thousand years. The record consists partly of pollen grains embedded in peats, partly of relic plants interned in the rear of the battle, and there forgotten. The record shows that the forest front at times retreated almost to Lake Superior; at times it advanced far to the south. At one period it advanced so far southward that spruce and other "rear guard" species grew to and beyond the southern border of Wisconsin; spruce pollen appears at a certain level in all peat bogs of the region. But the average battle line between prairie and forest was about where it is now, and the net outcome of the battle was a draw.

One reason for this was that there were allies that threw their support first to one side, then to the other. Thus rabbits and mice mowed down the prairie herbs in summer, and in winter girdled any oak seedlings that survived the fires. Squirrels planted acorns in fall, and ate them all the rest of the year. June beetles undermined the prairie sod in their grub stage, but defoliated the oaks in their adult stage. But for this geeing and hawing of allies, and hence of the victory, we should not have today that rich mosaic of prairie and forest soils which looks so decorative on a map.

Jonathan Carver has left us a vivid word-picture of the prairie border in pre-settlement days. On 10 October 1763, he visited Blue Mounds, a group of high hills (now wooded) near the southwestern corner of Dane County. He says:

I ascended one of the highest of these, and had an extensive view of the country. For many miles nothing was to be seen but lesser mountains, which appeared at a distance like haycocks, they being free from trees. Only a few groves of hickory, and stunted oaks, covered some of the vallies.

In the 1840's a new animal, the settler, intervened in the prairie battle. He didn't mean to, he just plowed enough fields to deprive the prairie of its immemorial ally: fire. Seedling oaks forthwith romped over the grasslands in legions, and what had been the prairie region became a region of woodlot farms. If you doubt this story, go count the rings on any set of stumps on any "ridge" woodlot in southwest Wisconsin. All the trees except the oldest veterans date back to the 1850's and the 1860's, and this was when fires ceased on the prairie.

John Muir grew up in Marquette County during this period when new woods overrode the old prairies and engulfed the oak openings in thickets of saplings. In his *Boyhood and Youth* he recalls that:

The uniformly rich soil of the Illinois and Wisconsin prairies produced so close and tall a growth of grasses for fires that no tree could live on it. Had there been no fires, these fine prairies, so marked a feature of the country, would have been covered by the heaviest forest. As soon as the oak openings were settled, and the farmers had prevented running grass-fires, the grubs [roots] grew up into trees and formed tall thickets so dense that it was difficult to walk through them, and every trace of the sunny [oak] 'openings' vanished.

Thus, he who owns a veteran bur oak owns more than a tree. He owns a historical library, and a reserved seat in the theater of evolution. To the discerning eye, his farm is labeled with the badge and symbol of the prairie war.

from

The Secret Family: Twenty-four Hours Inside the Mysterious World of our Minds and Bodies

David Bodanis

THE family enters the cool, air-filtered sanctum of the mall. A great deal of thought has gone into designing the entryway. The entry has to seem inviting, so people will be happy to come in, but it can't be too inviting, for then they'll linger and block it. There are likely to be benches attractively set down just inside the entrance, about as welcoming as a shopping arena can be, but look closely and you'll see that they're usually placed so that a sitter will have his back to the main traffic—a position that's psychologically all but impossible to keep for long. Tiny muscles tighten up on the family's forearms and back, forming the miniature air-slowing windbreaks we call goosebumps, as they try to orient themselves in the suddenly chilled air.

Uncomfortably hard tiles clack under the family's shoes for the first yards in, and this almost certainly makes them walk faster—about 10 percent faster, in one study—than if there had been a carpeted walkway. To be extra sure that there's no slow-down, faint clouds of ionone and other molecules are likely to be spraying out from the recessed cooling ducts farther along. Ionone is easily produced—it's just the result of breaking down common carotene molecules. It gives off the delectable odor of fresh hay. There are companies that sell these chemicals in liquid vats for mall managers to use in air-cooling systems. The unembarrassed can usually confirm this use by going up to an exposed duct—perching on someone's shoulder is sometimes necessary—and taking a close-up sniff. Farther on there will be different vapors. Shoe stores are likely to spray out a liquefied leather extract to draw in passing browsers; for sports stores, wisps of floral essence work best.

As they walk, the family almost certainly follows a reflex to veer toward the right. Children do it and adults do it—whether they're left- or right-handed—and it's so powerful an instinct that stores often pay higher rents for locations at the right-hand side of the entrance where the speed-controlled temperature-dazed shoppers are most likely to be piling in. Fluorescent lights above add to the initial disorientation, for these lights exhibit a constant slight flickering, which can create detectable nerve-cell spasms inside the brains of our family. The problem can be avoided when the fluorescent lights are perfectly adjusted, but with the hundreds of lights around, and janitors who have other things to do, that's not likely to happen.

To get upstairs, the family heads toward the elevator. The mall managers may keep one elevator on the ground floor always open. People march in, and even though they wait there exactly as long as they would had it not been standing open, they almost always feel better huddling inside rather than out. The next trick to appease restless waiting shoppers is to put mirrors on the wall of the elevator. We all tend to glance at ourselves when there's a full-length mirror nearby, be it the discreet side-glances at hair partings or shirt tucks which men are allowed, or the full-out, face-to-the-mirror, inch-by-inch makeup examination which certain Scarlett O'Hara wannabees engage in. (The observations are universal, but the admission of them isn't. In one comprehensive British poll, virtually all men said that they never looked at themselves when they passed a store window. But observers discreetly stationed at a number of mirrored posters observed a rather different truth: men were twice as likely as women to glance at themselves as they walked by, though, in mild fairness to that vainer sex, they were briefer in their mirror-assuring glances.)

A final distraction to impatient elevator waiters—though this one is expensive—is to staff an information desk across from the elevators. Up to one-third of the people coming by will then be curious enough or nervous enough or just polite enough, to stop and check on location details even if they already know perfectly well where they're supposed to be going. That further reduces the buildup of people waiting for the elevators.

(Will we accept anything when we're being led around? At one airport, passengers were annoyed at how long it took to wait for their luggage. The walk to the luggage area took one minute, and the wait there took eight minutes. The solution was elegant, if disturbing when you think that most of the people who fell for it can vote: the airport staff laid out a path that incorporated arbitrary twists and turns so that it now took eight minutes to get to the luggage area. Only one minute had to be spent in front of the empty luggage carousel. Even though the total wait was still the same, there were now fewer complaints.)

The boys are fidgety here in front of the elevator. The friend reaches into his back pocket, and extracts a plastic-wrapped storage device that has been there for several weeks, and contains a mixture of pigs' fat, rubber, Vaseline, Elmer's glue, and other tasty substances. The son looks over with interest, despite the parents' disapproving glances, and as friends are nothing if not generous at age ten, he is offered a piece: it's chewing gum.

Most substances that you can put into your mouth fit into one of two categories. Either they compress and break and become a mushlike slurry you can swallow—apples, steak, and toast are notable in this category—or they don't compress, and you would be strongly advised not to put them in your mouth at all. Those are the nonfood items, such as rocks, twigs, and their like. It's very hard to get items which are in between, both destructible yet not terminally compressible. The engineers of the modern gum product, however, have managed it. Their solution is to get substances that are soft enough for chewing—that's why all the Vaseline and animal fats such as lard and beef tallow are there—pour them into a tough rubber matrix, and manipulate it in such a way that no one is going to guess what's hidden inside. Something like the Elmer's glue we saw on the stamps is used, but there are also dollops of soap, polyethylene (the stuff that makes up plastic bags), and even some soil stabilizer to keep the gum bound tight.

As the boys chomp away, Vaseline and sheep's fat drip out. It is all swallowed, and will be worked on by the liver's detoxification systems in the hours to come. Sugar oozes out too, but this is also defended against, at least in part, for teeth aren't the passive chunks we generally take them for. Their surface chemicals constantly pull in fresh minerals from saliva, and use those minerals to help toughen the regions coming under acid attack from bacteria. At the same time, your saliva does its bit to help. Saliva is not a simple watery fluid, good for spitballs and other boyhood treats. It's constantly changing through the day, as the inside of your mouth monitors what's going in, and the saliva glands readjust their chemical output to help. Here, with the boys doing their best to harm their teeth, the glands detect the need for something to destroy acid. Simple bicarbonate of soda is excellent for this purpose, and so, within a few moments of the gum chewing starting, that's what the saliva glands pump in. It binds with and neutralizes the acid that the bacteria in the mouth are producing.

Saliva glands are truly intricate chemical factories, with a blood flow that's ten times greater than an equal mass of actively contracting arm or leg muscle would produce. The boys' saliva glands are pumping out another chemical, called sialin. This is even more cunning, for it floats over to the teeth-hugging bacteria already in place and subverts the way they use amino acids to make energy. As a result, those bacteria start producing alkali chemicals, that neatly quench most of the threatening acid.

A chime rings, and the family steps forward. Even in enclosed spaces we try to keep our personal distances, and here the girl has one advantage: a single woman is almost always given more space in a crowd than anyone else. (Though as social psychologists have ungenerously observed, the more plain looking she is, the less the deferred space.) The elevator doors close, and the parents and everyone else trust that the little cable above will lift the elevator to its destination. In 1854 the original Mr. Otis stood inside an open elevator three stories up, and had visitors at a New York exhibition cut its cable with an ax. It started to fall, and everyone shrieked, but then the little retracted rollers he had invented sprang out to grip the metal tracks, stopping the elevator, and everyone applauded. A device using the same principles is on all elevators now. Even simple escalators were considered fearful devices once, which is why when Britain's first escalator was installed at Harrods in 1898, a uniformed attendant was assigned to stand at the top with a glass of brandy at hand to revivify any traveler overcome by the mechanical ascent.

The elevator box jolts up, and as it does music plays, almost unnoticeably, which is just what the American Muzak Corporation likes. The sounds they project over an estimated 400 million people worldwide each day are designed *not* to be noticed. High notes are screened out by Muzak engineers, as well as low notes and volume shifts and even most minor chords—anything that might hint at some world beyond the major-chord mush, the amiable hushed bounciness, which is all that is left. The result is a product unique in musical annals: a harmonized sound sequence *entirely without musical content*. It is even transmitted in mono—one of the last nonstereo sources around—to enhance the screened-out simplicity.

Our biorhythms fade a little twice in each day. The major tiredness collapse occurs about four or five P.M., and the other, a lesser dip, at about 11 in the morning. The Muzak that's sent out from the company's North Carolina headquarters is designed to counter these lulls. The sequences that early-morning shoppers will hear are fairly slow, but speed up toward 11 A.M., then slow and later speed up again to counter the afternoon dip, too.

It works, as Muzak corporation brochures cheerfully point out. Cows produce more milk and army staffs watching radar screens make fewer errors and cardiac patients in intensive care units recover better when they hear these counterfatigue sounds at these times. The ten-year-olds chewing gum, not quite realizing what is happening, will find their rate of chomping goes up slightly.

Teenagers especially dislike it, so when the owners of a 7-Eleven store in Thousand Oaks, a city near Los Angeles, found that they couldn't get rid of teenagers hanging out there, they took the gloves off and used a "Muzak Attack." The store let the warbles and glissandi and woodwind arpeggios pour happily forth. The teenagers vanished.

Examining Documents

Jenny Tesar

FROM the viewpoint of the forensic lab, documents are anything on which there is handwriting, typewriting, printing, or other symbols of communication. Questioned documents are ones that need to be proven to be genuine or fake. Medical prescriptions, checks, contracts, passports, wills, ransom notes, letters, application forms, gambler's slips, driver's licenses, hotel registration cards, writing on walls or clothing—these are some of the more common types of documents that arise in criminal investigations.

In addition to analyzing handwriting, document examiners look for erasures and changes in a document. They piece together torn and shredded papers. They restore charred and water-soaked documents. They make typewriter, copying machine, and checkwriter comparisons. They determine whether or not a certain rubber or steel stamp was used to make a certain impression. They make spectrographic analyses of inks to learn if a document has been back-dated.

A critical aspect of document examination is comparing the questioned writing with other writings that are known to be genuine. If a person is suspected of writing a ransom note, then samples of that person's handwriting are needed. Preferably, the samples use the same words as those appearing in the questioned document. Similarly, examiners try to find the exact typewriter on which a threatening note was typed, the exact checkwriter used to prepare fraudulent checks, or the exact stamp used to make an impression on a suspicious will.

Sometimes, it is desirable to check a document for latent fingerprints and palm prints. But the chemical processing used to find latent prints may dissolve ink and cause paper to discolor. Therefore, document specialists generally complete their examinations before the document is checked for prints.

Document examiners use a broad range of equipment in their work. Microscopes are essential for studying handwriting and typewriting. They also enable examiners to determine if paper fibers were disturbed by erasures. And they are used to decipher type impressions left on typewriter ribbons. Infrared or ultraviolet light are used to show additions and deletions to documents. Spectrophotometers can be used to study the chemical composition of ink, to learn whether or not the same pen was used to prepare two documents—or to prepare all parts of a single document. Chromatography and infrared photography can also be used to compare inks. Infrared photography and reflected light photography are sometimes able to reveal and decipher writing on documents that have been charred in a fire.

As people learn to write, they develop special peculiarities in how they form letters. Ask friends to write this sentence and you will find many variations in the appearance of the letters. You will also notice that people write at different slants, use varying stroke widths, exert differing amounts of pressure on the pen or pencil, have different amounts of spacing between letters, and use different flourishes at the ends of words. Such peculiarities give each person a unique handwriting.

A forger tries to imitate another person's writing so accurately that the fake document cannot be distinguished from the genuine. One common method used by forgers is tracing. The document to be forged is placed on top of the genuine document. Strong light is shone through both papers, enabling the forger to see and trace the genuine document. Another common method is freehand imitation. The forger practices the person's handwriting, trying to perfect the peculiarities in that person's writing.

Creating a good copy of another person's writing is extremely difficult. It is almost impossible to make a forgery that cannot be detected by experts. The forger may correctly duplicate the letter forms, but there will be easy-to-spot differences in how the pen was held, how it moved across the paper, and when it was lifted from the paper.

Sometimes, writers are intent not on forging someone else's writing but in disguising their own. This may occur when people are writing ransom notes or obscene letters. Often, however, document experts can see through the disguise. Except for beginning writers, the movements made in writing are habits. When people write, they think about the subject matter, not about how to form the letters or how to combine the letters into words. Even people who are trying to disguise their handwriting will unconsciously use some of their unique writing peculiarities.

Document examiners always try to obtain as many samples of a person's genuine writing as possible, to use as standards of comparison against the questioned document. For example, a document that purportedly is a suicide note can be checked against personal letters, diaries, employment applications, and other writings of the dead person.

Dead Men Do Tell Tales

William R. Maples, Ph.D.
and Michael Browning

THE television show "Quincy" has caused me no end of vexation and amusement. When people learn that I am a forensic anthropologist, the first thing they usually say is: "Oh, like Quincy?" Quincy was a medical examiner whose whole career was one long string of dramatic successes. Born under a lucky star, Quincy solved his cases within hours or days. If Quincy had a problem, he telephoned his brilliant assistant, Sam, back at the lab, and Sam had the answer for him in seconds. Sam! How I envied Quincy his faithful and unerring Sam! Any one of us could shine like the morning star if we only had a Sam working for us. In one episode Quincy and Sam actually determined the hair color of a skeleton by examining its femur—a complete scientific impossibility. A bunch of us forensic anthropologists later cornered the technical advisor of this episode at the annual convention of the American Academy of Forensic Scientists. Up against the wall, needled and jabbed by our merciless questions over this hair-color episode, he finally admitted that he had taken "dramatic license" to "move the plot forward."

I am not Quincy. The difference between forensic pathologists and forensic anthropologists is quite simple. Pathologists have medical degrees. They are doctors who have received residency training in pathology. If they are fortunate, they also have some training in courtroom procedures. All the medical examiners in the state of Florida are forensic pathologists with medical degrees. In some states they may also serve as county coroners, legally determining the cause of death. But in others, the coroner may have no medical background at all; he may simply be a local person with a reputation for shrewdness and honesty. I have known coroners who were filling station owners, or funeral parlor directors, or even furniture salesmen. Why furniture salesmen? Because in the old days these merchants stocked coffins in their shops.

A forensic anthropologist is not a medical doctor, though he has a Ph.D. and has studied anthropology in college. We specialize in the human skeletal system, its changes through life, its changes across many lifetimes, and its variations around the world. We are part of the larger field of physical anthropology, or biological anthropology as it is known today, which is concerned overall with the human body and all its variations. My specialty, physical anthropology, is distinct from other fields, such as cultural anthropology and archaeology. The cultural anthropologists are the ones who go out and study the exotic tribes, the *"fluttered folk and wild,"* as the poet Rudyard Kipling called them. The archaeologists look for tools and other evidence of ancient and recent man in the folds and hollows of Asia, Africa and Europe.

My field of expertise is the human skeleton. Though some pathologists insist on doing their own skeletal examinations along with autopsies, I can confidently say that there are very few cases in which a forensic anthropologist—someone like me—could not add a great deal of useful information to what a pathologist can discover. I have had pathologists exclaim frankly in my hearing, when confronted with a skeleton: "Gee, I'm not used to looking at these without the meat on them!"

But long and lean were the years from the time I entered graduate school, in 1959, to the time I got my first case, in 1972. There was a spot of work from time to time in McKern's lab. There were occasional formal examinations of skeletons in Africa. But apart from these cases, the annals of my professional life in this period are rather parched and poor.

When I open my filing cabinets the gaunt memories of those starveling years come back to me vividly. In 1972 I had but a single case. In 1973 hope blazed up like a bonfire: a scatter of buried bodies was found less than a quarter of a mile away from where I live in Gainesville. These remains turned up when new utility lines were being laid, and for a while it was feared that we were dealing with the grisly spoils left by a serial killer. The former owner of the house in whose backyard these bodies came to light was an attorney who had committed suicide years earlier. All sorts of wild theories were floating about.

The police asked me and three university archaeologists to investigate. We all piled into a van and drove to the site. Within a few hours we had turned up casket hardware, nails, screws, etc., that indicated we were dealing with nothing more sinister than an early twentieth-century graveyard. The whole thing was a fiasco, a false alarm.

In 1974, I had two cases. In 1975, two more cases; in 1976, two cases; in 1977, three cases; in 1978—twelve cases! And from then on things began to snowball.

When the Florida Museum of Natural History was endowed by the state legislature in 1917 as the Florida State Museum, one of its functions, as spelled out in the original wording of the law, was that the museum would provide assistance to the state in "identifying specimens." I doubt the original framers of the law imagined that among those "specimens" would be human remains, still less that those remains would be the ghastly leavings of murderers and maniacs. But over the years I have tried to do my part to repay the generosity and vision of those state legislators of long ago. My first opportunity to do so—my first case—came in April 1972, when a Washington County sheriff's deputy brought me a peat-encrusted skeleton that had been found in the woods and asked me to analyze it.

The skeleton had been found in a swamp near Chipley. There was no name, no identifying information accompanying it at all. I took the skeleton down to the steam tables at the end of my laboratory in the basement of the anthropology department and started cleaning away the vegetable matter. Meanwhile a class nearby broke for coffee and the professor brought his pupils over to see what I was doing. This professor was a bit of a twit. He said to the students, very jocularly: "You see, science has its uses in the real world." I was irritated at his condescension but concealed it. I invited the students to have a look at the skeleton. They crowded over.

"Here are his socks," I said. "And you can see the feet are still in the socks."

At that point the twit vanished from the scene and so did most of his fainthearted students. I learned the power of cold reality, how it acts like a fly whisk to chase idle minds away; and I admired those students who stayed behind.

You always have a fondness for your first cases, and I found this skeleton very interesting. Under analysis, it turned out to be that of a toothless elderly man with a lot of union or fusion of bones in his back, due to old age. The really fascinating thing was that he had a large opening where one ear would have been on the skull. It was all hollowed out and eaten away. Obviously he had been deaf in that ear. But there was more: a penetration from this area up through the thin bones above, which meant that this perforation went into the cranial vault, the brain case. Finally, along the inner surface of that brain case you could see pitting, where an infection had eroded the bone during life.

I went to the University of Florida Medical School library, researched the problem and found abundant literature that described the condition. It was a middle ear infection. Such an infection, if not treated, will cause hearing loss and excavation of the bony surface in the area. Sometimes this gnawing will penetrate the brain case, leading to infection that would cause disorientation, nerve problems and death. In its earlier stages the infection produces a dripping exudation from the ear that would be foul-smelling.

Armed with this information, I asked the sheriff if there were any local people who fit this description. It turned out there was a man, a retired farm laborer living on Social Security, who was well known in the vicinity and who had been missing for two years. His name—there is no need to give his name; he was subsequently identified beyond doubt. Toward the end of his life a foul odor hung about him, so oppressive that people shunned him. From his tottering gait, he also seemed to have motor nerve problems. People thought he had suffered a stroke and was partially paralyzed. Neighbors and acquaintances confirmed that he seemed increasingly disoriented toward the end of his days. Finally he wandered off and disappeared, not to be seen again until the skeleton was retrieved from the swamp.

But the skeletal remains that had moldered for two years in the wild could still speak to me. The perforated skull with the pitted brain case yielded up information that agreed very well with reports of the man in life. It could even describe to me the last hours of the unfortunate farmhand, shunned and alone, stumbling into the swamp in pain, his brain swarming with infectious invaders that gnawed away at his balance, his reason and the very bone that encased his brain.

I handed the skeleton back over to the sheriff's office, together with my findings. Once, long afterward, I was traveling through Chipley and stopped in at the sheriff's office to ask about the final disposition of the case. The deputies told me that the coroner had ruled the farmhand had been clearly identified and had died a natural death.

Social Studies

Brady and Lincoln

George Sullivan

IN February, 1860, not long after Mathew Brady had opened his gallery on Broadway at Tenth Street in New York, Abraham Lincoln paid a visit. The meeting of Brady and the tall lawyer from Illinois, then fifty-one and who later in the year was to be elected to his first presidential term, resulted in one of the most famous portraits ever taken by Brady.

Lincoln had been invited to New York to address the congregation of Henry Ward Beecher's church in Brooklyn. Several leading Republicans, however, persuaded him to deliver the speech at Cooper Institute, a free school of arts and sciences in Manhattan, instead of in Brooklyn. Once the Reverend Beecher approved, Lincoln agreed to the change.

On Monday morning, February 27, members of the Young Men's Central Republican Union met Lincoln at the Astor House, where he was staying, and escorted him up Broadway to Brady's studio, where Brady had begun making preparations for the sitting. Lincoln's physical appearance presented problems. The *Houston Telegraph* described the future President as ". . . the leanest, lankest, most ungainly mass of legs and arms and hatchet face ever strung on a single frame," then added, "He has abused the privilege . . . of being ugly."

Brady decided to pose Lincoln standing, with one hand placed on a book, the other at his side. But Brady had trouble getting what he called a "natural" picture. Finally, he asked Lincoln if he would "arrange" his shirt collar.

Lincoln grinned, realizing what Brady had in mind. He then began pulling up his loose collar. "Ah, I see you want to shorten my neck," Lincoln said.

"That's just it, Mr. Lincoln," Brady replied. The incident served to relax Lincoln.

That night at Cooper Institute, Lincoln was introduced to an audience of some 1,500 by the famous poet and editor William Cullen Bryant. The huge throng was absorbed by Lincoln's words of reason and good sense. He did not call for the elimination of slavery overnight, but he did propose that slavery should not be extended into the new territories of the expanding nation.

Lincoln closed with these words: "Let us have faith that right makes might, and in that faith, let us, to the end, dare to do our duty as we understand it."

Less than twelve weeks later, Lincoln was nominated by the Republicans as their presidential candidate. The photograph that Brady had taken was used extensively during the campaign. It appeared as an engraving in *Harper's Weekly* and in countless other publications. It was duplicated by the tens of thousands as a card photograph and was also reproduced on banners and buttons. Currier and Ives made lithographs from it. Later, when Brady visited the White House, Lincoln is said to have remarked, "Brady and the Cooper Institute made me President."

In the years after his election in 1860, Lincoln became something of an industry for Brady. Not only did Brady and his operators photograph the president on many occasions, they also photographed members of his family, his close friends, the members of his cabinet, the members of Congress at the time, and even Lincoln's enemies. John Wilkes Booth, who assassinated the president in 1865, was about the only well-known individual with a connection to Lincoln who managed to escape Brady's cameras.

According to Charles Hamilton and Lloyd Ostendorf, authors of *Lincoln in Photographs, An Album of Every Known Pose*, Lincoln, during his lifetime, sat for thirty-three different cameramen who produced 126 different photographs.

Alexander Gardner photographed Lincoln thirty times, more than anyone else. Many of Gardner's photographs were taken at Brady's Washington studio on Pennsylvania Avenue, while he was employed by him.

Anthony Berger, who joined Brady in Washington in 1863 or 1864, is second to Gardner, with thirteen Lincoln photographs, all posed at Brady's studio. Brady or his camera operators are believed to have photographed Lincoln eleven times.

The first session in Washington involving Lincoln took place at Brady's gallery on February 24, 1861. *Harper's Weekly* had assigned Brady to photograph the newly elected president upon his arrival in Washington from his home in Springfield, Illinois. It was a long, exhausting journey, covering nearly two thousand miles through seven states. At various stops during the trip, Lincoln shook hands with admirers. The thousands of hands he shook caused his right hand to swell. During the photo session, Lincoln kept the swollen hand closed or tucked out of sight.

Alexander Gardner, who was in charge of Brady's studio at the time, took five poses that day. A young artist, George Story, a friend of Brady's who had taken a studio in the same building as Brady's gallery, once recalled the session: "A day or two after the President's arrival [February 23, 1861], Mr. Gardner, Mr. Brady's representative in Washington, came to my room and asked me to come and pose Mr. Lincoln for a picture. When I entered the room, the President was seated in a chair wholly absorbed in deep thought . . . I said in an undertone to the operator, 'Bring your instrument here and take the picture.'" Gardner used a two-lens and then a three-lens camera in taking the pictures.

During the session, Lincoln, who dressed in his best attire for the occasion, scarcely moved. John G. Nicolay, Lincoln's private secretary, described the president as having a "serious, far-away look." *Harper's Weekly* published an engraved reproduction of one of the photographs in its issue of April 27, 1861.

Lincoln's inauguration was scheduled for March 4, 1861. Brady himself made plans to photograph it and applied to authorities for credentials that would enable him to get close enough to the oath-taking ceremony to make a clear picture of it.

But Allan Pinkerton, who had guarded Lincoln on his trip to Washington, believed the president's life was in danger. To guard against an assassination attempt, sharpshooters had been stationed along Pennsylvania Avenue and troops were posted near the Capitol steps on the morning of the inauguration. A few hours before the inauguration, a report was received that a bomb would be exploded under the wooden platform on which the ceremonies were to take place.

When Brady and two of his operators arrived that morning to set up their equipment, they were given no special privileges and had to station themselves a long distance from the ceremonies. While their photographs captured part of the crowd and the Capitol Building (with its unfinished dome), it was impossible to make out the figure of Lincoln.

Lincoln made his second visit to Brady's Washington studio in 1862. This time Brady and his assistants made an Imperial photograph of the president, which now ranks as the largest known Lincoln photograph. The image is recorded on a glass plate that measures 18½ by 20⅜ inches. After the Imperial photograph was taken, Brady used a multi-lens camera to take other photographs, which were very similar to the first.

When Lincoln visited Brady's gallery on April 17, 1863, Brady's operator at the time, Thomas Le Mere, told him that there was quite a demand for a new standing portrait of the president. Lincoln, who often joked about his height, said, "Can it be taken with a single negative?" Apparently, the answer was "No," for Le Mere's photograph cuts off the president at the ankles.

A number of photographs of Lincoln were produced as stereographs, or stereo cards, as they are sometimes called today. Stereographs are paired photographs of the same image taken from slightly different points of view. When the paired images are viewed through a special optical instrument called a stereoscope, the viewer sees a single image in three dimensions. At one time, virtually every American family had a collection of stereographs and a stereoscope. Home viewing was almost as popular as television is today.

Special stereo cameras, each with two lenses mounted several inches apart, were developed that could photograph the paired views simultaneously. Besides portraits, all kinds of scenic views were photographed for stereo cards. Many Civil War photographs were also produced for stereo viewing.

During the period from 1858–1865, Edward Anthony and Frederick and William Langenheim were the leading publishers of stereo cards. In 1862 alone, Anthony sold several hundred thousand of the doublephoto, rectangular cards with rounded corners. The cards remained popular well into the 1900s.

What have become perhaps the best-known photographs of Lincoln were taken at Brady's gallery in Washington on February 9, 1864. Anthony Berger was the photographer. Brady is believed to have been there that day, helping with the posing and performing other chores.

In one series of photographs taken that day, Lincoln appears in profile. Sculptor Victor D. Brenner used this pose to model the portrait of the president that appears on the Lincoln-head penny. In another pose, the president is seated, looking stern and serene. This portrait served as the basis for the engraving of Lincoln that appears on the five-dollar bill.

Yet another picture taken by Anthony Berger at Brady's gallery on February 9, 1864, included Lincoln's son, Thomas, known as "Tad," who was ten years old at the time. The two are pictured looking at a big photograph album. The photograph was published in many different forms—as a card photograph, an engraving, lithograph, and painting. Copied by other photographers, it was turned out in enormous quantities.

Late in April, 1864, Lincoln returned to Brady's studio for another photo session. Again, Anthony Berger was the photographer. Berger also photographed Lincoln at the White House that month.

The last formal portraits of President Lincoln were taken by Alexander Gardner in 1865. Several years before, Gardner had left Brady and established his own studio in Washington not far from the White House. On February 5, 1865, Lincoln visited the studio.

After the president had posed for several pictures, Gardner moved in for a final portrait, a close-up. The glass plate bearing the image cracked during processing. After a single print had been made, Gardner discarded the damaged plate. After all, he may have figured, the president, who had been reelected the previous November, would be in office for four more years. There would be plenty of opportunities to make photographs. But on April 14 of that year, Lincoln was shot at Ford's Theatre. He died early the next morning.

Not long after Lincoln's assassination, Andrew Johnson, who had taken office upon Lincoln's death, went to Brady's gallery to sit for a portrait. Brady posed him in the same chair that had been used for Lincoln's sittings.

On May 5, 1865, the Washington *Daily Chronicle* noted that Brady had taken the first picture of Johnson as president. "Like all of Brady's works," said the newspaper, "it is easy in position, bold in outline, clear in finish, and true as life itself."

Monticello

Stephen Gardiner

MONTICELLO, Charlottesville, Virginia-Monticello was designed from c. 1769 by Thomas Jefferson (1743–1826), third president of the United States, for his own use. In this original form the house was perhaps the finest example of the Colonial style, but it was completely remodeled by Jefferson in a Palladian manner between 1796 and 1808. The building is a most original, imaginative and unacademic heir to the European Classical tradition. No wonder, then, that Monticello, together with the University of Virginia, Charlottesville (1817–26), also by Jefferson, had a huge influence on American architecture of the times.

Monticello is one of a number of great houses which took their inspiration from Palladio's Villa Rotunda (begun c. 1550). Among the others were Colen Campbell's Mereworth Castle, Kent, England (1722–5), and Chiswick House, London (1725) by Lord Burlington and William Kent. Monticello is, however, an improvement on its rivals. It was not in a valley or on flat ground, as are Mereworth and Chiswick, but on the top of a gently rounded hill, giving views in all directions and bringing it closer to the Italian original. Jefferson's first building, of 1778, was a simple Greek cross with porticos back and front; the remodeled design follows Palladio's Rotunda more closely, with porticos on all four sides, and flights of steps leading up to them.

But the second design for Monticello was not a slavish imitation of the Rotunda—as Mereworth was—another reason why Monticello is better than Mereworth or Chiswick. Although it reflects a scholarly understanding and reverence for the past, Monticello was designed to suit the present. Its plan is, in fact, a good deal more complex and functional than the Rotunda's; for example, all ground floor rooms have access either from the central hall or from corridors, and every foot of space is carefully used. Jefferson's design was exceedingly clever. The porticos were seen as tools to help simplify the complex plan, by producing an elevation with a domestic scale. The free forms of the library, study, drawing-room, tearoom, and octagonal bedroom become delightful variations within a strong symmetrical composition, governed and expressed by the presence of the porticos: and two stories appear to be one. Thus Palladio's conception—of a hill crowned with a dome—is followed, but not in such a way as to deny domestic proportions for modern requirements. A test of greatness is the degree to which the work of a genius can be absorbed by the disciple without ill effects. Monticello illustrates this form of greatness, which was Jefferson's.

Digging Down to Sterile Ground

Joyce Hansen and Gary McGowan

SEPTEMBER 30, 1991, was a breezy and sunny day in New
York City, with a little nip in the air—a reminder that winter was
on its way. Cranes picked up chunks of rubble, while dump
trucks and backhoes whizzed and pounded. Construction workers, in their orange hard hats swarmed like a colony of ants
throughout the construction site that included Broadway,
Duane, Elk, and Reade streets.

Just off Reade Street, another group of men and women also
worked busily. They were members of the archaeological team
hired by the United States government to analyze the site before a new thirty-four-story federal office building could be constructed. The excavated area exposed old gray stone walls, once
the foundation for two tiny nineteenth-century streets, known
as Republican and Manhattan alleys.

The archaeological crew was aware that the site, shown on
eighteenth-century city maps as the "Negroes Burying Ground,"
had once been a cemetery for people of African descent, paupers
(poor people), and British and American prisoners of war during
the American Revolution. They expected to find, if anything, about
fifty burials and a few bone fragments. What else could remain
after centuries of building and changes in the original landscape?

The archaeologists worked sixteen feet below the surface of
the southeastern section of the construction site. They had dug
down to sterile ground—a point where humans, with their
buildings, streets, and walls, had not touched. It was quieter
here. Honking horns and screeching sirens from the city traffic
were muffled and distant. The air was still, contained, and
fresh—not like the air above the surface, thick with fumes from
hundreds of cars and other motor vehicles.

The earth here was different, too. A wet, blood-red clay (alluvial clay) had been deposited throughout this region by glaciers
during the Ice Age. Hundreds of small rocks and pebbles, like
those found in the woods and forests of upstate New York, pep-
pered the ground.

As the crew carefully dug into the damp, fine, silty alluvial clay, tiny particles began to seep into their clothes and the creases of their skin and body. If there was a heavy downpour of rain while they worked in this soil, the workers could begin to sink; if the ground became unstable, holes could fill up and the earth cave in.

While they dug, it became apparent that there were graves here that had been underneath this bustling part of the city for two centuries or more.

At 10:00 A.M. one team member noticed a dark outline in the earth. Since the clay was soft, it was fairly easy to dig around the outline. Using a trowel similar to a gardening tool, the team meticulously scraped away the dirt. One of them spotted a large, bright brown, oddly misshapen nail, nothing like the nails we are accustomed to seeing today.

After being buried in the earth and exposed to the elements, this nail had undergone a process called oxidation. Oxygen, salt, water, and other chemicals had corroded the metal, causing it to expand from the inside out. Thus the nail had not only enlarged in spots, but twisted like a bloated overgrown worm.

Lying on their stomachs, separated from the moist, rocky earth only by thick plywood boards, flattened boxes, and a protective covering, the team slowed down the pace of their work. What might look like an old useless object was an important discovery. The nail might have come from a colonial coffin. Perhaps they had discovered a burial site.

Using a dental pick, a soft brush, and a rubber aspirator (often used as a baby's ear syringe) the excavators spent the rest of that day carefully removing the soil around the outline. For the next two and a half days they painstakingly pecked, pushed, and gently blew away the earth around the outline until they saw a dark stain.

They were correct about the nail, for a coffin lid was emerging. As the crew removed a rectangular, uniform portion of earth, a row of similar nails began to appear. The hexagonal shape of a casket could be made out. It appeared to be fairly typical for the eighteenth century—a modest pine or cedar coffin. The lid had melded almost completely into the red earth and the coffin had turned the dirt, with which it blended, a dark brown color, rich with the tannic acid found in wood bark.

Almost completely deteriorated, and as delicate as old parchment, the lid was only a quarter of an inch thick. The archaeologists collected tiny fibers from what remained of the wood.

For hours they brushed and peeled the lid away, hoping to find some skeletal remains. This was the most crucial part of the excavation. If the archaeologists weren't careful with their trowels and brushes, they might accidentally change the appearance of any remaining bone fragments, which could lead to false interpretations when the bones were studied and analyzed. For example, damage to the bone during a dig could falsely be interpreted as a wound, disease, or fracture from a previous injury.

The archaeologists didn't think, though, that they would find much. As they continued to brush away the soil, they realized that the weight of the earth above had caused the left side of the coffin to buckle and cave in, probably destroying the skeleton inside.

The excavation was completed by October 1. As the sun was setting and the autumn temperature dipped down to forty degrees, they finally reached the burial. The crew gazed in amazement. Instead of pieces of bone, eroded and destroyed by time, they saw a complete skeleton, face up with its arms at its sides.

Miraculously there was no serious damage, even though the water table was high here. (The water table is the level below which the ground is saturated with water.) The skeletal remains of this early New Yorker were slowly becoming part of the red earth. The remains were wet and gelatinous—almost the consistency of butter—yet the skeleton was completely intact and in remarkably good condition.

As the crew packed up and prepared to leave, it was clear to them that this well-preserved skeleton under the streets of lower Manhattan was one of the most important archaeological discoveries of our time.

What they did not know as yet was how much spiritual, cultural, historical, and archaeological treasure Republican Alley and Manhattan Alley would yield.

Underwater Gold Rush

Review of *Ship of Gold in the Deep Blue Sea*
by Gary Kinder
Susan Hall-Balduf

ONE minute, you're standing beside gallant Captain Herndon in 1857 on the deck of the S.S. Central America, laden with booty from the California Gold Rush but storm-tossed and taking on water. The next, you're trailing after ingenious and ingenuous engineer Tommy Thompson, who has simply wondered all his life how performing delicate technical tasks in the deep ocean could best be accomplished and who has chosen a treasure ship for experimentation just because it is the target for which he could most easily raise funding.

"Ship of Gold in the Deep Blue Sea" runs the gamut from high drama in the low-tech waters of pre-Civil War America, where the only distress signal a ship had available was an upside-down flag (virtually invisible in heavy rain), to low comedy in the silicon chip-dominated 1980s, when a lump of coal plucked from the ocean floor by a multimillion-dollar robot has to be arrested by a U.S. marshal in order for a recovery outfit to take legal possession of a shipwreck.

The Central America was a three-masted side-wheel steamer that transported passengers and cargo home to the United States from the east coast of Panama after they had arrived on the west coast from San Francisco and traveled overland. It had just left its stopover point of Havana when it sailed into the storm of the century, a full-blown hurricane that damaged dozens of ships in its path and went on to batter the eastern seaboard.

The storm tore down the Central America's masts, and a leak in its heavily laden hold drowned its engines. The captain knew his only hope of saving the lives in his care, a responsibility he took very seriously, was to keep afloat as long as possible on the chance that another ship might come along and rescue them.

Unlike the famously panicked passengers of the Titanic, the men—crew and passengers alike—on the Central America fought hard to save their ship, bailing by hand more than 24 hours without rest, food or drink. The ladies, meanwhile, sat in the parlor, keeping the children quiet and pretending not to worry about the waves crashing over their feet.

When it was time to take to the lifeboats, oarsmen rowed the terrified, half-drowned women more than a mile in high seas to another ship in marginally better condition. Then they returned to the Central America for another boatload. Not one woman or child was left on the doomed ship, and only one of those rescued died, probably because at one point she was crushed between her lifeboat and the side of the ship.

The captain ordered every flat surface to be detached: doors, hatches, sections of floorboard—anything he thought might be used for a raft. The last anyone saw of him, he was standing on the bridge when it was ripped away by a wall of water.

Few survivors were taken from the sea. Many were dragged under when the ship went down, and most who did find something to float on gradually succumbed to exposure and delirium. It was the United States' worst shipping disaster. Of the nearly 600 souls aboard, only 149 men, women and children survived the sinking of the S.S. Central America.

And all that lovely gold from California, too heavy for pockets, less valuable than a chance at life, went straight to the bottom of the ocean, somewhere off the coast of North Carolina in 8,000 feet of water.

Tommy Thompson was educated as a mechanical engineer at Ohio State University. He wanted to be an inventor; the first thing he invented was his own course of study, as the only ocean engineer in the middle of Columbus, Ohio. Fly somebody else to the moon. Tommy wanted to explore the riches of the water on 71 percent of the Earth's surface.

The trouble was, nobody had figured out how to send down equipment that wouldn't crash into the bottom, snap its electronic cables or do anything more useful than photograph, scoop or grab. The famously photographed Titanic rests in 12,500 feet of water; whether anything can—or should—be removed from it for historical examination remains debatable. A clumsy clutch at debris was all very well if pieces were what you wanted; if scientific retrieval was the goal, something more sophisticated was in order.

And Tommy, starting in 1985, built a vast network of friends, allies, partners and investors, and managed to order the equipment he needed, conjure up by computer the most likely sites to search for the wreck and pull together the crew and other resources that let him go looking. There was gold in them thar bills. He could find people willing to pay them.

However, that wasn't his true goal. As Tommy's childhood friend and business partner Barry Schatz explained it, "We didn't go after the Central America as an end in itself, but as a way to learn how to work in the deep ocean and then to discover the resources there."

It took three years, $12 million and many twists and turns of fortune before Tommy Thompson came up for air with tons of the stuff that dreams are made of. It would not always have been fun to plow the ocean with him or to endure the flying guano when the lawyers hit the courtroom fans in the battle to determine just who owned this loot.

But if your feet are dry and the nearest waves are merely ripples in a glass of lemonade, "Ship of Gold" offers fascinating reading for a long afternoon.

from

Ship of Gold in the Deep Blue Sea

Gary Kinder

MEN have always pondered how they will act under fire, and mostly the reality when it comes is far more sober and sickening than imagined, and the acts are much less quick and noble. When a ship seemed destined to sink, the captain and his officers often had to hold the crew and the male passengers at gunpoint to keep them away from the lifeboats until they could safely remove all of the women and children. Sometimes not even the captain and crew acted nobly. Four nights earlier, Herndon had jokingly turned the dinner conversation from shipwrecks to topics more pleasant by declaring that if his ship ever went down he would be under her keel. It was a charming seaman's segue, and from the mouths of perhaps most men it would have remained no more than that. But the remark had been prompted by the sinking of another steamer three years back, when the captain and crew had commandeered the lifeboats, and 259 of the 282 passengers, including all of the women and children, had perished. Herndon's friends knew that for three years the story had haunted him. He was now in the middle of an even bigger disaster, but he had already determined that surviving by less than honorable means was not worth a lifetime of scorn.

Customary for the day, but grossly inadequate, the *Central America* carried six lifeboats, five of wood, one of metal. The night before, one of the wooden boats had been smashed against the wheelhouse. The remaining boats each normally held four oarsmen, a helmsman, and forty to fifty passengers, but with the strain on the oarsmen in seas such as this, Herndon could load no more than fifteen or twenty. As soon as the *Marine* rounded to, he ordered the first officer to clear away two of the lifeboats, one on the port, one on the starboard, and to get the port boat to the lee side of the ship. Then he ordered all women and children below to don life preservers.

Although the sea nearly swamped the first lifeboat under the guards of the steamer, the crew launched it and the second boat safely. Then they lowered a third lifeboat, and as soon as it hit the water, a heavy sea quickly sucked it away, then rose up and smashed it against the hull of the ship, the planks shattering and the remains of the boat hanging from its block.

Two boats were now in the water, the oarsmen trying to keep them away from the sides of the steamer. Two boats remained on the upper deck, one wood, one metal. The crew lowered the wooden lifeboat safely into the water. Chief Engineer Ashby helped launch the metal boat, riding it down into the waves, but a heavy sea caught the boat, drove it hard under the lee guard, stove it in, swamped it, and sank it immediately. Ashby disappeared with the boat, and the crew had to pull him from the water.

Below in the main cabin, the women and children gathered to prepare for the trip to the *Marine*. To give them as much freedom as possible and as little weight, the women were instructed to strip off their undergarments and layers of skirts, everything but the outside dress, then put on a life preserver. They also wrapped the older children in life preservers and the babies in blankets to be held in their arms.

Many of the women traveled with a great deal of money they had not registered with the purser. All of them were now advised not to carry more than two twenty-dollar gold pieces with them. Two women retrieved a satchel from their stateroom and upon returning to the cabin, opened the satchel, and weeping, shook eleven thousand dollars in gold onto the floor. Through tears, they said that anyone who wanted the money could take what they pleased. "That money is all we made in California," they added. "We were returning home to enjoy it."

As the women discarded their extra clothes and put on life preservers, the captain's boy appeared at the entrance to the cabin and shouted, "The captain says all the ladies must go on deck!"

The few who had managed to ready themselves and their families for the trip made their way across the room and started climbing the steps to the hatchway, their dresses long and sagging from lack of hoops and petticoats, their upper bodies covered in cork and tin life preservers, their hands holding or pushing forward small children, until they reached the deck. There the water crashed around them and the wind blew the spray over them, and they were wet through in an instant. By the time Ashby was hauled from the sea, women and children were struggling their way to the lee side of the ship, where the five-man crews fought to keep the lifeboats from being smashed against the ship or swamped under her guards. Herndon ordered Ashby and his first officer not to let a single man into the boats until all of the women and children were off.

"While they were getting into the boats," observed one man from the bailing lines, "there was the utmost coolness and self-control among the passengers; not a man attempted to get into the boats. Captain Herndon gave orders that none but the ladies and children should get into the boats, and he was obeyed to the letter."

In line to be transferred to a lifeboat, Annie McNeill glanced at Captain Herndon as he stood on the rain-soaked deck. She thought he seemed saddened. She talked with him briefly, and he said he would not try to save himself, that he would go down with his ship.

"Nevertheless," she remembered, "he did all that lay in his power to save others. He was a very kind, generous, gentlemanly man, and if he had any fault it was that he was not severe enough to his own hands."

The only way Captain Herndon could get the women and children into the boats was to lower each by rope one at a time from the upper deck, while the oarsmen tried to fend off, and the lifeboats crested close to the ship's hull. He and his men had fashioned a rope chair. "A noose was passed around our feet and dress," recalled one of the women. "There was nothing to support our backs, but we held a rope, which came down in front, with our hands. The boat could only approach the steamer between the waves, so we had to remain suspended sometimes while the wave passed. These waves would also drive us under the side of the steamer."

The water sucked away from the steamer's hull, then rose up and slammed against it, sending salt spray high into the air and hissing back into the sea. The oarsmen fended off, trying to keep the boat steady, close enough to catch the women and children dropped from the deck, yet far enough away to avoid the waves smashing the boat to splinters. Already the storm had claimed half of the lifeboats.

The women and children had to jump from the deck as far out over the water as they could, dangling on the rope, and then drop suddenly when the waves pushed the boat higher and toward the ship. In that instant, the men holding the ropes often just let go. Some women fell into the boat, others hit the water, and then either the hands on deck raised them hanging from the rope to try again, or the oarsmen grabbed ahold and hauled them in over the gunwale. The sea moved suddenly and with great force, seemingly in all directions at once, and a body slammed against the hull of the ship or dropped suddenly into the boat found them both hard and unforgiving. Many of the women were bruised and cut; some sprained shoulders or twisted ankles. Most of them fell into the sea at least once, several of them twice, and one disappeared beneath the surface three times. As soon as a woman or child had dropped to the boat and an oarsman could free the rope, the men on deck snapped it up and quickly began rigging the next passenger.

Some women being herded toward the rope looked around wildly for their children and called to their friends, but their voices were drowned in the confusion. Some got shuffled forward so quickly and found themselves in the sling and over the side so suddenly that they ended up in a boat without their children. Some watched after the children of other women. Captain Herndon supervised the evacuation, constantly moving from one part of the ship to another, ensuring that only women and children got into the first boats.

Jane Harris started up the gangway from the saloon to the upper deck holding her baby in her arms, but she could barely move because the steps under her feet slid sideways then suddenly dropped away or rocketed upward as the ship pounded in the trough of the waves. Herndon saw her trying to negotiate the stairs and sent one of the passengers to help her. Moments later, as she stood on deck prepared to descend to the first boat, Herndon assisted in loading her into the rope swing.

"The captain tied a rope around me," she remembered, "and I think he was one of the men that had hold of it when I was lowered down. He was a noble man, and I shall never forget him as long as I live. When I began to slide down, a great wave dashed up between me and the little boat, which threw the boat off from the ship and left me hanging in the air with the rope around my waist. I was swung hither and thither over the waves by the tossing of the ship, then I was dropped suddenly into the boat when it happened to come directly under me. As soon as I got into the boat, I looked up and saw the captain was fixing a cape around my child, and a few moments afterward he lowered her down to me."

The minstrel Billy Birch had left the bailing lines, found his wife, Virginia, and helped her with her life preserver. Then the two of them went to their cabin to find a cloak for Virginia. Amid the water and debris, Virginia saw something she could not leave behind: the canary she had carried aboard in a cage. "It was singing as merrily as it ever did," she remembered, and she hated to think of the small bird being drowned or crushed as the steamship broke apart.

"On the spur of the moment I took the little thing from its prison and placed it in the bosom of my dress. My husband remonstrated with me, hurrying me to leave the vessel, and telling me not to waste time on so trifling an object."

Together they hurried through the crowds of people belowdecks and up through the hatchway, trying to keep their footing as they made their way against the wind. They prepared Virginia quickly, and she bid her husband of three weeks good-bye. "I expected that it was the intention to transfer all the passengers to the brig, otherwise I would not have left while my husband remained behind. But he told me to go and he would soon follow, and so I went." The canary stuffed into her dress, Virginia swung over the side of the steamer and disappeared beneath the waves before she could be hauled, soaked and gasping, into the first of the small boats.

Many of the women expected their husbands to accompany them in the lifeboats, or assumed that their husbands would follow soon in another boat. But every man refused to leave with his wife until all of the women and children had been safely ferried to the *Marine.*

Mary Swan was a young wife traveling with a baby not yet two. When the order came for the women and children to prepare for lowering to the lifeboats, her husband left his place at the pumps and came to her. "About an hour before I left, he took me aside and bade me, 'Good-bye.' He said, 'I don't know that I shall ever see you again.' He was very glad to think that I could be taken off. He wanted me to go, and said that he did not care about himself, if it were possible that I could be saved, and the little child. He told me that he would try to save himself if an honorable opportunity should present itself after all the women were taken off. He had been sick for three or four days before the disaster, but notwithstanding this, he persisted in keeping his place at the pumps."

Behind Virginia Birch in the first boat came the only black woman on board, the stewardess, Lucy Dawson, known affectionately as Aunt Lucy. A stout, older woman, Aunt Lucy fell into the water three times before they could land her in the boat. On one of the dunkings, a wave lifted the lifeboat, which slammed into Lucy, then smashed her against the side of the steamer.

Three more women and five or six more children left the deck of the *Central America*, swung out over the water, and descended into the first of the lifeboats. Four crewmen manned the oars and at the helm stood one man Herndon knew he could trust above all others, the bos'n, John Black. As the oarsmen pushed off and dug in their oars, Virginia Birch heard Captain Herndon yell to Black, "Ask the captain of the brig to lay close by me all night for God's sake, as I am in a sinking state, and have five hundred souls on board, besides a million and a half dollars!"

Awaiting the women and children, two more lifeboats now remained at the sides of the steamer, each already beginning to fill, fore and aft, as crews on deck prepared the rope slings, loaded them with passengers, and swung them out over the water.

Before boarding in San Francisco, Thomas Badger had given his wife $16,500 in twenty-dollar gold pieces, which she had sewed up in toweling, in three parcels, and laid flat in a trunk. The trunk sat in their stateroom, now in water up to Jane Badger's knees as she picked her way among the "rubbish which strewed the cabin." She found the trunk, unlocked it, took out the gold, placed it in a carpetbag, threw a crepeshawl on top, locked the bag, then had to leave it sitting on the lower berth: It was so heavy, she couldn't lift it.

In his coat hanging in the stateroom, Badger also kept a memorandum book containing notes and other records of debts owed to him in New York, the sum of which was several thousand dollars. Wading through the water, Jane Badger retrieved the book "with all its contents," secured in a small bag about $1,500 worth of diamonds, bracelets, and rings, together with a purse containing $40, and made her way back to the deck. When she found her husband and told him what she had done, he told her to throw away the jewels, anything with any weight to it, but she declined, insisting she would keep them in her pocket.

On deck, Badger helped rig his wife for her descent to the next lifeboat. He bid her good-bye, and Jane Badger swung out over the water; a wave sucked the small boat away from the hull, and she dropped into the sea. On the second try, she landed in the boat but at first could only crouch in the bottom, her legs too unsteady and the sea too unpredictable for her to risk moving to a seat. When she finally moved to a bench, "a lady of remarkable stoutness" dropped from the deck above onto her neck and shoulders so hard she thought the blow had broken her neck. Some of the women in her boat took up buckets to help bail, though their haste, the wind, and the motion of the sea combined to keep much of the water from ever making it over the gunwale.

The men knew they were unlikely to leave the ship, but to coax their wives into the sling ready to be lowered, many allowed their wives to think they soon would be reunited on the brig. Annie McNeill, an orphan of nineteen when she married a man of thirty-three, had retrieved seventeen thousand dollars, chiefly in drafts, plus her diamonds and jewelry. "I am sure I should never have left the steamer had I known that the men were not coming," she said. "I should never have left my husband." They had been married five months, and she had no other family. "He constantly assured me that he was going with me until he got me on deck and the rope tied around me, when he said he could take care of himself and wanted me to be safe first."

In their stateroom preparing to leave, Ada Hawley asked her husband if he would go with her to the brig. He took his money out of their trunk and said not a word. She had been ill for several days, and she needed help with DeForest and little Willy. Her husband grabbed the baby, and a friend carried the older child, and they hurried on deck. Mrs. Hawley looked for the *Marine,* and it appeared to lie about a mile and a half away. She went over the side first, and there she waited in the boat.

"The little children were passed down," she recalled, "the officers lowering them by their arms, until the boat swung underneath, and they could be caught hold of by the boatmen. It was frightful to see these helpless little ones, held by their tiny arms above the waves. My babe was nearly smothered by the flying spray, as they were obliged to hold him a long time before he could be reached by the boatmen, but when I pressed him once more to my bosom, and covered him with my shawl, he soon fell asleep. I took nothing with me except a heavy shawl and my watch."

The instant the boat filled, the order came for the crew to shove off, and Herndon again shouted to the helmsman, "Tell the captain of the brig, for Heaven's sake, to lay by us all night!"

As the oarsmen set their oars to, Ada Hawley saw her husband. "He stood on the wheel-house and kissed his hand to me as the boat pulled away from the ship."

With her husband on deck working, Addie Easton went to their stateroom and put on a "dress skirt to cover my night dress and wrapper, which I afterward took off, as I thought I might get in the water and it would cause me to sink. Then I went to my small trunk which was in the room and took my dear mother's miniature, also one of my brother James, and some money. Taking a shawl and putting on a life preserver, I started to go above."

Just as she reached the door, Ansel came in and told her to hurry. "We shall be saved," he said, "but the women and children are to be taken off first."

"I can't go without you," said Addie.

At the thought of leaving her husband on the ship, her courage vanished. Ansel told her she had to go, and that he should follow very soon. Then their friend Robert Brown came to the door of their cabin.

"Come, Easton," he said, "you must hurry. They are taking another boatload now."

Ansel quickly reached into the trunk, took out a coat, stuffed the remainder of his money, about nine hundred dollars, and some valuable papers into the pockets, and rolled it into a bundle.

When the Eastons and Brown got to the deck, the second boat was nearly full. Ansel found Captain Herndon and asked him how many boats were left. The captain replied, "Only one. We had five but two were dashed to pieces as they were being manned, so we have but three." He calculated, however, that the three boats could make several trips before dark.

"I left in the third boat," Addie later remembered. "I said however to Ansel, 'I don't want to go till you do.' He said, 'You had better go now,' or something of that kind. I then kissed him and said, 'I'll pray for you.' In a moment I was swinging from the deck, and when a swell brought the little boat underneath, the rope was lowered and I dropped in the bottom of the boat. It was a dreadful moment for we were in great danger of swamping or being stove to pieces. And just then the contents of one of the barrels they were bailing with came down on my head, completely drenching me. Ansel threw me his coat containing the money and also took off the coat he was wearing and threw it to me to put about my shoulders."

One passenger described the evacuation of the women and children as "a dangerous, heroic and almost superhuman effort" that "can scarcely have a parallel." But the passenger also noted that "through some strange and mysterious influence there were several young and unmarried men taken in the life-boats to the brig, leaving behind those men who had wives and children."

Virginia Birch had pleaded with Ashby to allow her husband, Billy, to go with her. "But he refused," she recalled, "using insulting language."

Lynthia Ellis, a woman of delicate constitution, dehydrated, and suffering acutely from four days of seasickness, asked that her husband be allowed to go with her to help care for their four children, two of whom were sick, all of whom were young. But the hands refused. "No men would be allowed to go until all women and children were safely off."

Other women, too, had pleaded with the officers to let their husbands go with them and were refused, yet somehow in the confusion single men now sat at their side. With Addie safely in the lifeboat, Ansel Easton and Robert Brown returned to the bailing gang, but before that lifeboat filled, several men got in with Addie and the other women and children, the crew unaware that three women and at least as many children remained on board the steamer.

One of the men who boarded a lifeboat early was Judge Monson. He had applied to the first officer to allow an elderly gentleman, Albert Priest, to board that third boat. Perhaps realizing the judge was a friend of the captain, the first officer agreed, and the crew lowered the old man.

"I gave Mr. Priest a message to my brother in New York," Monson said later, "in case I should not be saved myself. Mr. Priest said, 'Never mind the message, come, Judge, yourself.' The first officer said, 'Certainly, Judge, it is your turn—all right, jump in.' I immediately was lowered into the boat. A moment previous I had not the slightest idea of leaving the steamer then."

Ann Small was the last of the passengers loaded into the third boat. Mrs. Small was a new widow with a two-year-old daughter. A few weeks earlier, her sea captain husband had died at sea, and she had buried him in Panama. When she boarded the *Central America* in Aspinwall, the American consul had asked Captain Herndon to deliver her and her child to New York. Herndon replied he would personally guarantee their safety. Now as the officers placed her in the rope swing, Herndon came up to her.

"Mrs. Small," he said, "this is sad. I am sorry not to get you home safely." Then he turned away, and she saw no more of him.

The boat, tossing at the side of the steamer, waited below for its final passenger. The crew quickly wrapped Ann Small into the harness, swung her out, and paid out line on the harness. Twice she fell into the sea. When at last she made it into the boat, wet and shaken, the oarsmen pushed off to begin the long journey to the brig. Seated in the lifeboat, Ann Small now looked up: On the deck of the steamer high above her she saw her little girl. The crew had wanted the mother lowered to the lifeboat first, so she then could receive her child. But the men in the boat below did not realize that one more tiny passenger remained for them to rescue; they had pushed off immediately, and they couldn't go back now. As the small boat pulled into the high seas, Ann Small saw her little girl on deck still in the arms of a crewman.

A Christmas Sermon on Peace

Martin Luther King, Jr.

PEACE on Earth. . . .

This Christmas season finds us a rather bewildered human race. We have neither peace within nor peace without. Everywhere paralyzing fears harrow people by day and haunt them by night. Our world is sick with war: everywhere we turn we see its ominous possibilities. And yet, my friends, the Christmas hope for peace and good will toward all men can no longer be dismissed as a kind of pious dream of some utopian. If we don't have good will toward men in this world, we will destroy ourselves by the misuse of our own instruments and our own power. Wisdom born of experience should tell us that war is obsolete. There may have been a time when war served as a negative good by preventing the spread and growth of an evil force, but the very destructive power of modern weapons of warfare eliminates even the possibility that war may any longer serve as a negative good. And so, if we assume that life is worth living, if we assume that mankind has a right to survive, then we must find an alternative to war—and so let us this morning explore the conditions for peace. Let us this morning think anew on the meaning of that Christmas hope: "Peace on Earth, Good Will toward Men." And as we explore these conditions, I would like to suggest that modern man really go all out to study the meaning of nonviolence, its philosophy and its strategy.

We have experimented with the meaning of nonviolence in our struggle for racial justice in the United States, but now the time has come for man to experiment with nonviolence in all areas of human conflict, and that means nonviolence on an international scale.

Now let me suggest first that if we are to have peace on earth, our loyalties must become ecumenical rather than sectional. Our loyalties must transcend our race, our tribe, our class, and our nation; and this means we must develop a world perspective. No individual can live alone; no nation can live alone, and as long as we try, the more we are going to have war in this world. Now the judgment of God is upon us, and we must either learn to live together as brothers or we are all going to perish together as fools.

Yes, as nations and individuals, we are interdependent. I have spoken to you before of our visit to India some years ago. It was a marvelous experience; but I say to you this morning that there were those depressing moments. How can one avoid being depressed when one sees with one's own eyes evidences of millions of people going to bed hungry at night? How can one avoid being depressed when one sees with one's own eyes thousands of people sleeping on the sidewalks at night? More than a million people sleep on the sidewalks of Bombay every night; more than half a million sleep on the sidewalks of Calcutta every night. They have no houses to go into. They have no beds to sleep in. As I beheld these conditions, something within me cried out: "Can we in America stand idly by and not be concerned?" And an answer came: "Oh, no!" And I started thinking about the fact that right here in our country we spend millions of dollars every day to store surplus food; and I said to myself: "I know where we can store that food free of charge—in the wrinkled stomachs of the millions of God's children in Asia, Africa, Latin America, and even in our own nation, who go to bed hungry at night."

It really boils down to this: that all life is interrelated. We are all caught in an inescapable network of mutuality, tied into a single garment of destiny. Whatever affects one directly, affects all indirectly. We are made to live together because of the interrelated structure of reality. Did you ever stop to think that you can't leave for your job in the morning without being dependent on most of the world? You get up in the morning and go to the bathroom and reach over for the sponge, and that's handed to you by a Pacific islander. You reach for a bar of soap, and that's given to you at the hands of a Frenchman. And then you go into the kitchen to drink your coffee for the morning, and that's poured into your cup by a South American. And maybe you want tea; that's poured into your cup by a Chinese. Or maybe you're desirous of having cocoa for breakfast, and that's poured into your cup by a West African. And then you reach over for your toast, and that's given to you at the hands of an English-speaking farmer, not to mention the baker. And before you finish eating breakfast in the morning, you've depended on more than half of the world. This is the way our universe is structured, this is its interrelated quality. We aren't going to have peace on earth until we recognize this basic fact of the interrelated structure of all reality.

from
Memories of Anne Frank: Reflections of a Childhood Friend

Alison Leslie Gold

ON November 12, 1945, Hanneli turned seventeen. On December 5, Mr. Frank came to fetch her by taxi. On the way to the airport he picked up Gabi at the orphanage and two other children who had an aunt in Switzerland. Hannah had never been on an airplane before but was not scared at all. Instead she was curious about what it would feel like to fly up into the sky.

The small airplane stood on the tarmac. While the little group waited, Mr. Frank handed Hannah and the others Dutch coins on a chain. He slipped them over their heads. On one side was the face of the queen. On the other side was engraved the date of their journey—December 5, 1945.

Hannah and Mr. Frank spoke quietly together.

Hanneli remembered that when she and Anne were small, she was as guilty as Anne of chattering at school but because Anne was so peppery, and Hanneli so sugary, it was always Anne who caught the sharp edge of the teachers' anger. Never Hanneli, whose reputation was that she was shy, sweet, and obedient. But Anne had always said that Hanneli was shy on the outside but spunky with people close to her. Anne knew Hannah better than anyone, and had loved to tease her.

Mr. Frank told Hannah that when they were in hiding Anne had often talked about Hannah. He told her that Anne regretted so much that she hadn't said good-bye to Hannah, that they hadn't sorted out all their differences before Anne went into hiding. Hannah was Anne's oldest friend and he hoped he and Hannah would be good friends and always stay in touch. He would like to be like a second father to her.

Hannah wished she knew what Anne's thoughts about her had been while Anne was in hiding and had had so much time to think and reflect. But how could she ever know Anne's thoughts? How could she ever know if Anne felt the rift between them had healed? How could she ever again come close to a friend in that same way? Already Hannah was seventeen, almost grown up, and Anne—forever—would remain a girl.

Mr. Frank walked Hannah and the children to the airplane. He wished them a good journey. He waited on the tarmac while they walked up the little stairway into the plane. Hannah quickly settled the little girls in seats, and put Gabi next to her. Shortly the engines began to growl, and the propeller to turn. The airplane rolled forward. Through the window Mr. Frank could be seen as he stood alone and waved. Then the plane taxied, and Hannah realized that it was flying up into the air.

Hannah's stomach jumped with excitement. She gripped Gabi by the hand. The earth seemed to fall away. Outside were red roofs, and green and brown fields striped by ribbons of water. Canals. Elm trees in a line. The Dutch countryside. There were the spires of small village churches, thatched cottages, redbrick houses. The airplane made a wide turn, and off in the distance was the irregular coastline, the dark green North Sea. Boats. An orange smudge of sunset.

In Hannah's suitcase was the photo album that Maya Goudsmit had saved from her family's apartment after the arrest. It was the only surviving remnant of her past, preserved for her by an act of kindness. In the book were photos of her parents. They were smiling, young, newly married. There were photographs of her grandparents, her uncle.

There were photos of her infant years in Berlin before Adolf Hitler was elected in 1933.

There were photos of Amsterdam, a photo of Hannah and Anne on the sidewalk in front of the apartment on Merwedeplein. Age four. This was the time when Mr. Frank often took Hannah and Anne with him to his office on Sundays.

Anne and Hanneli had played in the big room. They'd called each other on the telephone, played with a stamp that had the date, rolled paper into the typewriter, and wrote letters to each other. They dropped water on people who were on the street. What fun it was to be naughty with Anne!

While they played, the clear bell of the Westerkerk church down the street rang every fifteen minutes.

Though she had not known it at the time, this very office would be Anne's hiding place for over two years.

There was a photo of five little girls from school sitting in a sandbox. Hannah had a big bow in her hair, Anne had knobby knees. The year, 1937.

Another showed nine girls with their arms around each other, 1939.

There was a photo of Hannah and Mr. Goslar, 1935.

There was a photo of Mrs. Goslar.

There was a photo of the thatched cottage in which the Goslars rented rooms during the summer on the North Sea when Anne came to stay. There were photos of Gabi and Hannah. Gabi was born just as the German army had attacked and occupied Holland, 1940. The photographs demonstrated that the Nazis hadn't stopped them altogether from enjoying life.

Hannah and Anne had pushed Gabi's carriage, proud to be allowed to take Gabi for strolls up and down the neighborhood streets that bordered on the Amstel River. They had pretended that Gabi belonged to them, had taken turns pushing the carriage, and sometimes both pushed at once. They'd always have the same conversation on these walks.

Hannah clearly remembered every word of this conversation:

"How many children do you want?" Anne would ask her.

"I want ten children," Hannah would reply. "What about you?"

"I don't know how many, but I'm planning to be a writer."

"I know. And Margot wants to be a nurse in Palestine."

"Right. And you want to sell chocolates in a shop, or teach history. Right?"

"Right."

Another time, walking along the elm-lined park path, Gabi had fallen asleep and they'd decided to sit for a while. They'd walked on toward the bench but when they'd come to it, the bench had a new sign: FORBIDDEN FOR JEWS.

At that moment it seemed like the Nazis had declared war on them. But why? What had they ever done? Baffled, angry to be persecuted so unfairly, they had left the park, and never went back after that.

While so many people had not survived, the photographs were safe in her suitcase. Though memory might blur, the photos would remain unchanged.

The earth fell away further as the airplane veered and climbed into rain-filled Dutch clouds. A confetti of silvery raindrops streaked the little windows. The plane began to bump and shake and flew through thick, dark clouds. It took a while to fly through the rainstorm.

By then night had come and the plane flew into the dark. Outside were strewn clusters of shining stars. There was the Little Dipper constellation, like an upside-down kite. It had seven pulsating stars. To Hannah the stars had names: Sanne, Ilse, Jacque, and Hannah. At the tip of its tail was the bright Pole Star that the first sailors once used to navigate at night. This star was Anne.

As Hanneli's plane flew on toward Switzerland, the constellations gradually climbed. The plane climbed, too. New stars rose over the earth's horizon and the pulsating old stars moved majestically, eternally across the heavens.

from

Zlata's Diary

A Child's Life in Sarajevo

Zlata Filipović

Saturday, October 19, 1991

YESTERDAY was a really awful day. We were ready to go to
Jahorina (the most beautiful mountain in the world) for the
weekend. But when I got home from school, I found my mother
in tears and my father in uniform. I had a lump in my throat
when Daddy said he had been called up by the police reserve. I
hugged him, crying, and started begging him not to go, to stay
at home. He said he had to go. Daddy went, and Mommy and I
were left alone. Mommy cried and phoned friends and relatives.
Everyone came immediately (Slobo, Doda, Keka, Mommy's
brother Braco, Aunt Melica, there were so many I can't remember them all). They all came to console us and to offer their
help. Keka took me to spend the night with Martina and Matea.
When I woke up in the morning, Keka told me everything was
all right and that Daddy would be home in two days.

I'm home now, Melica is staying with us and it looks as
though everything will be all right. Daddy should be home the
day after tomorrow. Thank God!

Tuesday, October 22, 1991

Everything really does seem to have turned out all right.
Daddy got back yesterday, on his birthday. He's off again tomorrow, and then every two days. He'll be on duty for ten hours
each time. We'll just have to get used to it. I suppose it won't
last for long. But, I don't know what it all means. Some reservists from Montenegro have entered Herzegovina. Why? For
what? Politics, it seems, but I don't understand politics. After
Slovenia and Croatia, are the winds of war now blowing toward
Bosnia-Herzegovina??? No, that's impossible.

Wednesday, October 23, 1991

There's a real war going on in Dubrovnik. It's being badly

shelled. People are in shelters, they have no water, no electricity, the phones aren't working. We see horrible pictures on TV. Mommy and Daddy are worried. Is it possible that such a beautiful town is being destroyed? Mommy and Daddy are especially fond of it. It was there, in the Ducal Palace, that they picked up a quill and wrote "YES" to spending the rest of their lives together. Mommy says it's the most beautiful town in the world and it mustn't be destroyed!!!

We're worried about Srdjan (my parents' best friend who lives and works in Dubrovnik, but his family is still in Sarajevo) and his parents. How are they coping with everything that's happening over there? Are they alive? We're trying to talk to him with the help of a ham radio, but it's not working. Bokica (Srdjan's wife) is miserable. Every attempt to get some news ends in failure. Dubrovnik is cut off from the rest of the world.

Wednesday, October 30, 1991

Good news from my piano teacher today. There's going to be a school recital and I'll be playing in it!!! I have to practice. I'll be playing Kabalevsky, *Six Variations on a Slovak Song.* All the variations are short, but difficult. It doesn't matter, I'll do my best.

Nothing new at school, it's the half term soon and we're working on our grades. The days are shorter, it's colder, which means it'll snow soon—HOORAY! Jahorina, skiing, two-seaters, one-seaters, ski-lifts—I can hardly wait!!! I'm pushing it a bit, there's still some time to go, but we've already bought ski tickets for the whole season.

Tuesday, November 5, 1991

I've just come back from choir practice. I'm hoarse! Imagine, our choir teacher told us today that we would be giving a performance soon. What a "public life" I'm having! We'll be singing "Nabucco," "Ave Maria," "When I Went to Bembaša," "I Sing of Thee" and "Ode to Joy." All the songs are wonderful.

Friday, November 8, 1991

I'm packing and I'm putting you, dear Diary, in my backpack. I'm spending the whole weekend with Martina and Matea (M&M). Super!!! Mommy is letting me go. In my backpack I've got my school books, my pajamas, my toothbrush . . . and as soon as I put you in—off I go.

CIAO!!!

Sunday, November 10, 1991

It's now 4:30 and I've just come home from M&M. It was wonderful. We played tennis, watched MTV, RTL, SKY . . . went out, walked and had fun. I took you with me, dear Diary, but I didn't write anything. You're not cross with me, are you?

I've done my homework and now I'm going to have a bath, watch TV and then go to bed. A weekend like any other—wonderful!

Tuesday, November 12, 1991

The situation in Dubrovnik is getting worse and worse. We managed to learn through the ham radio that Srdjan is alive and that he and his parents are all right. The pictures on TV are awful. People are starving. We're wondering about how to send a package to Srdjan. It can be done somehow through Caritas. Daddy is still going to the reserves, he comes home tired. When will it stop? Daddy says maybe next week. Thank God.

Thursday, November 14, 1991

Daddy isn't going to the reserves anymore. Hooray!!! . . . Now we'll be able to go to Jahorina and Crnotina on weekends. But, gasoline has been a problem lately. Daddy often spends hours waiting in the line for gasoline, he goes outside of town to get it, and often comes home without getting the job done.

Together with Bokica we sent a package to Srdjan. We learned through the ham radio that they have nothing to eat. They have no water, Srdjan swapped a bottle of whisky for five liters of water. Eggs, apples, potatoes—the people of Dubrovnik can only dream about them.

War in Croatia, war in Dubrovnik, some reservists in Herzegovina. Mommy and Daddy keep watching the news on TV. They're worried. Mommy often cries looking at the terrible pictures on TV. They talk mostly politics with their friends. What is politics? I haven't got a clue. And I'm not really interested. I just finished watching *Midnight Caller* on TV.

Wednesday, November 20, 1991

I've just come home from music school. I had my school recital. I think I was good. I tried. I made only two mistakes which they might not even have noticed. Matea was in the audience. I'm tired because it was nerve-racking.

Wednesday, November 27, 1991

It'll be November 29th, Republic Day, soon. Mommy and Daddy are going shopping and are getting everything ready to go to Jaca's (a family friend) and Jahorina.

HOORAY!!! I can hardly wait. Jahorina will be wonderful and unforgettable as always.

Friday, November 29, 1991

We're on Jahorina. Jaca has warmed up the house, there's a fire burning in the fireplace. As usual, Zoka (Jaca's husband) is making something special to eat, Daddy is talking politics with Boža (our friend and Daddy's colleague). Mommy and Jaca keep jumping into the conversation, and we children, Branko, Svjetlana, Nenad, Mirela, Anela, Oga and I, are wondering whether to take a walk, play a game, watch a movie on TV or play the unavoidable Scrabble. This time we've decided to play a game. We always have fun and laugh in our games, we have our own sense of humor. It's cold but wonderful. I'm so happy, I'm having such a good time. The food, drink and company in Jahorina are so nice. And at night, my favorite moment—Oga and I are the first to go to bed—for a long, long talk before going to sleep. We talk, we make plans, we tell each other secrets. Last night we chattered about MTV and the new music video.

Monday, December 2, 1991

It's my birthday tomorrow. Mommy is making a cake and all the rest, because we really celebrate in our house. One day is for my friends, that's December 3, and the next day is for family friends and relatives. Mommy and I are getting a tombola [a basket of party favors] together, and thinking up questions for the children's quiz. This year we have birthday cups, plates and napkins all with little red apples on them. They're sweet. Mommy bought them in Pula. The cake will be shaped like a butterfly and . . . this time I'll be blowing out eleven candles. I'll have to take a deep breath and blow them all out at once.

Tuesday, December 3, 1991

Today is the big day—my birthday. Happy Birthday to Me!!! But, alas, I'm sick. My sinuses are inflamed and some kind of pus is trickling down my throat. Nothing hurts really, but I have to take an antibiotic—Penbritin, and some disgusting nose drops. They sting. Why did this have to happen on my birthday? Oh, I am unlucky! (Don't be such a pessimist, Zlata, things aren't so bad.)

All right, I'll get well and celebrate my birthday later, with my friends, I mean, because the "grown-up" guests (family and family friends) are coming to wish me a happy birthday today. And here I am in my nightgown! Mommy and Daddy gave me a wonderful birthday present—Head skis, new Tyrolia bindings and new poles. Super! Thank you Mommy. Thank you Daddy!!

We've just seen off some of the guests, and I'm tired, I have to stop writing, I've run out of ideas and inspiration. Good night.

Wednesday, December 4, 1991

I'm writing to you from bed, dear Diary. Another day in bed awaits me. Bimbilimbica (my favorite doll) is snoozing on the little table, and Panda just keeps looking and looking at her . . . Let him look.

7:45. I'm in bed again, listening to the rattle of our washing machine. The repairman came to fix it. Poor thing, it's a hundred years old. I should treat it with respect. The repairman has gone and I'm now listening to Michael Jackson, "Man in the Mirror." I just had a crazy idea. I'm going to try to join Madonna's Fan Club. I really am crazy!

Thursday, December 5, 1991

I woke up very late. Then Azra, Minela and Bojana came by to see me. Bojana is having a birthday party on Saturday. Lucky her! WHY AM I SICK??? Boo-hoo! Boo-hoo!

Saturday, December 7, 1991

The weekend in bed. Bojana's having her birthday party today and I can't go. I feel sad. I can't even read or watch TV anymore. I want to get well!

Every night Mommy and Daddy keep trying to get Srdjan on the phone. It's impossible to get through to Dubrovnik. God, there really is a war going on down there. Today I saw pictures of Dubrovnik on TV. Horrible. We're worried about Srdjan and his family. Mommy managed (because she was persistent) to get him on the phone at eleven o'clock last night. He's hungry and thirsty, he's cold, they have no electricity, no water, nothing to eat. He's sad. Mommy cried. What on earth is happening and why? God, is it possible that there's a war going on down there? Dubrovnik is being destroyed, people are dying. Sad but true.

Take care of yourself, Srdjan, I'll keep my fingers crossed for you. We'll be sending you another package in a few days, through Caritas.

On Monday I'm going to Auntie Mira's (the doctor's) for a check-up.

Ciao!!!

Monday, December 9, 1991

I went to see Auntie Mira. She says I can go back to school tomorrow. Whoopee! We bought a pair of gray trousers at "KIKA's" (the children's boutique). I like them. Well, *Murphy Brown* is going to be on TV now. I have to watch!!!

Ciao . . .

Wednesday, December 11, 1991

I'm back at school. There's a lot to learn, it'll be the end of term soon. I've got a math test tomorrow. I have to practice. I got an A in history today. On Saturday I'm celebrating (a bit late) my eleventh birthday.

Saturday, December 14, 1991

Today, eleven days later, I celebrated my eleventh birthday with my girlfriends. It was like the real thing. We had the tombola, the quiz, the "butterfly" cake. I blew out all the candles on my first try. We had a good time. Being sick stopped me from having my party on December 3, but this was nice too. Once again—Happy Birthday to Me, and may I never get sick on this big day again. Oh yes, I got wonderful presents—most of them from "Melanie's" (a boutique with wonderful knick-knacks). They fit in perfectly with everything in my room.

Thursday, December 19, 1991

Sarajevo has launched an appeal (on TV) called "Sarajevo Helps the Children of Dubrovnik." In Srdjan's parcel we put a nice New Year's present for him to give to some child in Dubrovnik. We made up a package of sweets, chocolates, vitamins, a doll, some books, pencils, notebooks—whatever we could manage, hoping to bring happiness to some innocent child who has been stopped by the war from going to school, playing, eating what he wants and enjoying his childhood. It's a nice little package. I hope it makes whoever gets it happy. That's the idea. I also wrote a New Year's card saying I hoped the war in Dubrovnik would end soon.

Thursday, December 26, 1991

5:45. I haven't written to you for a long time, dear Diary. Okay, let's start from the beginning. I got a B in my piano exam, an A in solfeggio and an A in general music, so I finished with an A average. Super. Mirna did the same as me. I wrote to *Sa-3-Ći-ci* [a children's program] TV show and won a ticket for the Ninja Turtles.

It was Christmas yesterday. We went to M&M's (Martina and Matea's). It was wonderful. A big Christmas tree. Christmas presents and the proverbial Christmas table. And Bokica was there with Andrej. And there was a surprise. Srdjan phoned. Everyone was happy and sad at the same time. There we were all warm, surrounded by Christmas decorations and presents, with lots of wonderful food and drink in front of us. And there he was, like everybody else in Dubrovnik . . . in a war. This war will pass, Srdjan, we'll all be together again! You've got to hold on!!! I'm keeping my fingers crossed for you and for all the people and children in Dubrovnik.

It'll be New Year's Eve soon. The atmosphere seems different than before. Mommy, Daddy and our friends and family aren't planning a New Year's Eve party this year. They don't talk about it much. Is it because of the war in Dubrovnik? Is it some kind of fear? I don't know or understand a thing. Mommy says we'll decorate the tree tomorrow.

Today was my last day at music school this year. And school?! I'm hoping for straight As. YO, BABY, YO!, as The Fresh Prince of Bel Air would say. That's one of my favorite programs on TV. PHEW! I certainly do talk a lot. Just look at all these words. PHEW!

Just one more thing: my class is going to the cinema tomorrow. We're going to see *White Fang*. It's a wonderful book by Jack London, I hope the film is as good.

Ciao!!!

Outsider

Lensey Namioka

MY fiction for young people falls into two distinct types: One set of stories consists of mystery-adventure stories set in feudal Japan or Song dynasty China. The other set consists of contemporary stories about Chinese immigrants adjusting to a new life in America. Both types of stories share one theme in common, however. The protagonists are usually outsiders.

In the series of adventure stories set in feudal Japan, the main characters are two *ronin*, or unemployed samurai. They wander around the country looking for work, and in almost every case they arrive as newcomers at some locality. The Song dynasty China adventure story is about a band of outlaws, and of course nobody can be more of an outsider than an outlaw.

The stories about immigrants describe outsiders trying to fit into a new country and a new society. In one book, *Yang the Youngest and His Terrible Ear,* the hero is an outsider even in his own family. Everybody in his family is a talented musician, except for Yang the Youngest, who can't play the violin to save his life.

My preoccupation with outsiders may have originated from my parents' families. Both my father and mother came from the families of officials in China (called mandarins by Westerners). It was the policy of the government to move their officials around constantly. For if they were too closely connected with any one region, they might accept favors from some local faction and lose their impartiality.

My father said his memories of his childhood were filled with packing up and traveling to a new home. He became really efficient at packing his little bag of toys and favorite books. All his life he remained an expert at packing.

On one occasion Father's family started to cross a river by ferry. After the boat pushed off, they heard a pitiful yowling from the bank. It was the family cat, who had been left behind because cats were supposed to be more attached to a place than to people. But this cat was exceptionally loyal, and it started to swim after the boat! They managed to rescue the cat and took it with them. My father's love for cats dated from that incident. Wherever our family lived, we always kept a cat. Years later, I wrote a book titled *The Loyal Cat,* and cats appear in several other of my books (one of them a vampire cat, however).

When my father was old enough to go to college, he went to America and attended Cornell University, which is situated in a small, upstate New York city. There was no Chinese community there, and no Chinese groceries for sale. For four whole years he ate solid meat-and-potatoes American food. He was truly an outsider, although he made good friends from those days and never lost touch with them.

My mother's family also traveled. They went all over China by riverboat, sedan chair, and train. They also went abroad by ocean liner. My maternal grandfather went to Europe, spending three years in London at the Chinese legation. He visited the Paris Exposition in 1889 and saw the newly erected Eiffel Tower.

My mother studied medicine in Japan for seven years. Again, she was an outsider in a foreign country. At least she could eat rice, not meat and potatoes. In China it's not safe to eat anything raw, even salads, but in Japan Mother finally got used to raw fish.

I still remember how she tried to serve Japanese food to us at home. I hated it at first, but finally learned to like it. This was fortunate because I later married a Japanese and spent time living in Japan. Now I love raw fish.

My parents continued their roving lives after they got married. They traveled to America in the 1920s, and my two older sisters were born in Boston. My parents even took their children to Europe with them. They soon found that it was hard work carrying two infants around, and they stashed the two girls with a French family. That was why my sisters spoke French as their first language. They were outsiders in France, and when they returned to China they were still outsiders because none of our family friends could speak French.

I was born in Beijing after my parents returned to China. But they didn't stay long in Beijing. They went back to America in 1933 and spent a year in Washington, D.C. My sisters were speaking Chinese by then, and they found themselves outsiders again in America. Returning to China, my parents moved to Nanjing, which was the national capital at that time.

In our family we grew up speaking the northern dialect (called Mandarin by Americans). In Nanjing, which means "Southern Capital," people spoke a different dialect, although not so different that we couldn't understand.

But when Japan started invading China in 1937, we had to move out of Nanjing and go inland. My father, who worked for a research institute, followed the institute to the interior away from the invaders.

The farther we moved away from the coastal cities, the harder it was for us to understand the people we met. In Changsha I went to a local school, where I couldn't understand the teacher at all. Soon enemy planes began bombing the city, and there were scary times when we had to scatter and look for air-raid shelters. Strangely enough, my more vivid memories were of struggling to understand my teacher and of trying to eat the school lunch, which was very, very HOT. (Changsha was the capital of Hunan, a province notorious for its spicy hot food.)

My father was a linguist, and his work involved traveling up and down China studying various dialects. Because of the war, it became impossible for him to travel around. When he was offered a teaching job at an American university, he decided to go to America with his family. His idea was to stay there until the war ended. He didn't expect at first that our family would settle in this country and become immigrants.

Naturally we were outsiders when we arrived in America. My sisters and I went to school speaking hardly any English at all. But like baby ducks thrown into the water, we had to keep our heads above water by learning English as fast as we could. In fact my father was more worried about our forgetting Chinese. He made a rule that we should speak only Chinese at home and not mix English words into our conversation. He fined us a penny for every English word that slipped in. After a while he gave up the rule because my mother refused to pay the fine. Besides, there were words that just had no Chinese translation. How do you say "cheeseburger" in Chinese, for instance?

Eventually we all learned English pretty well, and we also made friends in school. But I never felt that I really belonged. At first it made me unhappy always to be an outsider. Gradually I began to accept the fact. We enjoyed our social lives, and what did it matter if we looked or sounded differently from our friends and neighbors? Several of my books, in particular *Who's Hu?* and *Yang the Third and Her Impossible Family,* discuss this gradual acceptance of one's differences and becoming resigned to being an outsider.

In some ways my husband, Isaac, is just as much of an outsider as I am. We met when we were graduate students at the University of California in Berkeley. I noticed that he looked a bit different from most Asian boys, and later he told me about his family.

He came from Japan, and his grandparents grew up at a time of great changes in the country. After centuries of being closed off, Japan finally opened its doors to the outside world. Some Japanese were excited at the prospect of going abroad and investigating foreign countries. Among them was Isaac's maternal grandfather, who managed to get on a ship to America. After many adventures, he wound up in Brooklyn, New York. There, he met a girl whose family had just immigrated from France. They fell in love and got married. Several children were born to them in Brooklyn, one of them being Isaac's mother, my future mother-in-law. Eventually the family moved back to Japan.

Japan was—and still is—a country of great homogeneity, where the people came from pretty much the same racial stock. Being half French, Isaac's mother and her siblings all looked different from other children. They were immediately marked as outsiders.

Isaac's mother grew up to marry another outsider: Saburo Namioka, who was a Christian. In Japan Christians formed a small minority of less than 1 percent. In the 1930s and 1940s they were systematically persecuted by the militaristic government then governing the country. My future father-in-law was a suspect in the eyes of the authorities for another reason: He was opposed to Japan's war of aggression, and he spoke out about it. As a result he was arrested and sent to prison, and his health never completely recovered from the harsh conditions there. The rest of the family became outsiders, and for them the last years of the war were grim.

After the war, Isaac received a fellowship to study at a Christian college in America. He did graduate work at the University of Kansas, and later went to Berkeley, where we two outsiders found each other.

We moved around quite a bit after we got married. Even after we moved to Seattle in 1963 and bought a house, we still traveled whenever we could. Isaac teaches at the University of Washington, and during his sabbaticals, we manage to live abroad. Like my parents, we feel that traveling is not only enjoyable, but the normal way to live.

On Isaac's first sabbatical, we spent a year in Kyoto, Japan. Our daughters went to the local public school, and they found out what it was like to be outsiders. They started school without speaking any Japanese, and like me, they had to swim hard to keep their heads above water. Aki, our elder daughter, initially suffered bullying from some of the boys in her class. Bullying is common in Japanese schools where there is little tolerance for diversity, and anyone who seems different gets picked on. The teacher finally took a hand and told the class they should be more hospitable toward their guest from America. Things improved, and our daughters began making friends in school.

During our stay I found that in Japan you get better treatment as an outright foreigner than as a Japanese who was somehow different. Although my face could pass for that of a Japanese, I found it paid to let people know right away that I was a Chinese who was only visiting their country.

Once I was traveling alone on my way back to America from China, and I had to change planes in Tokyo. Because of bad weather, the flight was canceled, and I had to spend the night in Tokyo. I hadn't planned for this extra stay in one of the world's most expensive cities. It was long past midnight, and I stood forlornly in front of the air terminal, holding an untidy shopping bag printed with the characters for "China." Immediately a policeman and a taxi driver came over. When they heard my story, they kindly called up an inexpensive hotel nearby and arranged for me to stay. That was one time when it paid to be an outsider.

In Seattle there is a large Asian community, and we have friends among both the Chinese Americans and the Japanese Americans. We enjoy the firecrackers during Chinese New Year celebrations, and we go to the local Cherry Blossom Festival. Yet, because we are a mixed couple, we don't belong completely to either the Chinese or the Japanese ethnic groups. In a sense, we are still outsiders. And, like Mary Yang in *Yang the Third and Her Impossible Family*, we have learned to be content.

Math

A Horse Named Hans

Stanislas Dehaene

AT the beginning of this century, a horse named Hans made it to the headlines of German newspapers. His master, Wilhelm von Osten, was no ordinary circus animal trainer. Rather, he was a passionate man who, under the influence of Darwin's ideas, had set out to demonstrate the extent of animal intelligence. He wound up spending more than a decade teaching his horse arithmetic, reading, and music. Although the results were slow to come, they eventually exceeded all his expectations. The horse seemed gifted with a superior intelligence. It could apparently solve arithmetical problems and even spell out words!

Demonstrations of Clever Hans's abilities often took place in von Osten's yard. The public would form a half-circle around the animal and suggest an arithmetical question to the trainer—for instance, "How much is 5 plus 3?" Von Osten would then present the animal with five objects aligned on a table, and with three other objects on another. After examining the "problem," the horse responded by knocking on the ground with its hoof the number of times equal to the total of the addition. However, Hans's mathematical abilities far exceeded this simple feat. Some arithmetical problems were spoken aloud by the public, or were written in digital notation on a blackboard, and Hans could solve them just as easily. The horse could also add two fractions such as $\frac{2}{5}$ and $\frac{1}{2}$ and give the answer $\frac{9}{10}$ by striking nine times, then ten times with its hoof. It was even said that to the question of determining the divisors of 28, Hans came out very appropriately with the answers 2, 4, 7, 14, and 28. Obviously, Hans's number knowledge surpassed by far what a school teacher would expect today of a reasonably bright pupil!

In September 1904, a committee of experts, among whom figured the eminent German psychologist Carl Stumpf, concluded after an extensive investigation that Hans's feats were real and not a result of cheating. This generous conclusion, however, did not satisfy Oskar Pfungst, one of Stumpf's own students. With von Osten's help—the master was fully convinced of his prodigy's superior intelligence—he began a systematic study of the horse's abilities Pfungst's experiments, even by today's standards, remain a model of rigor and inventiveness. His working hypothesis was that the horse could not but be totally inept in mathematics. Therefore, it had to be the master himself, or someone in the public, who knew the answer and sent the animal a hidden signal when the target number of strokes had been reached, thus commanding the animal to stop knocking with its hoof.

To prove this, Pfungst invented a way of dissociating Hans's knowledge of a problem from what its master knew. He used a procedure that differed only slightly from the one described above. The master watched carefully as a simple addition was written in large printed characters on a panel. The panel was then oriented toward the horse in such a way that only it could see the problem and answer it. However, on some trials, Pfungst surreptitiously modified the addition before showing it to the horse. For instance, the master could see $6 + 2$ whereas in fact the horse was trying to solve $6 + 3$.

The results of this experiment, and of a series of follow-up controls, were clear-cut. Whenever the master knew the correct response, Hans got the right answer. When, on the contrary, the master was not aware of the solution, the horse failed. Moreover, it often produced an error that matched the numerical result expected by its master. Obviously, it was von Osten himself, rather than Hans, who was finding the solution to the various arithmetical problems. But how then did the horse know how to respond? Pfungst eventually deduced that Hans's truly amazing ability lay in detecting minuscule movements of its master's head or eyebrows that invariably announced the time to stop the series of knocks. In fact, Pfungst never doubted that the trainer was sincere. He believed that the signals were completely unconscious and involuntary. Even when von Osten was absent, the horse continued to respond correctly: Apparently, it detected the buildup of tension in the public as the expected number of hoof strokes was attained. Pfungst himself could never eliminate all forms of involuntary communication with the animal, even after he discovered the exact nature of the body clues it used.

from
The Magical Maze: Seeing the World Through Mathematical Minds

Ian Stewart

WELCOME to the maze.

A logical maze, a magical maze. A maze of the mind.

The maze is mathematics. The mind is yours. Let's see what happens when we put them together.

What is mathematics? What mathematicians do.

What is a mathematician—someone who does mathematics?

Not exactly. That's too easy an answer, and it creates too simple a maze—a circular loop of self-referential logic. No, a mathematician is more than just somebody who *does* mathematics. Think of it this way: what is a businessman? Someone who does business? Yes, but not just that. A businessman is someone who sees an *opportunity* for doing business where the rest of us see nothing: while we're complaining that there's no restaurant in the area, he's organizing a telephone pizza delivery service. Similarly, a mathematician is someone who sees opportunities for doing mathematics that the rest of us miss.

I want to open your mind to some of those opportunities.

I don't want to convince you that mathematics is useful. It is, but utility is not the only criterion for value to humanity. I *do* want to convince you that mathematics provides a lot of fascinating insights into the natural world—including bits of it that most of us seldom connect with mathematics, such as the shapes of plants, the markings on animals' coats, and how living creatures move around. Above all, I want to convince you that mathematics is beautiful, surprising, enjoyable, and interesting. You can get a lot out of mathematics for its own sake, and historically, that's where a lot of it came from. The rest came from a two-way trade between the natural world and the human mind.

Some famous mathematicians (no names, no pack drill) have argued that the only good mathematics is what they call "pure" mathematics, which they praise for its lack of utility. I think that's nonsense, as well as being an intellectual pose of the worst kind. Being useless is nothing to be proud of. But to me, nuts-and-bolts applications to human affairs are the icing on the mathematical cake: they enhance the interest, the surprise, the fun, and the beauty—but they're not the *reason*. As far as *The Magical Maze* is concerned, the idea is to appreciate the cake *as* cake, whether or not there's any icing—and whether or not you get a bit of icing on your plate.

The title *The Magical Maze* sums up many of my feelings about that kind of approach to mathematics. It is a maze because being a mathematician involves navigating, with confidence, through an intricate network of logical possibilities. At every step in a mathematical investigation you are faced with choices. Some choices lead in fruitful directions; most do not. So mathematics is a maze: a logical one.

It is also magical. In fact, mathematics is the closest that we humans get to true magic. How else to describe patterns in our heads that—by some mysterious agency—capture patterns of the universe around us? Mathematics connects ideas that otherwise seem totally unrelated, revealing deep similarities that subsequently show up in nature. Even though mathematics is "just" a creation of the human mind, it has given us enormous power over the world we inhabit. In mathematics, you can set out to understand the notes played by a violin, and end up inventing television.

That's *real* magic.

Mathematics

Lensey Namioka

WHEN I started going to school in America, one of the things I learned was that girls weren't supposed to do well in mathematics. In China, as well as in Japan and many other Asian countries, women are expected to be good at figures and regularly keep the household accounts and manage the budget. A husband hands over his wages to his wife. She pays the bills and gives him an allowance for going out with the boys.

My mother made the financial decisions in our family. Once when my parents were living in Berkeley, California, Mother attended a land auction with a friend. She went more out of curiosity than from any real desire to buy land. A plot of land near our house was up for sale, and just for fun Mother made a bid on it. She was sure somebody would top her bid.

She was stunned when nobody else said a word, and she found herself the owner of a large plot of land.

As she and her friend started to leave, a man rushed up to them. He was a realtor who was supposed to make a bid, but had arrived too late for the auction. Right on the spot, he offered Mother whatever she had paid, plus an extra $1,000.

"No, thank you," Mother replied. By then she was rather tickled by her purchase.

The realtor raised his offer to $2,000, but Mother still turned him down. He managed to get our address and phone number and called up our house.

When Father answered the phone, the realtor shouted, "Your wife just threw away $2,000!" "I'm sure she had her reasons," Father answered calmly, confident that Mother knew what she was doing.

As it turned out, the land increased in value, and my parents had a comfortable nest egg in their old age.

I didn't know at first that in America girls weren't supposed to be good in math. When I got good grades in math, I found out the other kids thought I was weird. My first book with a contemporary setting was *Who's Hu?* which dealt with the subject of an immigrant Chinese girl who was good at math and discovered that this made her a freak in the eyes of her classmates. Later, I wrote an article for an anthology about my own experiences with mathematics, titled "Math and After Math."

There were reasons why math was my best subject. My English was still pretty shaky at first, but in math we used the same Arabic numbers as my Chinese schools did. Moreover, Chinese schools were (and still are) way ahead of American schools in math. But even in China, I had been ahead of other students in arithmetic because I sang the multiplication table.

"You can remember a tune more easily than a string of numbers," Father would tell us. "To remember the multiplication table, it's better to sing it." To teach musical notation in Chinese schools, numbers were given to the notes of the diatonic scale: do was one, re was two, mi was three, and so on. Therefore to remember that two times seven was fourteen, all I had to do was hum the tune re-ti-do-fa. It wasn't a very pretty tune, but it stuck in my mind a lot better than a bunch of numbers. Even today, I multiply in Chinese. I hum when I try to figure out how much two candy bars cost, for instance.

I maintained my reputation as a freak in high school when we started algebra. The reason was that I loved story problems, something most of the other kids loathed. To this day, I don't understand why students hate story problems. When I taught calculus in college, it was the same. Kids moaned and groaned if they were assigned story problems.

As for me, multiplying (even with music) or dividing long columns of figures was terminally boring. Differentiating or integrating formulas in a calculus class was equally boring. In story problems, however, I found color, excitement, even romance.

I remember problems involving an army column marching toward the enemy. A messenger was sent to the rear with a message warning of an imminent ambush. Given the length of the column, the speed of the messenger's horse, etc., would the warning arrive on time? Some of the ambushers might even be outlaws wearing baggy pants, or a princess with a bamboo sword.

Although I received good grades in math throughout my school and college years, I came to the conclusion finally that I was not cut out to be a mathematician. It took more than simply doing all the homework assignments.

My parents reproached me when I told them I was giving up mathematics and going into writing. "You spent so many years studying math!" they said. "How can you give up such a beautiful subject?"

"Enjoying beauty is not the same thing as being able to produce it," I told them.

They were still disappointed, however, especially my father. He had a double major in mathematics and physics when he was a student, although he ultimately became a linguist.

My mother was afraid that by giving up a teaching job with a regular salary and becoming a freelance writer, I would lose my independence, for she knew that very few writers were self-supporting. Mother was a strong believer in women having independent careers. My parents had four daughters and no sons, but they saw no reason why their daughters couldn't be just as successful as any son.

In her autobiography (*Autobiography of a Chinese Woman*, published by John Day), Mother described how her parents, with strong support from her remarkable grandfather, had broken with Chinese tradition by allowing her to obtain a medical degree and to start a hospital in Beijing. She gave up her career when she got married, and she said she regretted it for the rest of her life.

At least my parents should be glad to see that my sisters became a musician, a chemist, and an astrophysicist respectively. My husband and I have two daughters, no sons, and my daughters are in computers and engineering respectively. None of them gave up a career upon getting married.

The attitude toward women in math and science seems to be gradually changing in America, and my daughters say that it's possible to be a scientist, engineer, or mathematician without being considered weird—atypical, maybe—but not outright freakish.

There are times, though, when I think over my parents' words and wonder if all my years of studying and teaching mathematics have been wasted.

Maybe not. I married a mathematician, and my social life revolves largely around mathematicians and their spouses. In some respects this shows.

Mathematicians never lose a sense of fun, and even at a ripe old age they still play games. A less flattering description is that they never reach maturity. So far, I have never lost my juvenile capacity to enjoy myself.

Another trait that most mathematicians share is that of thrift. They are not actually mean with money, and they give generously to causes they believe in. But they *hate* unnecessary spending. I think this attitude first develops when they learn to prove theorems. A theorem is strong if you spend very little on the hypothesis and get a lot as a conclusion: In other words, you want the best bargain possible. Mathematicians, in their quest for a strong theorem, are avid bargain hunters.

I've gone dutch to lots of restaurants with mathematicians. After the waiter presents the bill, there is a prolonged discussion of how much each person pays.

"You had the chef's salad with cheese, so you pay a dollar more than I do," or "I had the house wine, not French merlot," and so on.

The waiter stands there, looking very patient. If you're not used to this, you might curdle with embarrassment and want to crawl under the table. Nobody objects to paying his proper share, but nobody wants to pay a *penny* more than he has to.

A related characteristic is the mathematician's attitude toward elegance. An elegant proof is a short one, and when two mathematicians obtain the same result, the one with the shorter proof is declared the winner. The aim of mathematicians when improving their papers is to get rid of all unnecessary baggage.

Maybe these traits show in my writing. I don't throw in something just for color or to jazz up my writing. A character, an incident, a locality—these are used to advance the plot or to make a point. In reading other people's work, or—especially—listening to public speeches, I dislike long-windedness more than anything else, even more than pretentious terminology.

This makes my writing sound rather plain and bleak. Perhaps it is. But I truly believe that suspense, pathos, or humor can be conveyed economically. It takes skill to accomplish this, and I'm still working at it. In every book, there are places where my editors tell me, "This passage is slow. Can't we tighten it?" Then I know that there is more work to do and, like my husband and his colleagues, I have to get rid of the extra baggage.

The Importance of the Computer

John McLeish

ALL calculating aids, from algorithms to log tables, from *quipus* to electronic spreadsheets, were constructed to speed up and simplify our handling of numbers. They assist us in all the aspects of human living, that is, in our practical activities as well as our research into the construction and working of the universe and ourselves, and in the ordering and manipulation of abstract ideas. These activities are possible—and indeed have been accomplished in earlier times—without sophisticated number-tools and computer hardware, but also without the modern panache. Throughout history, there has been a direct connection between the level of number-work in societies (its sophistication and speed) and the level of "civilization." Of course, the existence of number expertise, and of the tools that assist it, is no guarantee of "high" civilization, but their absence has proved an effective barrier against it.

At a simple level, the computer (both in its "mainframe" and "desk-top" forms) is the latest in a long line of such calculation aids. It allows number-work and, by extension, all alpha-numeric activities to proceed at a speed and with an accuracy unimaginable in any previous generation. One computer (located in an office or bank, say) can do the work that previously took the time and energy of hundreds, sometimes thousands, of clerks. In 20 minutes, a computer can perform calculations that once required as many years (for instance, creating logarithm tables). Yet, when computers were invented they were the object of considerable suspicion, not only from laypeople but from those who should have known better, including teachers and professional mathematicians. Now that most of us routinely accept computers, we use our reliance on their speed and accuracy to let us "spin off" into hitherto inaccessible or awesomely complex realms of number-work, and of the science that depends on it.

But computers are far more than mere calculation tools. They differ from every other previous device in a way that gives them infinite potential. They can "understand," and manipulate, anything at all so long as it can be turned into numbers. They can be programmed to process words, charts, graphs, and images of every kind. They make decisions (for example, when to buy or sell stocks and shares). They run sequential operations of every kind, from manufacturing processes to space flights. They store records, help with medical examinations and diagnoses, and facilitate work in design, engineering and the arts. In a computer-oriented society, almost no aspect of human life is left untouched. To take a simple example, in the USA, using a computer service, you can dial from home to access all the airlines in North America for the cheapest return fare to, say, Hawaii, and book a seat. Doing this costs less than taking a taxi downtown to a travel agency, with its severely limited facilities—and is obviously more convenient.

In short, in the last 40 years or so, computers have speeded up and facilitated human life to an unprecedented degree. In that time, the human race has developed intellectually more than in the whole of the previous millennium. Whether this means that we have reached some kind of pinnacle of civilization, compared to our computerless ancestors, is a question as imponderable as what will happen next. Only one thing seems certain about future generations: that they will think of us now, in computer terms, in much the same way as we look back on the megalith-builders with their neolithic inch and neolithic yard.

Programmers

Michael Fulton

PROGRAMMERS form the backbone of their cyberspace companies. Their responsibilities cover all the bases in the daily operations of their company. Alan S. Ellman, owner and president of Interactive Connection, says, "Programmers are some of the most confident people in the world. I come from a family of doctors and surgeons, and I feel that programmers are more confident than doctors because each day programmers come to work, they solve new problems. Programmers can do anything; it's just a question of time and resources."

Programmers are the shop foremen of cyberspace. They keep the office productive and efficient. They develop new programs and adapt old ones. They troubleshoot and problem-solve. And programmers are compensated generously for their work. An experienced programmer can command anywhere from $70,000 to $100,000 a year. At the entry level a programmer can expect $30,000 to $45,000, depending on his technical skills and college coursework. Keep in mind, however, that the hours may be grueling.

Interactive Connection is a company that creates Web pages. It also sells syndicated content to major corporations, which add this material to their own Web pages. Interactive Connection's client list includes such household names as Ralph Lauren, Sports Channel, the *New York Times,* Univision, and Weider Publishing.

The offices of Interactive Connection are located in an expansive seventh-floor space on Fifth Avenue in New York City. Only antique columns interrupt the massive open space that would more resemble a roller rink than an office, if it weren't for the cubicles that form a maze for the visitor.

Upon closer examination the room begins to fit into the realm of cyberspace. I wouldn't try rollerblading there after all. Wires run everywhere. New hardware pops up in corners, and a lot of equipment is still in boxes. The atmosphere runs toward the eclectic. A few walls are decorated with jointed compound sculptures that seem to burst from inside the walls. The space provided for client and staff meetings contains dark wood furniture with aubergine upholstery.

The cubicles are decorated to fit the personalities of the people who work within them for the extended hours they spend there. A giant stereo system with tower speakers is found in Aryeh Goldsmith's space. Plastic toys and figures adorn Amy Yang's cube. One of the "walls" of Jinnah Hosein's cubicle is a plastic sheet because the wall was constantly being taken down to run more and more wires to keep up with the need. The sheet is somehow emblematic of the constantly changing world that is cyberspace. Posters and photos are the wallpaper elsewhere.

The programmers belong in this funky atmosphere. Jinnah, whom I met first, is the picture of Generation X grunge. With his shoulder-length hair and baggy clothes, he could easily be confused for one of the generation's minions. However, at nineteen, and already an indispensable summer employee with Interactive Connection, he is far from displaying the lack of direction that sometimes characterizes his generation. He is currently attending Vassar College and is, for the most part, a self-taught technician. To him, self-discipline is a key factor in being a successful programmer.

Jinnah began working with computers when he was ten years old. He had mastered the MS-DOS (the old Microsoft disk operating system) soon after. By the time he was thirteen, he was working summers with computers at his father's company. Each summer after that, he gathered more and more experience and knowledge. When his high school began installing its computer system, he worked with the company contracted for the job and was eventually hired by them.

The combination of networking and maintenance that the company taught him, and the self-taught expertise he had with UNIX and the system's administration, led him to study computer science at college. At Interactive Connection, he is involved with the daily maintenance of the server, and he provides programming for the Web pages the company develops. When the full-time staff runs into difficulties, he is called upon to assist them in developing programs to solve the problems.

Jinnah says that in order to become a programmer, you have to play around and ask yourself, "I have a task that I want to do. How do I get it done?" This curiosity is what makes for a successful programmer.

"You have to want to understand," Jinnah adds. "You have to ask questions and find people who can answer those questions."

He believes that the computer has a rather basic methodology and that when you begin to understand it, all the pieces fall together. From that point on, you can begin to anticipate what another programmer might have done to achieve the result you want.

"There are things you can do to place yourself in the right place at the right time," he says, and I believe him, seeing how fast and far he has come. Almost a decade younger than me, he is in a position of responsibility at Interactive Connection. He recommends getting involved with your school's computer department and talking with your service provider's technicians to find solutions to any questions you have.

As for education, he believes that his liberal arts background at Vassar College has been most appropriate for his work. He thinks that having only a technical background is often limiting. Most helpful to him, outside of his technical expertise, have been discipline and his teaching skills. "The discipline that I need for this career comes from all ranges of education. My technical knowledge is useless unless I can assist others and explain to them what's going on." He is constantly being called upon to share his knowledge with the staff, so his language and writing skills are just as important as the programming languages he works with.

Christopher Park's involvement with cyberspace began as a surfing hobby, and he rode the wave to a position of leadership. As systems operator at Interactive Connection, Christopher is top dog of the programmers. He has his college degree, is well-spoken, and at the ripe old age of twenty-three is a senior figure at the company. In no other industry can you find this combination of youth and success.

To break into a career in cyberspace, he recommends, "Set up an account with a Web service provider, take a look at what's out there, source other pages, and have fun with it." To make the transition from a hobby to a career, he just stuck to his own advice. Like so many others, Christopher is for the most part self-taught. "Computer science is largely like math, in that practice is the only way to get familiar with it. Don't be afraid or intimidated by it. Follow a logical pattern and keep plugging away at it."

Christopher arrives at work around 8:30 each morning and immediately begins his maintenance and troubleshooting regimen. He checks to see that each of the servers is up and running smoothly. He then turns his attention to whatever scripts and programs he has been working on. Any problems that arise during the day are also his responsibility—and, believe me, they arise. Christopher's was the one interview that was continuously interrupted as his coworkers came to him for answers to their troubles.

He told me about a program that he recently wrote that will make his life as systems operator a little easier. They have a "chron" at his office. It's a clock that keeps all of the computers and electronic devices synchronized, so that the entire operation runs together.

Christopher wrote a program to check that the ticker feeds, another element of their business, were always in sync with the rest of the system. (A familiar example of a ticker feed is the stock market quotes feed. When you watch the news on some television channels you can see the prices of stocks racing by as they are posted with up-to-the minute changes.) Since Interactive runs syndicated sites such as the *New York Times* Web page, they need ticker feed information to update their pages. If Christopher's program spots a ticker feed that is out of sync with the chron, it means that the ticker feed has been interrupted. Christopher's program will then e-mail him and cause his computer to beep to notify him that an e-mail message has been received.

Christopher enjoys his position because of the excitement and challenge of it. He feels that his job is new every day, and he's thrilled when he learns something new. The only drawback to his work has been the public's lack of familiarity with what the Web is best suited for. He thinks that many of Interactive Connection's clients have seen too many movies about the Web and that these businesses don't understand its limitations. His clients want real-time video and audio and fancy graphics work, which cannot always be done and usually isn't practical. Computers that most consumers have would not be able to download these pages because they would simply take up too much memory.

Programmers remind me of the independent filmmakers that you see on public television. They have better and more important things to think about than their own appearance. They are not slovenly or untidy, but most cannot be bothered with maintaining a corporate image. They are simply too busy getting and keeping things running to worry about such things. Neckties will not make them better thinkers, and with the hours that they sometimes work, their ties would simply get mangled.

Joe Schwartz, a cyberspace programmer with NPS Associates, *www.npsa.com/npsa/*, says that the freedom that programmers are given to dress as they choose lends a certain credibility to their work. "Scuzzy guys who are just into the machines lend credibility to the job, because that's what people expect to see. It's weird. . . . Because clients can't read computer code, they want to see computer trendiness in the programming pit."

Joe's job is currently situated in his boss's apartment in Brooklyn. He is the Windows programmer in a five-person office. His main responsibility is to write programs that allow a client's computers to work with cyberspace browsers. He enables a company's intranet (their internal computer network, linking computers in the office) to be plugged into the Internet, allowing office-wide access to cyberspace.

When I asked how he developed his computer skills, he joked that it was a result of a "lack of friends." He added, "If you're a kid that takes everything apart and puts it back together, you'll turn to computers sooner or later."

If the programmers are modest about the energy they pour into their work, their coworkers definitely are not. Amy Yang, a project manager with Interactive Connection, told me a story about a programmer who spent the better part of four days producing a Web site to get it done by the deadline. He couldn't be found on the day of the meeting with the client. Amy kept handling the phone calls from the client as calmly as possible, assuring the person at the other end of the line that the programmer would be in soon. Later that afternoon she spotted the groggy programmer walking by her cubicle. It turns out that he had spent the past three nights at work completing the project. He had just awoken from a much-needed rest following his third consecutive all-nighter. The client was well-satisfied with the work, but it took a rather steep physical toll on Amy's coworker.

Are you ready to help form the infrastructure of a company? You can be your own person and express yourself as you see fit. But you also have to possess the facility to put in grueling hours. In cyberspace you are given a lot of responsibility and then sometimes left on your own to pioneer your own answers. Discipline, diligence, curiosity, creativity, and practice are all required.

Digital Reality

Martin Gay and Kathlyn Gay

Date: June 1994
Source: America Online/Mobile Office Manager
Subject: Who's Gonna Drive You Home?
Eighteen-year-old Kevin Chang developed a software program
that automatically controls acceleration and braking in cars. An
infrared sensor mounted on the front of each automobile moni-
tors its distance from the vehicle ahead and surrounding objects.
"Since computers can react faster than human beings," explains
Chang, "cars can drive faster and you can fit more of them on
the freeway. You can tailgate closer safely." The Institute for
Transportation Studies at UC Berkeley is already knocking on
Chang's door.

PERHAPS Chang's great new idea as described in the America Online (AOL) electronic magazine will be a standard feature
on future cars produced in Detroit. Already there are many
computer devices installed in the latest models. Temperature is
kept constant for passengers by an environmental computer.
Other information processors determine when injectors should
shoot fuel into piston chambers. Mechanics can't even adjust
the new engines without first reading the output of their shop's
diagnostic computers. Eighty years after the Model T, Henry
Ford probably wouldn't recognize today's high-tech vehicles.

Automotive technology is only one place where information
has been used to transform a product. A little closer to home,
the American Standard people have developed a "smart bath-
tub," in which "the bather selects the temperature, humidity,
music, air, and water flow with the touch of electronic buttons.
The unit has a communications linkage that allows its owner to
contact the tub from a remote location and ask it to have the
right environment ready at a certain hour," according to Stan
Davis and Bill Davidson, authors of *2020 Vision.*

Most of us are frequently surprised and sometimes amazed
by the reports of fantastic new products and services being
tested and marketed for every aspect of our lives. However, we
seldom think about the way the methods for delivering the reports have changed.

Long ago, messengers delivered news by word of mouth or handwritten documents. Then new communication technology spawned newspapers and magazines that could be delivered by motorized vehicles, trains, and airplanes. Continued advances in technology made radio, telephones, and television common delivery systems for information.

Today the personal computer is a common fixture in the workplace and the home. An estimated 60 percent of U.S. households will have computers by the year 2000, and electronic networks and various online services link computers and users around the world. Information can be distributed rapidly to millions of people, although there are fears that the vast majority worldwide who do not have access to computers will not be able to obtain the information available.

Sports

Eulogy for Mickey Mantle

Bob Costas

YOU know, it occurs to me as we're all sitting here thinking of Mickey, he's probably somewhere getting an earful from Casey Stengel, and no doubt quite confused by now.

One of Mickey's fondest wishes was that he be remembered as a great teammate, to know that the men he played with thought well of him.

But it was more than that. Moose and Whitey and Tony and Yogi and Bobby and Hank, what a remarkable team you were. And the stories of the visits you guys made to Mickey's bedside the last few days were heartbreakingly tender. It meant everything to Mickey, as would the presence of so many baseball figures past and present here today.

I was honored to be asked to speak by the Mantle family today. I am not standing here as a broadcaster. Mel Allen is the eternal voice of the Yankees and that would be his place. And there are others here with a longer and deeper association with Mickey than mine.

But I guess I'm here, not so much to speak for myself as to simply represent the millions of baseball-loving kids who grew up in the 50s and 60s and for whom Mickey Mantle was baseball.

And more than that, he was a presence in our lives—a fragile hero to whom we had an emotional attachment so strong and lasting that it defied logic. Mickey often said he didn't understand it, this enduring connection and affection—the men now in their 40s and 50s, otherwise perfectly sensible, who went dry in the mouth and stammered like schoolboys in the presence of Mickey Mantle.

Maybe Mick was uncomfortable with it, not just because of his basic shyness, but because he was always too honest to regard himself as some kind of deity.

But that was never really the point. In a very different time than today, the first baseball commissioner, Kenesaw Mountain Landis, said, "Every boy builds a shrine to some baseball hero, and before that shrine, a candle always burns."

For a huge portion of my generation, Mickey Mantle was that baseball hero. And for reasons that no statistics, no dry recitation of facts can possibly capture, he was the most compelling baseball hero of our lifetime. And he was our symbol of baseball at a time when the game meant something to us that perhaps it no longer does.

Mickey Mantle had those dual qualities so seldom seen—exuding dynamism and excitement, but at the same time touching your heart—flawed, wounded. We knew there was something poignant about Mickey Mantle before we knew what poignant meant. We didn't just root for him, we felt for him.

Long before many of us ever cracked a serious book, we knew something about mythology as we watched Mickey Mantle run out a home run through the lengthening shadows of a late Sunday afternoon at Yankee Stadium.

There was greatness in him, but vulnerability too.

He was our guy. When he was hot, we felt great. When he slumped or got hurt, we sagged a bit too. We tried to crease our caps like him; kneel in an imaginary on-deck circle like him; run like him, heads down, elbows up.

Billy Crystal is here today. Billy says that at his Bar Mitzvah he spoke in an Oklahoma drawl. Billy's here today because he loved Mickey Mantle, and millions more who felt like him are here today in spirit as well.

It's been said that the truth is never pure and rarely simple.

Mickey Mantle was too humble and honest to believe that the whole truth about him could be found on a Wheaties box or a baseball card. But the emotional truths of childhood have a power that transcends objective fact. They stay with us through all the years, withstanding the ambivalence that so often accompanies the experience of adults.

That's why we can still recall the immediate tingle in that instant of recognition when a Mickey Mantle popped up in a pack of Topps bubble gum cards—a treasure lodged between an Eli Grba and a Pumpsie Green.

That's why we smile today, recalling those October afternoons when we'd sneak a transistor radio into school to follow Mickey and the Yankees in the World Series.

Or when I think of Mr. Tomasi, a very wise sixth-grade teacher who understood that the World Series was more important, at least for one day, than any school lesson could be. So he brought his black-and-white TV from home, plugged it in and let us watch it right there in school through the flicker and the static. It was richer and more compelling than anything I've seen on a high-resolution, big-screen TV.

Of course, the bad part, Bobby, was that Koufax struck 15 of you guys out that day.

My phone's been ringing the past few weeks as Mickey fought for his life. I've heard from people I hadn't seen or talked to in years—guys I played stickball with, even some guys who took Willie's side in those endless Mantle-Mays arguments. They're grown up now. They have their families. They're not even necessarily big baseball fans anymore. But they felt something hearing about Mickey, and they figured I did too.

In the last year, Mickey Mantle, always so hard on himself, finally came to accept and appreciate that distinction between a role model and a hero. The first he often was not, the second he always will be.

And, in the end, people got it. And Mickey Mantle got from America something other than misplaced and mindless celebrity worship. He got something far more meaningful. He got love—love for what he had been, love for what he made us feel, love for the humanity and sweetness that was always there mixed in with the flaws and all the pain that wracked his body and his soul.

We wanted to tell him that it was OK, that what he had been was enough. We hoped he felt that Mutt Mantle would have understood and that Merlyn and the boys loved him.

And then in the end, something remarkable happened—the way it does for champions. Mickey Mantle rallied. His heart took over, and he had some innings as fine as any in 1956 or with his buddy, Roger, in 1961.

But this time, he did it in the harsh and trying summer of '95. And what he did was stunning. The sheer grace of that ninth inning—the humility, the sense of humor, the total absence of self pity, the simple eloquence and honesty of his pleas to others to take heed of his mistakes.

All of America watched in admiration. His doctors said he was, in many ways, the most remarkable patient they'd ever seen. His bravery was so stark and real, that even those used to seeing people in dire circumstances were moved by his example.

Because of that example, organ donations are up dramatically all across America. A cautionary tale has been honestly told and perhaps will affect some lives for the better.

And our last memories of Mickey Mantle are as heroic as the first.

None of us, Mickey included, would want to be held to account for every moment of our lives. But how many of us could say that our best moments were as magnificent as his?

This is the cartoon from this morning's *Dallas Morning News*. Maybe some of you saw it. It got torn a little bit on the way from the hotel to here. There's a figure here, St. Peter I take it to be, with his arm around Mickey, that broad back and the number 7. He's holding his book of admissions. He says "Kid, that was the most courageous ninth inning I've ever seen."

It brings to mind a story Mickey liked to tell on himself and maybe some of you have heard it. He pictured himself at the pearly gates, met by St. Peter who shook his head and said, "Mick, we checked the record. We know some of what went on. Sorry, we can't let you in, but before you go, God wants to know if you'd sign these six dozen baseballs."

Well, there were days when Mickey Mantle was so darn good that we kids would bet that even God would want his autograph. But like the cartoon says, I don't think Mick needed to worry much about the other part.

I just hope God has a place for him where he can run again. Where he can play practical jokes on his teammates and smile that boyish smile, 'cause God knows, no one's perfect. And God knows there's something special about heroes.

So long, Mick. Thanks.

from

Football for Young Players and Parents

Joe Namath

FOOTBALL is a wonderful game. I love it. I'll tell you one reason why: it's an honest game. It's true to life. It's a game about sharing.

I believe that most of life is sharing and working together. There isn't too much you can do in life all by yourself. For instance, I'm sometimes on TV. Well, *I* don't do TV. *We* do TV. We've got directors and camera people and production people—a whole *team* that let's me stand up there and be on TV. Or maybe you want to get in your car and drive downtown. Well, somebody else made the car, somebody else keeps it running, somebody else keeps up the roads. It's the truth, man. You don't do very much on your own.

Playing football, you learn this better than any way I know. In football, the best quarterback or the best halfback in the world isn't going to get much done if his buddies up front don't block people. Football is a team game, and that's why I love it. In fact, I like that part of it so much that even when I wanted to name my fishing boat, I called it *Team Game.*

The thing is, a team game is just so much fun. You're working together. You're sharing an adventure. You've got your buddies there with you when times are good—and also when times are bad. When things get tough, it's awful to be alone. A time like that, you're lucky to have your teammates to reach out to. When times are good, when you've won a big game and you're feeling great, it's much more fun to celebrate and share the accomplishment with your friends.

So football is a team game, and life is a team game. That's one reason I like to help boys learn to play this sport. We can learn what *life* is about by learning the game. As soon as the boys start arriving at our summer football camp, we start to eliminate that "I" word and start putting in the "We" word. *We* can do this. *We* can do that. Each boy has to work hard himself, master the basic techniques, get good at his own down the field and score some points. You do get great individual efforts from time to time, sure. But it's by working together that you get to know the real fun of the sport.

I'll tell you another thing that teamwork means in football. It means listen to your coach. I see some youngsters come to play football who aren't used to being bossed around. Maybe at home they get to do nearly anything they want. They might be a little pampered. When those kids first run into a football coach, they may be a bit shocked.

But football isn't a democracy. The game is so complicated that somebody has to be in charge. That somebody is the coach. The thing for you to do is adjust to the situation and learn what you can from it. You may not agree with everything the coach is doing, and sometimes you may be right. Coaches make mistakes like everybody else. But if you waste your time being mad at your coach, you won't be able to learn from him. You won't be able to help your team. If you think your coach is really a bad man, ask your parents to come see him work. But otherwise, let the coach be the coach. You be a player. That's the way a football team works.

Football is a hard-knocking sport. This isn't ping pong or checkers we're talking about. It's a tough game, and if you want to play, you have to show some courage.

But I'll tell you something else. Once you learn some of the skills of blocking and tackling, once you've hit some big guy and lived to tell about it, it doesn't seem so bad anymore. The rules of the game protect you. You wear good equipment. You learn how to handle yourself. Pretty soon you're a football player and holding up your end for your teammates.

You learn something about yourself in the process. You learn you can do your best even when it's hard, even when you're tired and maybe hurting a little bit. You're going to get your share of bumps and bruises. You're going to get your foot stepped on or your knuckles cut up. Then you'll find out you can still play hard, still do your job.

I don't mean you act stupid. If you really get hurt—if you strain a muscle or sprain an ankle—you come right out of the game and let a doctor look at you. But the little bumps and bruises, it's a good feeling when they don't stop you. A man feels good when he shows some courage, some toughness.

Two things can help you handle the combat. First, choose a position that makes sense for you. If you're a little guy, you don't belong in the middle of the line. A little guy should show his courage as a wide receiver, maybe, or a safety.

Second, you need some self-discipline. The only way to do well during a game is to work hard during practice. Learn the right techniques. Practice until you have them perfect. Come early to practice, get as much out of every minute as you can, then stay out afterward and do a little extra.

I've got a piece of paper in my wallet with a sentence I wrote on it years ago. It says, "I believe a necessary quality of one's good character is discipline." I do. And if you show some discipline—if you learn how to block and tackle right—it also gives you courage. Discipline and courage go together.

Arthur Ashe

Bruce Brooks

BY the time this appears in print, it is unlikely that Arthur
Ashe, who died yesterday at the age of forty-nine, will be getting
much ink or airtime. At the moment tributes sing out all over,
mostly from people in the worlds of sports and journalism.
Ashe's tributes are better than the ones most of our heroes get
in the few days after they leave us, even Dizzy Gillespie and Au-
drey Hepburn, two universally loved idols who also died in recent weeks. You always have to say grandiose things about a
public figure who has died, but this time people don't have to
rely as much on the somber clichés of admiration and grief.
This time the mourning admirers can be honest and sponta-
neous; they can say what they mean.

This is appropriate, because Ashe always said what he meant.
Probably not since Jim Thorpe—except perhaps for the young
Muhammad Ali—has there been a champion athlete who never
recited one of the standard lines in response to one of the standard questions, who never resorted to the easily uttered expression of easily understood joy, disappointment, determination,
sportsmanship, pride, humility, etc., etc., etc. If he found himself with an opportunity to speak when speaking would mean
something, Ashe did not waste his chance by using words or
ideas others had already worn out.

Why were we able to perceive Ashe's honesty so easily? Because on some intuitive level we recognize that to state frankly a
unique, individual feeling requires a unique, individual use of
language, and we could not mistake Ashe's discourse for anyone
else's. Whether he was analyzing the strategy he used to bam-
boozle Jimmy Connors in the 1975 Wimbledon final, relating the
controversial reasons for visiting South Africa in 1991, or admit-
ting that he had AIDS and fiercely resented being forced to share
the "news," Ashe spoke in sentences the form of which seemed
to have been invented for the immediate purpose of giving us a
startling but unquestionable insight into things.

He said a lot of startling things, but the only thing about him
that was ever truly difficult to believe (though you believed it,
you believed it) was the magnitude of his intelligence and in-
tegrity. Such intelligence is a great gift, enjoyed by very few

human beings, even fewer of whom find themselves in the spotlight as often as Ashe did. Especially the spotlight on a playing field. One had to keep reminding oneself: "This guy's a *jock!*" It was always revealing but completely unfair to compare, for example, an Ashe postgame interview with a similar series of quotes from anyone else in the world of sports—or, for that matter, from practically anyone in the world of politics, or science, or any other field in which we expect to find bright people. There are some smart persons out there, and some honest ones, but often their brains seem to run on gasoline while Ashe's ran, magically, on white light.

Ashe leaves us with a good lesson: There is a place in sports for smart people. Intelligence—used well, in analysis, study, practice—helps you in anything you try to do, whether it's a backhand lob at a surprising moment or a moral stand on a complex issue. He was a very talented tennis player, blessed with extraordinary reach and power and touch, but his victories were victories of the wits.

Horseshoes

George Plimpton

THE atmosphere was very relaxed. The interview went well. The president-elect talked a lot about fishing—how it gave him time to relax from the rigors of work, and to do some contemplative thinking. He quoted Izaak Walton's line that says the day a man spends fishing ought not be deducted from his time on earth. He'd had only one long spell of government duty without fishing and that was when he served as chief of the U.S. Liaison Office in Beijing from 1974 to '75. At a Soviet embassy party he was invited to sit in a boat at one end of a ceremonial pool. At the other, an army of beaters got in the water and started driving a school of large carp toward him.

"Scary," President Bush said. "Hundreds of these gigantic carp crashing around in the water. We waited for them with nets on the end of poles."

Barbara Bush remembered that what was caught was immediately cleaned by the Russian kitchen staff and prepared to take home. "The Russians had a beautiful complex built during the time of Peter the Great," she said. "They entertained a lot."

"Hockey games," the president-elect said. "On the lake. I was never much of a skater so I didn't go out on the ice. I don't like to do things I can't do well. I don't dance well, so I don't dance.

"See this scar here?" he asked suddenly. He pointed to the back of his hand. A six-pound bluefish off Florida had nipped him. "Then I've got a scar here close to my eyebrow from a collision trying to head a ball playing soccer at Andover. Can't see it? Well, how about *this* one?" He pulled his shirt away from his neck to reveal a prominent bump on his right shoulder blade. "Got that one playing mixed doubles with Barbara at Kennebunkport. Ran into a porch."

"His mother always said that it was my shot," Barbara Bush said. "I didn't run for it, so he did. She was probably right."

The president-elect smiled and shrugged his shoulders. "Popped the shoulder out," he said. "Separated."

"After that they moved the porch," his wife said with a smile.

Bush said that he had been playing tennis since he was about five. He had stopped singles not long after grade school and concentrated on doubles, largely because his ground strokes were "terrible" except for a backhand chip return of service that drops at the feet of the oncoming server and which he referred to as the "falling leaf."

"The what, sir?" I asked.

"The falling leaf." He went on to say that at the net is the only place where he feels completely at home and he will come in at every opportunity, even behind a second serve. "Or even the falling leaf," he added with a laugh.

A number of other homegrown phrases had developed in the Bush family over the years, and I was told what some of them were. A weak shot elicits the disdainful cry, "Power outage!" The most esoteric is "Unleash Chiang"—from the hue and cry in government circles to allow Chiang Kai-shek to invade the Chinese mainland from Taiwan and which, on the Bush court, refers to a potential source of power.

"George will look over his shoulder," Barbara Bush explained, "and urge his partner to 'unleash Chiang!'"

"The interesting thing about these phrases," she went on, "is that they get exported; people take them with them, and off in the distance, from someone else's court, you'll suddenly hear, 'All right, now, unleash Chiang!'"

When the interview was over, the president-elect looked at me and asked, "Hey, how about a game of horseshoes? You've done all these things . . . football with the . . ."

"Detroit Lions."

"Right. And the Boston Bruins and all that. You gotta try some horseshoes."

I nodded and said it would be a great honor.

On the way out to the horseshoe court, Barbara Bush stopped me. "You'll have to wear a cowboy hat," she said. "No one with any self-respect plays horseshoes without a cowboy hat." She rummaged around in a closet just inside the front door. On a top shelf sat an assortment of Bush's hats. I tried on a few of the western variety. His head is a lot larger than mine, so the hats tended to slide down my forehead nearly to my eyes.

"These hats all seem to be the same size," I remarked, a somewhat lunatic observation since it implied Mr. Bush wore hats of different head measurements.

I finally picked a tall-crowned model with the president-elect's name stamped in gold on the inside. I wore it out to the horseshoe pit at a curious, raked angle so that I could see where I was going. The president-elect stared briefly at it. His was decorated with a braided Indian cord that supplemented the hat-band. He held out some horseshoes.

"You got a choice," he said. "The drop-forged eight or the ten."

"I'll take the . . . ah."

The president-elect laughed. He looked down at the horse-shoes, hefting them to judge their weight. "I don't know the difference myself," he said. "They tell me the harder the metal, the more it tends to be rejected by the stake."

Then he explained the rules—one point for the shoe closest to the stake and three for the ringer; the winner would be the first to reach fifteen. We took some practice throws. I threw my shoes so that they revolved, parallel to the ground, toward the opposite stake. This somewhat startled the president-elect since that is the style (though I was unaware of it) used by most top-flight pitchers.

"Hey, what have we got here?" he asked suspiciously. He prefers to hold the shoe at its closed end and toss it so it turns once as it goes down the pitch.

"You played this game before?"

"Not for thirty years," I said truthfully.

The game began. The president-elect was supported loudly by his granddaughter Jenna, who is seven, seated at courtside bundled up in a bright orange parka. There was considerable chatter during play—needling and a plethora of the homegrown expressions: "power outage" for a halfhearted toss, "SDI" for a throw with a higher arc than usual, and "It's an ugly pit" for those times when no one's shoe was close to the stake. Once, it was impossible to tell which of the two shoes had landed closer; the president-elect shouted, "The tool! Get the tool!"—a request that was echoed by those standing around watching.

The tool, which was fetched from the gardening shed, turned out to be oversized navigator's dividers. The president-elect knelt in the pit and brushed the dirt away from the two horse-shoes. He handled the gadget with great relish. In fact, all aspects of the game were carried on with great élan. On occasion he would turn to me and ask the rhetorical question: "Isn't this game great? Have you ever had a better time? Isn't this just great? *Heaven!*"

I *was* having a good time. The iron felt cool and comfortable to the grip. I peered out from under the brim of my hat and suddenly, after a number of one-pointers, threw a ringer. I found myself with fourteen points and only one to go to win. The president-elect had thirteen. Cries of alarm rose from Jenna's chair.

I began to worry about winning. What would it do to the

president-elect's confidence to lose to someone who hadn't thrown a horseshoe in thirty years? Would he brood? Suddenly slam the heel of his hand against his forehead at cabinet meetings? Stumble into the bushes in the Rose Garden? Talk out loud to himself at state dinners? Snap at Sununu?

I decided that I would credit my victory to the hat. "Beginner's luck," I was going to say. "And this hat of yours. If it hadn't been for this cowboy hat . . ."

It seemed the perfect solution. Gracious. Self-effacing. Just the thing to say.

"Listen, we can't let this happen," the president-elect was saying as he stepped up to throw. He sighted down the pitch. As he swung his arm back he produced one of his homegrown motivators; it wasn't "Unleash Chiang!" in this case. "Remember Iowa!" he called out, in reference to his recovery from political adversity there during the primaries. We watched the red horseshoe leave his hand, turn over once in flight, drop toward the pit with its prongs forward and, with a dreadful clang, collect itself around the stake. A ringer! Sixteen points and the victory for the president-elect. He flung his arms straight up in triumph, a tremendous smile on his face. From her chair Jenna began yelping pleasantly.

I said as follows: "Nerts!"

I can't recall the last time I had used that antique expression. The president-elect came toward me, his hand outstretched. "Isn't that great!" he said as I congratulated him. He wasn't talking about his win but the fact that the game had been so much fun. I agreed with him. *"Heaven!"* he said.

We walked back up to the residence. Up on the porch, Mrs. Bush suggested that we leave our shoes, muddy from the horseshoe pitch, by the front door so we wouldn't track mud on the carpets. I stepped out of my loafers. One of my socks had a hole in it. My big toe shone briefly until I pulled the sock forward so that it dangled off the front of my foot, flopping as I followed the president-elect into the house. He wanted to give me a tour of the premises. I followed him upstairs, first to his closet-sized office with its photographs of the cigarette boat *Fidelity,* which he takes out for bluefishing, and a mounted bonefish (TEN POUNDS, EIGHT OUNCES, reads the plaque under it), a little rubber shark riding its back, tossed up there by a grandchild.

We went up to a dormitory-like room at the top of the house where the older Bush children bunk out on the floor in sleeping bags when they come to visit. The nearest thing to a trophy case is up there—a shelf cluttered with the kind of shoebox mementos one might find in the back of a teenager's closet: scuffed baseballs, one of them, I noted, signed by Joe DiMaggio with the inscription, "You make the office look great"; a football autographed by Roger Staubach, who wrote, "Thanks for giving a darn about friends"; a Keith Hernandez-model first baseman's mitt; a Chicago Cubs pennant; a 1988 Dodgers World Series baseball cap; an NASL soccer ball; two construction worker's hard hats; and a blood-red Arkansas Razorback novelty hat shaped like a boar's head. The president-elect took the hat off the shelf and tried it on, the snout poking over his forehead.

"I'm not sure it suits you, sir," I said. "It would startle your constituency."

"Not in Arkansas," he said, putting it back.

He picked up one of the baseballs and began tossing it in his hand. "Now the only time I handle these is throwing out ceremonial balls." He began describing one of his more embarrassing moments when—apparently hampered by a bulletproof vest—at an opening-day ceremony he had bounced a ball halfway to the Houston Astros' catcher. "You tend to forget the distance," he said. "It's a question of raising your sights. You learn. Next time it's going to be right on target."

As we came down the stairs a small group was standing in the foyer—members of his cabinet-elect. I recognized Quayle, Sununu, the chief of staff, and Nick Brady, the secretary of the treasury. Scowcroft. Apparently the president-elect had scheduled a staff meeting. The toe of my stocking hung over a step. Sununu apparently knew something about my career as a participatory journalist. "Hey," he called up merrily. "A new cabinet member?"

The president-elect came to the door with me. As I stepped back into my loafers he urged me to come back for a rematch. "When the White House horseshoe court is ready, there'll be a ribbon-cutting ceremony. Got to come down for that."

I said I would. "I'm bringing my own cowboy hat this time," I said.

A Sense of Horses

Michael J. Rosen

WHEN I was younger, the whole of summer hinged on those
few hours each week at the camp stable, just as the whole of
the school year merely anticipated summer vacation.
I devoted myself to horseback riding. That, and swimming.
Team competition left me anxious on the sidelines, but at the
stables, the horse and I faced greater opponents: We outmaneu-
vered gravity, vanquished separate fears, and attempted a me-
diating language of touch and balance, where words were
hardly uttered.

Did I love riding because I was good? Was I good because I
loved it? I'd climb in the saddle, and gradually, other riders,
other horses in the ring, whatever it was I didn't want to do
after camp or beginning junior high—it all ceased to exist, along
with the rest of my life on the ground, shrinking, fading behind
our dusty trail.

That last summer of camp, Sparky was my own horse. It
never dawned on me that each morning she was some other
camper's, since I rode in the afternoon. I chose her from my in-
structor Ricki's description of Sparky's ideal rider: self-assured,
consistent, with enough authority so the horse wouldn't take
control. I wanted that challenge. Maybe I just wanted a beautiful horse with what Ricki called "a flea-bitten gray" coat. Or
maybe it was Sparky's eyes: blue, like a sapphire, that made
stars of sunlight.

Each session, we'd saddle up, practice maneuvers, and then
parade out of the ring and across a plank bridge that, like a
colossal xylophone, echoed the horses' hooves as they struck
each board. We'd trail-ride in the forest for twenty minutes or
so until we reached the meadow, where we'd have "open practice," meaning a chance to break loose. Though Ricki hadn't
taught any gait faster than a canter, some horses, Sparky included, had to gallop. Suddenly the *one, two* and *three, four* of
her hooves vanished into a liftoff, a levitation I felt the way you
can feel the instant a plane lifts off or a roller coaster dips, and
I'd be weightless, hardly resting in the saddle, my heart clop-
clopping its own rapid gait as I hovered at a velocity only the
tears that the wind jerked from my eyes revealed. In those

moments—no more than a minute or two—the earth vanished entirely beneath us: She had become Pegasus, the winged Greek horse, and by some miracle, a twelve-year-old mortal had been chosen to ride her.

Sparky performed as no other horse I'd ridden. Each session, I sensed improvement. I settled into her trot. Reined more clearly. The moment I signaled to canter, she responded. Before Sparky, I'd never appreciated what Ricki meant about how horse and rider work toward a harmony that merges powers and thoughts.

One day, Gibby the stable owner's son replaced Ricki. She'd been injured, he explained. A horse had kicked her, crushed four ribs. "See, even experts can't be too careful." Though we vaguely knew Gibby, he didn't know us. For two solid weeks, he had us circle him in the corral while he pelted dirt clods at horses that weren't minding.

Someone besides us kids must have complained. For his final session, Gibby walked us to the meadow. "You're on your own," he said, "just don't run 'em." Then he dismounted and gathered up dirt clods.

"I said, don't race her," Gibby shouted at someone, just as I leaned into a canter.

A moment later, something whizzed past my chest. "You, for crying out loud! Listen!"

I jerked Sparky to a halt. "Me? You want me?"

"Yes, you! Too many holes to be running a blind animal! Trot her. Got it?"

"What? Sparky's not blind."

"Right. She's not blind, and you're not stupid." Then Gibby turned to yell at another camper.

I jumped down and stood in front of Sparky. Her eyes gazed, blinked, wondering no doubt why we weren't flying, why I was on the ground. I stared into her left eye, at the reflected clouds that were as much within her eye as in the sky. I stared at her other eye, at the receding herd of tiny horses and riders. I pressed my face to her muzzle and held my breath trying not to cry, then trying to stop.

Before long my counselor returned. No, I wasn't hurt. No, nothing happened. No, I don't care if the other kids see me crying. Ultimately, I said that I hated him . . . Gibby . . . camp . . . and everything else in a world that was this unfair. I wanted to stand in that field of rabbit warrens and groundhog burrows and tractor-wheel ditches and cry at least until camp ended, and maybe until summer ended, and quite possibly until I turned thirteen or thirty and this sadness, this overwhelmingly sorry feeling—for Sparky, for myself?—had run dry with the tears.

But it didn't take that long. The bus was waiting. I took Sparky's reins and led her across the field, retracing a path my own two feet had never touched.

Her chest bandaged, Ricki returned the last day of camp to present achievement awards. She handed me a yellow card with a blue ribbon: the camp's top honor, the Pegasus Award. "Just don't hug me," she said.

I never saw Sparky after that summer. But I continued to think of that moment in the meadow, standing, stunned, forced to admit that true and impossible knowledge. And while that twelve-year-old boy, and, no doubt, that mythic horse, are long gone, it's only now I can see—instead of the sun, the woods, or other riders—my own reflection in that horse's cloudy, uncomprehending, sparkling eye.

A Letter To My Daughter

Florence Griffith Joyner

DEAR Mary,

I've been running since I was five—just your age now. Pointing to my early start, people often say to me, "Why don't you start your daughter running track?" I know they mean well, but that's not my style. If you do choose to run track or do gymnastics, you'll have 100 percent of our support. But it has to be your choice.

When I was a kid, I gave my heart to running because it made me feel free, and it didn't matter to me whether I won or lost. In college, when other kids were arguing politics in the student union or going to parties, I was running. Missing out on those things didn't really bother me—frankly, I wanted to go to the Olympics a lot more than I wanted to party. But missing out on family things—well, I cried many tears for many years when I couldn't make it to a birthday party or a graduation because I had a meet.

Sometimes the cost was more than I was prepared to pay. Once, at a track meet in Japan, I called my mother, as I always did, to let her know when I'd be home. One of my brothers answered the phone and told me she'd gone back to North Carolina. That's where my grandpa lived. I'd talked to him on the phone, but I'd never met him. I loved him, though. I loved the way he said my nickname, Dee Dee. He made me laugh. I swore to my mother that I'd save up enough money so that she and I could take a trip to North Carolina.

It never happened. Grandpa died that day. Mama didn't tell me how sick he was because she didn't want to distract me from the competition. To this day, I would give up every medal, record, title, award, certificate and ribbon to be able to spend time with my grandfather.

There were other things that hurt. In 1984, when I finally made the Olympic team for the 200 meters, I knew beyond doubt I was going to win.

But I was wrong. I came in second. Lots of people thought I should give up track then and move on. But I gazed at that top podium and vowed I'd stand on it in four years.

No one else had that confidence in me. To everyone else, I

was second best. In fact, my nickname was The Silver Queen, for all my second-place finishes. It took a lot of energy to ignore those opinions of me.

When I made the Olympic team in 1988, I said my prayers and concentrated on the finish line. In spite of the thousands of cheering people in the stands, when the race started, it was as if I had gone deaf: I heard nothing except the wind rushing past my ears. When I burst through the tape, I felt that rush of glory. This was what I had worked so long to prove, what I had sacrificed for, and I felt blessed that I could do it on the day that it counted.

I loved running, and I got the glory. But, Mary, only you can decide if the reward is worth the effort. It's not my duty, nor is it my right, to make sure you do everything I missed out on, or that you become a superstar. What I want for you is to grow up happy, healthy, confident, strong and determined to reach your goals. Whatever they are, it starts with a dream.

Love, Mom

Hoop Dreams

Ebony Magazine

IN past years, the U.S. Olympic women's basketball team was assembled just a few weeks before the start of the Summer Games. National teams won gold medals in 1984 and 1988, but in 1992 the U.S. came in a disappointing third place. So, this time around Olympic officials decided to try something different, and for the first time, the nucleus of the team—the USA Women's National Basketball Team—was selected in May, more than a year before the start of the 1996 Olympics.

Comprised of 11 of basketball's most gifted athletes, the team is preparing for the Olympics by participating in a grueling nine-month tour. Before they are finished in June, they will have played 26 exhibition games with some of America's finest collegiate women's teams as well as several games abroad. Although no one on the national team is guaranteed a spot, women's basketball enthusiasts agree that the 11 players have the best chance of making the Olympic team.

Eight African-Americans—Sheryl Swoopes, Lisa Leslie, Teresa Edwards, Katrina McClain, Carla McGhee, Nikki Mc-Cray, Ruthie Bolton-Holifield and Dawn Staley—are members of the team. Leading the charge is head coach Tara VanDerveer, who is assisted by Reneé Brown and Nell Fortner. The trio will also coach the Olympic team.

"By playing together for an extended period of time," says VanDerveer, "the players on the National Team can learn each other's idiosyncrasies. That is what this year is for—learning the nuances of the game. It is not X's and O's, ball handling and shooting. It's anticipating what a teammate will do."

Depending upon the outcome of the 1996 Olympics, "I want to be like Sheryl" could very well become the catch-phrase of the late '90s for young girls who aspire to play professional women's basketball. That's because last fall Sheryl Swoopes became the first woman—Black or White—to have a basketball shoe, the *Air Swoopes*, named after her. "I was honored," she says, "because that's something I never thought would happen."

Swoopes certainly has earned the honor. In her first season with Texas Tech University in Lubbock, the 6-foot forward scored double digits in all but one of the 31 games in which she started. Then in 1993, she almost single-handedly led her team to an 84-82 win over Ohio State in the NCAA Division I Championship game. With a game score of 47 points, Swoopes broke records as the first player—male or female—to score that many points in an NCAA Championship game.

Now the 24-year-old athlete is determined to help the U.S. capture the Olympic gold medal this summer. "I think the idea of putting a women's team together that will train together and play together for a year, right up to the competition in Atlanta, is wonderful," says Swoopes. "I don't think [Olympic teams] had enough time in the past to get the chemistry right and to learn the style of play that coaches want. It's giving us the perfect opportunity to win the gold medal."

Shooting for Olympic gold has required a great deal of sacrifice from each of the team's members, including their leading scorer, Lisa Leslie. "Very little goes on outside of playing basketball right now," says the 6-foot-5 forward and center. "You give up your life when you choose to be with a team for a year."

Leslie hasn't always been so willing to make sacrifices in the name of basketball. Despite her height—she was already 6 feet tall by the sixth grade—she was not immediately devoted to the sport. Modeling on fashion runways, she says, not dribbling a basketball, was her childhood dream. "[My sisters and I] were really into modeling and being very feminine," she recalls. "We studied the rules of etiquette, did our hair, polished our fingernails and put on lip gloss."

Reluctantly, Leslie agreed to play but only as long as she did not fall on the team's concrete court. Eventually, she says, "I had to make the choice: 'Am I going to be cute or am I going to play sports?'" Her mother, Christina Leslie, told her she could do both.

Since then, Leslie has been making women's basketball history. She scored 101 points *by halftime* in 1990 before the other team walked off the court in self-admitted defeat. That accomplishment placed her just four points shy of breaking basketball legend Cheryl Miller's halftime high school record of 104 points. And when she graduated from the University of Southern California in 1994, Leslie was the Pac-10's all-time leading scorer and rebounder with 2,414 points and 1,214 career rebounds.

After graduation, Leslie signed with an Italian league, where she played professionally during the 1994-95 season. Since joining the national team, she has averaged 17.1 points per game and 6.3 rebounds and leads the team in blocked shots.

Leslie's ultimate basketball goal, she says, has always been to win a gold medal.

Guard Teresa Edwards can relate to such a goal. The University of Georgia graduate is the first American basketball player—male or female—to compete on three Olympic teams. She has also played overseas professionally longer than anyone else on the team—nine years—in Italy, Japan, Spain and France. "My attitude, the way I perceive things, the way I live my life, has come through basketball," says Edwards. "The travel and the different cultures; meeting people and dealing with people, the way I carry myself on and off the court. . . . Everything I could possibly talk about is going to be connected to basketball."

As the oldest of five children and the only girl, Edwards fell in love with the game more than 20 years ago. "[Basketball] was the only game growing up," she says, "where I could go up against the boys and beat them." During the 1984 Olympics, the 31-year-old was the youngest member on the U.S. gold medal-winning team. In 1988, Edwards was again instrumental in the U.S. gold medal win, finishing as the team's second-leading scorer with a 16.6 point average. She was also a co-captain on the 1992 team that won the bronze.

Beyond winning another gold, Edwards is hoping a role in a United States professional league is also in her future. "If not on the coaching level, then definitely as a general manager," she says. "And I would like to some day own a women's professional team here. I definitely would like to be involved in the growth of this sport here in America on a professional level."

Although others have tried and failed over the last 25 years, a professional women's U.S. basketball league finally appears to be on the horizon. "The timing is perfect," says Edwards. "The public is demanding it, and the attention is there."

Poised to take advantage of the attention being generated by women's basketball is the American Basketball League, which plans to field the first of its professional women's teams in October 1996.

The ABL was founded by a group of athletic administrators, educators and business executives, including Bobby Johnson, the owner of Pebble Brook Healthcare, Inc., in Atlanta. Johnson, who is also a certified public accountant, is the league's chief financial officer. "The acceptance of women's basketball on the amateur, college and professional levels is really exploding," he says. "And if they're able to have successful leagues of women basketball players overseas, then surely we can do it over here."

Collegiate attendance records, Johnson says, also support a professional league. Reportedly, attendance at NCAA women's Division I regular season games has more than tripled since 1982, with tournament attendance climbing from 67,000 in 1983 to 248,000 in 1995. And last season more television viewers watched the women's NCAA championship game, which drew some 18,000 fans, than an NBA game televised on the same day.

Unlike the NBA, the ABL will recruit players, negotiate and own their contracts and will pay player salaries, bonuses and benefits. Team operators will purchase the right to operate a team and have ownership interest in the league. However, team operators will independently manage their teams, hire team personnel, draft and trade players, negotiate local contracts and be responsible for marketing their teams.

The league will initially consist of eight teams, divided into eastern, central and western divisions and will be headquartered in the San Jose, Calif., area. Beginning in October, teams will play 42 regular season games, followed by the playoffs in late February and early March. And at mid-season the league's best will play an All-Star game.

"It has to be now," team forward Katrina McClain has said. "It's now or never. I really believe this is it. This is our chance to get everybody's attention by showing that we can play and that it's fun to watch women's basketball. People in this country don't realize that the best women's basketball is played *after* college."

Although the new league will give women's basketball more exposure in the U.S., it will be some time before women enjoy the kind of benefits that are common among men. Just ask Sheryl Swoopes. After graduation, her male counterparts began negotiating six-figure NBA salaries. However, she received a plane ticket to Italy for their 1993-94 season. She played only 10 games before returning home. "I know a lot of people who've had great experiences overseas," says Swoopes. "Unfortunately, mine wasn't a great one. So that's why I'm so determined to do something to help establish some kind of league in the United States."

Swoopes' efforts include her role on the ABL advisory board, where she and Edwards sit along with two other national team members. The four are also among the nine team members who have signed league contracts.

Thus far, 25 additional women, including former University of North Carolina star Charlotte Smith, have also signed agreements. Remaining roster spots will be filled this spring during the league's inaugural draft. "Women's basketball is really ready for this," Edwards has said. "We've been waiting for this. We're standing strong. We're standing together."

Players will own 10 percent of the league in the form of a Players' Trust and have a voice in league management via its advisory board. They will also earn an average of $70,000 per season and a minimum of $40,000, with premiere players earning anywhere from $100,000 to $125,000. However, ABL paychecks will be small potatoes compared to the huge salaries offered by many foreign teams, where American players command as much as five to six times that amount.

Despite the drastic pay-cuts, the opportunity to play at home, say many of the national team players, heavily influenced their decision to sign with the ABL. Dawn Staley, who has played professionally in France, Italy, Brazil and Spain, has said of her time abroad: "A lot of money went toward phone bills and bringing people over to keep me company, so it's not that much of a pay-cut. Hey, the only reason I played overseas was to get the international experience to help me make [the national team]. Overseas was my sacrifice. This is my reward."

First Strike

Gary Paulsen

IN reality it is not possible to draw an exact line and say here one kind of fishing becomes another, just as it is not possible to draw an exact line in any part of life to separate it from another.

Summer fishing came in so many different forms, became so many different arts, that there must be a start to it, a beginning and a middle and an end just to be able to see it.

The start was where the river passed a smaller stream that entered the river by the Ninth Street bridge.

Though summer had come, always lying back hiding was the cold snap—a late killing frost that caught everybody off guard so often that it seemed people would come to expect it and not set their garden vegetables out. But they are always surprised by the frost, and have to wrap paper around the plants in small cones until the backyards of everybody in town seem to be full of buried elves with only their hats showing.

But the frost does more than kill plants. Something about it affects the fish, and where the stream comes into the river just after the frost and even during the frost the northern pike come to feed. It is perhaps that they think it is fall, or perhaps the cold makes small fish come there and the big ones follow.

And they are truly big—some of them like twenty-pound green sharks, filled with teeth and savagery.

Fishing for them was done one way and one way only—casting lures. Two lures worked the best, and everybody who came to work where the stream flows into the river used one or sometimes both of them. The best was a red-and-white daredevil—a spoon that is silver on one side with red and white stripes on the other and a single triple-hook at the bottom, or business end. The new ones didn't seem to work very well until they were scuffed and scratched by teeth tearing at the paint on them. Most of us tried rubbing them on rocks or concrete to scuff them up a bit, but it didn't work as well as having it done by teeth. The other lure was called a plug—a simple cylindrical piece of wood painted red in the front and white in the back with two small silver eyes and a "lip" made of stamped metal to pull the plug under when it was reeled in.

The rigs used then would not be considered usable by modern

fishermen. This was all before glass or carbon rods and spinning reels or free-wheeling casting reels, and casting with them was a true art, a balance of coordination and luck. The line used was of a heavy braid—there were no monofilaments then either—rolled on a drum reel with thumb-busting side drive handles that had to spin with the drum when a cast was made.

Everything was in the thumb. The right thumb rested on the line drum, and the rod—a clunker made of spring steel and by modern standards about as flexible as casting with a tire iron—had to be whipped overhead and forward with great force at the same instant the thumb had to be lifted from the drum to allow the lure to pull the line out. But not all the way. If the thumb came up too much, the line would go too fast and cause a backlash—a tangle on the reel sometimes so hideous the line had to be cut from the drum with a pocketknife, hacked off, and replaced completely. But the thumb couldn't be pressed too hard either, or the lure wouldn't go anywhere.

And then, just as the lure entered the water the thumb had to act as a gentle brake and stop the line drum.

All to start just one cast.

And almost no casts produced a fish. It might take sixty or seventy casts to entice a northern to strike, and then it didn't always pay off.

If the daredevil was used it had to be allowed to wobble down into the water no more than a foot, and then the rod had to be put in the left hand and the right hand had to grip the handles, and the line had to be reeled in as fast as the hand could move to make the spoon roll and flip and flash silver and red. Then, just before shore the daredevil had to be stopped, cold, for half a second in case there was what was called a "follow-up" to give a fish time to hit it just then.

The plug was slightly different. Because it was of wood it floated and so the cast had time to be developed correctly. The cast could be placed with more time, the plug allowed to drift into position, and then the reeling started at one's leisure.

The lip on the front of the plug worked as a water scoop so that the faster the plug was reeled in the deeper it would dive, and the depth could be controlled that way. Some worked the tip back and forth to the right and left while reeling, but it didn't seem to help, just as spitting on the lure—another trick used by some—also didn't seem to help. Once somebody scrounged some blood from a butcher in a small bucket and dipped the lures in the blood, and that had some effect but made us stink for days of rotten blood and fish slime. It didn't bother us, but in school there was a noticeable reaction.

Again, as with the daredevil, when the plug was close to shore it was stopped for half a moment to allow a possible follow-up strike, but really the cast was always everything. And though many—most—casts did not catch fish, each and every cast had to be made with art and skill and the hope, the prayer was always there that it would work; that *this* cast would work *this* time.

The problem was the cold. It was necessary to work the line in just the right place, reeling the braided line through the fingers to be able to "feel" when the first hit came, if it came. Braided line soaked up water, and this squeezed out on the finger, ran down the wrist, and dripped on the waist or legs—depending on where the reel was held.

Wet, cold hour after hour, each perfect cast followed by each perfect cast waiting for that moment, that split part of a moment when it comes.

The strike.

They are never the same. Daredevil strikes are different from plug strikes as cold-weather strikes are different from summer strikes, and every fish seemed to strike differently.

Northern pike are the barracuda of fresh water and when the mood is on them they will hit, tear at anything that moves. Mother loons keep their babies on their backs so the northerns won't get them, and baby ducks get nailed constantly. Northerns eat anything and everything. In their guts we found bottle-caps, can openers, cigarette lighters, bits of metal, nails, wire, pieces of glass and once, complete, a pair of sunglasses that fit one of the boys perfectly.

But they're picky. Not always, but sometimes. And they must be coerced, persuaded, into biting—begged, enticed.

A cast can be "dropped," the lure allowed to settle, then reeled in fast, then allowed to settle again and once more reeled fast—to make it seem sick or wounded. It can be skittered across the surface, then suddenly stopped, skittered and stopped, teased and teased, looking, waiting for *the* moment:

The strike.

It always comes like lightning. Sometimes there is just the tiniest hint, a small grating of their teeth on the lure as they come in for the hit, but usually there is no warning. One second the reel is turning and the lure is coming in, and the next there is a slashing blow and the line stops, begins to sizzle out, cuts the finger, and the rod bends, snaps down, and in some cases, if it is a large fish and a steel rod, it stays bent in a curve.

It is impossible to judge size. Three pounds seems like six, six like twelve and over. One cold, clear morning a miracle came. A cast, one clean cast with a daredevil that slipped into the water like a knife, clean and in and halfway back, the reel spinning as fast as it would go; there was a small grating on the lure and then a tremendous slashing strike, a blow that nearly tore the rod away, and the line cut the water, sizzled off to the right so fast it left a wake.

Seventeen pounds.

A great green torpedo of a fish that tore the water into a froth, a fight that slashed back and forth until at last the fish was tired, until it nosed finally into the bank, where it could be dragged up onto the grass to lie, green and shining, the tail flapping, and a voice, a small voice notes the sadness of the fish and whispers in the mind and the words come out:

"Let it go."

"Are you crazy?"

"Let it go—it's too, too much fish to keep like this. Let it go. . . ."

"Nobody will believe it."

"We saw it. That's enough. Let him go."

And so it is.

Somebody has a scale, a spring with a needle that slides, and the fish is weighed, and the lure is removed, and it is laid in the shallows. It wiggles twice, a left and right squirm, and it's gone.

"It will learn," somebody says. "It will never strike again."

But he is wrong.

Four of us that day catch the same fish and release him, and each time he fights and each time he slides back into the river and disappears like a green ghost, and there are many other springs and thousands of other casts and hundreds of fish caught and eaten when it snaps cold, where the stream comes into the river, but never the same again.

Never that same slamming surge of the first large strike.

Seventeen pounds.

from
Circus: An Album

Linda Granfield

IT'S easy to forget that a circus show is approximately two hours of *live* entertainment. No matter how skilled and practiced the performers are, anything can happen. Someone has to be out front, keeping an eye on everything, anticipating problems and quickly dealing with an emergency if it arises. That's the ringmaster's job.

The ringmaster is a position that has changed throughout circus history. Early ringmasters like Philip Astley held the reins of the circling horses. Later ringmasters, who wore red jackets, white breeches and black hats, directed the show, becoming masters of ceremonies who announced the different acts.

Today, a ringmaster (male or female) still plays the "straight man" for the clowns, still watches for any problems in the ring, still introduces the various acts. Many of them sing as well. The uniform has changed, too. During the 1994 season, the ringmaster of the Moscow Circus wore a baggy black suit, spats and an oversized black top hat. American ringmasters may change costumes many times during the show, displaying one dazzling sequin-encrusted jacket after another. The ringmaster of the Big Apple Circus wears a traditional riding habit.

The ringmaster grandly introduces each act to the audience. He calls the performers back for their bows. He smiles and welcomes everyone as if they've entered his living room. And, in a way, they have. When he blows his whistle and slowly calls out "Laaadeeeeez and gentlemen, boys and girls, chilllldren of all ages . . ." the magic begins.

The members of a circus band are called windjammers. The music they play may include marches, reggae, calypso, barbershop, even rap—whatever fits the individual circus act. Some circuses, like Canada's Cirque du Soleil, perform to a completely original score that has been written especially for the show.

The band serves as a clock, too. Performers behind the scenes know which act is on by listening to the music. And while performing, they time their acts by the beats, and follow the pace set by the music.

The musicians must closely follow every move made by the circus performers. A turn of the performer's head, for example, may signal to the musicians that a change is coming. In fact, if you go to the circus night after night during an engagement, you will never see an act performed exactly the same way each time. The constant changes keep the routine fresh, as the performer finds tiny ways to refine the act.

The music tells the audience when to get noisy and when to hush. Loud, romping tunes highlight the livelier acts; gentler music (or no music) accompanies the intense concentration of a performer who is perched high above the crowd. The music can distract the audience, perhaps by playing loudly and making a funny sound when the juggler drops a club. If a horseback rider misses his leap onto the back of a steed and has to wait for another opportunity, the band has to continue playing until the act has "caught up."

Circus bands have been warning devices, too. If a disaster occurs, like the great Ringling Big Top fire in 1944, the band is prepared to play a certain song that signals rescue workers and the performers to help the audience exit.

The circus generally opens with a "spec," when the entire company parades around the ring. Then it's time for a carefully choreographed series of acts that generally fall into one of four categories—thrill acts, animals, ground acts and clowns.

Thrill, or daredevil, acts can make an audience hold its collective breath. In the 1800s, "Professor Baldwin's Great Drop from the Clouds" was a parachute act sure to make people gasp. Roman chariot-racing was another, as the air filled with dust pummeled from the ring floor by the noisy, dangerous hooves of the horses, and the riders desperately tried to keep from being thrown out of the carts. Or human cannonballs were fired with a loud boom and a flare that distracted the audience, while the "cannonball" hurtled through the air into a carefully placed net.

Today's thrill acts include the Globe of Death, a metal-mesh sphere containing three motorcyclists who dangerously drive at speeds of up to 60 miles per hour as they try to avoid crashing into one another. Or the Wheel of Death—twin metal-mesh cylinders that move constantly, circling high above the ring while a performer walks around the *outside* of the moving apparatus.

My First Experience in a Circus

Sonya St-Martin

WHEN I was four, I was pretty hyper. I was always jumping all over the place, so my mother enrolled me in a gym class. I stuck with it for seven years and then entered the National Circus School. There I did everything: acrobatics, juggling, trampoline and floor vaults. I stayed in school for eight months, then I appeared in the year's final show. My first time before the public—I was a wreck. I learned afterwards that Cirque du Soleil wanted to hire me for a tour. I immediately signed up.

Rehearsals started in July. When I saw the sets and equipment, I flipped. We rehearsed the acting and acrobatics for nine months. The day I finally got my costume, I was ecstatic. But when the premiere came, you better believe I was nervous. Once it was over, I shouted like a maniac—I was so proud of myself.

Leaving for San Francisco was a big shock for both me and my family. I miss my friends, mom, dad and brother a lot. It's tough on the morale but you survive. . . .

On the other hand, life on tour gives me a chance to make new friends, though these are adult friends. I love them and have a lot of fun with them. They respect me so I respect them back. I like the fact that I am not treated like a kid here but like a mini-adult. The only thing I regret is not having friends my age anymore.

While traveling with Cirque du Soleil, I also get to see a lot of cities throughout the world. That's really cool. In California, the scenery is gorgeous and the weather a lot more pleasant than in Montreal.

My typical day starts with school (from 10:30 am to 3:00 pm). I then practice on the Chinese poles (4:30 to 5:00 pm) and the Russian swing (5:00 to 6:00 pm). I help wash the poles and set them up on the stage (6:15 to 6:30 pm) then go eat till about 7:00 pm. I put on my make-up, get into my costume and do the show from 8:00 to 11:00 pm. It's a pretty heavy schedule but I like it.

Overall, I think life on the road is hard mostly because I'm away from my friends and family. However, it allows me to travel, make new friends and perform for 2,500 people a night, which makes it a unique experience.

Knowing

Bruce Brooks

ONE day while I was snorkeling around an island in the Caribbean Sea, I swam into a small bay and the clear, slightly turquoise water turned into mercury. Or at least that is how it seemed. One second I was slipping effortlessly through liquid crystal; the next second I was stuck inside a thick silver mass that pulsated on every side with the current. I felt I was about to smother, though I continued to breathe (or, to be honest, to gasp) perfectly well through my snorkel.

The sensation of being completely enclosed in some solid substance came largely from my sudden inability to see anything but pure silver: I had been used to seeing every little thing underwater brilliantly, but now the silver blocked out the bottom, the surface above me, and the busy coral reef that had been on both sides just a moment ago. What had happened? I forced myself to hang still in the water, breathing normally, trying to believe this was a weird illusion that would recede in a moment and leave me with an understanding. It took me a full half minute to figure out that I had swum into the midst of a huge school of small silver fish.

The fish were suspended in the water right up against me, like a mercury shirt. I focused on one, then the next, then the next, and saw that they held themselves apart by the smallest of margins, a few molecules of water winding between the scales and fins. The current was faint—a lilting in-and-out—but the mass of tiny fish made it oppressively visible as they moved with it in perfect unison. I pulled my head back, but my scalp touched nothing, and the fish in front of me still hung less than an inch from the glass of my diving mask. I swept my right arm upward in a slash, but not a fin did I touch, though there were fish surrounding every finger. I wiggled my fingers; the fish moved with the wiggles, always remaining the same short distance away.

After a while I made myself start swimming. It was the same eerie feeling of being encased in a solid mass, yet staying untouched and free-floating. No matter how sudden my movements were, the fish anticipated them and moved exactly the same distance in the same direction, as a unit.

I was just getting kind of comfortable with this odd communion when I felt something happen in the water. I wasn't at all sure how I perceived it—it wasn't a feeling that came from one sense over another—but I knew, in every part of my body, that something big was approaching. Something heavy. The fish around me seemed to thrum with alertness, and in that instant I was just one of them, waiting to see what came around the corner of the reef.

The tension in the water grew; my body, detached from my nice, cool intellect, got keen and rigid, ready to dart this way or that. The experience was fascinating; one part of me was amazed at the way I was picking up what the fish felt—and the way I was acting like them—while the other part was watching curiously (and tensely) for the arrival of this ominous newcomer. Then, like a roll on the tympani in an orchestra, a rumbling that begins below the threshold of hearing and gradually encroaches on perception until it is all we can feel, a huge presence boomed upon us, sweeping all the finicky tension before it. The small fish parted, leaving an alley two feet wide from surface to bottom, and into that alley swam three eighty-pound tarpon.

The tarpon is a grand fish. It has scales like silver dollars, eyes like a giant owl's, and a mouth that looks like a cave. The three of them that swam slowly through us now were like a trio of dinosaurs crashing a poodle show; they cast their eyes right and left with unmistakable superiority and disdain. (And if they noticed that I wasn't a two-inch fishling, they gave no sign. Perhaps my obvious awe made me just another member of the small fry to them.)

The fish and I kept our corridor respectfully open. The tarpon cruised through, waving their tails with slow, careless dignity. I (and no doubt the little fish) waited anxiously for one of them to dash suddenly into the throng and gulp down a few dozen snack bites, but it never happened. The big guys just idled along, leaving us behind holding our breath (at least some of us). As they moved away, a release of tension like a collective sigh swept through all of us watchers. Then, at the last moment, as the tarpon tails began to disappear at the far end of the alley, I remembered I *wasn't* one of the small fish, and hastily paddled after the tarpon to follow and spy. I never caught up, and when I returned to the silver bay fifteen minutes later, the little fish were gone, too.

In the years since that dive, I have wondered about my experience down there in the water with the jillion little fish and the three tarpon. How did the small fish stay so close together and yet never bump into one another? How did they stay so close to me, yet never allow me to touch them? How did they feel the approach of the big hunters? How did I feel the same thing? As I look back, what stands out most clearly is that in those few minutes we all seemed to know and feel a great deal. There was simply a lot of awareness.

How did this awareness come about? How did we all perceive the things we did, and know what we knew? Take the approach of the tarpon, for example. I cannot answer for the fish, but, if pressed, I would say that at the time there just seemed to be a kind of vibration in the water: nothing you could see rippling, nothing you could hear splashing, but something subtler, something you could feel in your skin and sense in your mind, the way you do when someone in a state of high excitation enters a room full of other people. The tension passes quickly through the crowd until everyone is alert, waiting.

I am fascinated by the fact that all of my supposedly superior human qualities of alertness and intelligence did not really set me apart from the fish in whose midst I had intruded—without whose perceptions, perhaps, I might not have even been able to sense what was going on. For there was no doubt that whatever I felt they felt first; it was then communicated to me. Not sent as a specific message, but definitely communicated.

Getting communication through vibrations from a bunch of fish! Imagine! Most of us would scoff at the idea: communication, we would say, is a decidedly human art, especially when the transmission and reception are subtle. Oh, sure, lions might snarl at each other and birds might cheep, but it takes human wits to design, deliver, and receive more elaborate messages. Doesn't it?

Well, maybe not. We boast the largest brains in the animal world, relative to body size, but communication involves more than just thinking. There is a physical side to the art: messages are sent and received by the body—especially in the senses. The five senses—sight, hearing, taste, smell, and touch—represent a mysterious mix of intelligence and physique: there is an apparatus in the nervous system that perceives a sound or odor or vision, and there is the brain (also a part of the nervous system), which translates the perception into thought. As we have noted, humans have superior brains. But when it comes to the physical equipment for sending and receiving messages, we are laughably inferior to thousands of animals. So, given the fact that birds, for example, have better sight and better voices than we do, that dogs and bears have better senses of smell and hearing, and that butterflies have a better sense of taste, is it logical for us to conclude that we own the field of communication? If so, what is all this sharp animal equipment for?

Perhaps we should begin to understand that animals are equipped as they are because they need to be alert for possible communication at all times—communication not just from other members of their flock but from their environment at large. Usually, we regard the act of *sending* a message as the definitive act of communication; we think carefully about what we are going to say or write or film, or what was behind the words or images cast toward us by someone else. But now we may do better by looking at the *receiving*, rather than just the sending. Getting a message requires intelligence and physical skill, too.

It will help if we try to see the environment the way an animal does; as a constant source of information about everything that matters in life. Where is the food? Where is the enemy? Where is my mate? These questions are constant, and the answers are always out there. Scents on the ground, sounds in the wind, a change of color among the leaves of the forest—all of these offer a tale of the moment to an alert animal. It is a tale the animal had better be ready for; any piece of information is ignored at peril. The lives of wild animals are dangerous, and efficient. Nothing is wasted, least of all information. An animal basically lives in an uninterrupted state of wariness, presuming—pretty accurately—that there is always a hostile animal nearby looking for it, or that it may never find another piece of food.

Humans don't need to be quite this careful all the time, so it is difficult for us to recognize and acknowledge the intelligence and almost athletic adroitness animals bring into play with their senses. We can more easily appreciate the wit and skill clearly involved in the many amazing ways animals *do* send messages—through song, gesture, display, dance, sign language, even chemical emission—because we are used to evaluating such behavior in ourselves. These actions are worthy of appreciation; they reveal how ingenious animals can be when they intend to say something. But the ingenuity is there in the waiting and watching and listening and sniffing, too—in the fabulous ears, tongues, noses, antennae, eyes, nervous systems. We can learn much about the world by trying to understand what sort of things animals are ready to perceive.

Of course, it is not possible for a human being to feel exactly what an animal feels when it perceives a certain sight, sound, smell, taste, or touch. We can only imagine. Scientists try to help out imagination by studying the physical mechanics of animals' sensory organs; they can describe precisely how sound waves strike a membrane in a fox's ear and set it atremble, or how the tissues lining a bear's nose absorb molecules from the air and pass electrical impulses on to the brain. And even though knowing how it happens mechanically is not nearly the same as feeling it happen directly, we can combine facts with observations and empathy to create a kind of understanding that lets us speculate pretty well.

The Arts

The Dancers

Mary Clarke and Clement Crisp

JUST as every recipe in a cookery book begins with the ingredients, a guide to the ballets should start with the essential raw material of the performance. Although ballets are sometimes danced without music or without decor—and sometimes without costumes—they simply cannot be danced without dancers. This is a rather *bald* statement but one which has to be stressed from the very beginning. Dancers are athletes; they are athletes whose training is harder, more demanding and much, much longer than any gymnast's or sprinter's. Like footballers, they must train throughout their career, but unlike most other athletes, dancers have no closed season. The daily class which usually lasts for an hour and a half continues right through their active careers. From their entry into the ballet school until the day they take off their dancing shoes for the last time, dancers know that every weekday will begin with the same sweating ritual of bending and stretching and teaching their bodies. The only time off is annual or public holidays and Sundays or another day of rest in the week. A dancer once said, 'If I miss class for one day I know it; if I miss class for two days the audience will know it'. And this applies to the greatest as well as the humblest members of a company.

On any level ballet training is good for the body. Boys or girls attending just a weekly ballet class will stand a little straighter, keep a little slimmer, look a little more alert. The physical discipline that is the essence of ballet training can bring mental discipline too. But there are no short cuts; either a limb is properly stretched, a foot properly pointed, or it is not. And for the child who seems gifted enough (physically and mentally) to take up ballet as a career there are no halfway houses. From the very beginning ballet training needs determination and dedication.

Ballet training can start with baby classes but these are gentle and do little more than encourage good posture and perhaps foster an understanding of music. By the time a child reaches the age of about eleven any chance of becoming a dancer will be apparent. The schools attached to the great national companies audition youngsters at this time. These auditions are not concerned with prior training, only with the intelligence and the actual physique of the candidate. Rigorous medical examination will show if the body is suitable for classical training because the least and smallest physical defect (a bone slightly out of alignment, a family tradition of exceptional tallness) can mean that ultimately the child will not be able to make a career in classical ballet. For example, a boy with a brilliant record in children's stage dancing competitions was turned down by The Royal Ballet School because weakness at the back of one knee could have resulted in serious injury when he came to the rigours of partnering. There was no reason, though, why he should not have made a career in other forms of theatre dance such as jazz or musical comedy.

Most schools attached to the national ballet companies throughout the world give their young pupils a combination of academic and ballet training during their first five years. The academic schooling is important since there is inevitably a weeding out of apprentice dancers whose promise is not fulfilled and it is essential even for the successful students to have a sound education.

Ballet training itself is a system of movement that has been developed over a period of three hundred years, but it is important to insist that the classical technique that students learn is an entirely logical and sensible method of movement. Its aim is to achieve maximum control and maximum mobility. 'Turn out' is the first basic principle of ballet training. The leg is taught to turn out from the hip socket to an angle of 90° to gain freedom of movement and pleasing line. By giving the legs the greatest possible flexibility it enormously increases the range of movement of a dancer's body. Good turn out is acquired easily and without strain, from the hip, never from the knee. All the other controls and disciplines aim at a similar command of the body's actions. All have been proved over the years. None can be ignored, though it would be foolhardy to suggest that they cannot be improved.

It is very important that even early training should be undertaken in a school where the teachers are properly qualified and have themselves been trained either by one of the several good teaching bodies—like the Royal Academy of Dancing or the Imperial Society—or by previous experience as a dancer from a major ballet company. Care in early training is absolutely vital. A bad muscular habit or bad positioning can result in physical injury and perhaps deprive a student of a later career as a professional dancer. Faults acquired at a very early age can only sometimes be eradicated; sound basic training, on the other hand, is the foundation for the dancer's entire career.

The degree of movement of which the human body is capable depends on the flexibility and strength of the muscles and on the length of the ligaments (bone-connecting tissues). Ligaments are not flexible, like muscles, but they can be lengthened by special training at an early age before they have had time to harden. This is one reason why the professional dancer needs to start training young. The least flexible part of the body is the skeleton, the bony frame. The structure of bones and joints governs the amount of bodily movement in any one direction. The ribs and chest can easily be bent to each side and forwards but will not bend back. The ball and socket structure of the shoulder and hip joints permit a degree of movement. Movement from the hip is easier in a forward direction; it is more difficult to swing the leg up to the side or the back than in front of the body. The ballet dancer must practise until it can be raised high in all directions without any loss of balance or control. The secret in dancing—as in, say, water skiing—is in the control of distribution of weight. Although the ballet dancer trains every part of the body, special care is given to the feet and legs. The dancer's foot is a springboard and only from the strength in the feet and legs can the body be propelled into the air, or achieve and maintain all the positions and movements required of it. For girls there will be the additional demands on pointe work. Girls are trained very carefully to prepare to go on pointe and only do so when strong enough (usually at about the age of thirteen) and in well chosen pointe shoes. First they do exercises to accustom themselves to balancing effortlessly on pointe and then they begin the actual steps and turns. In all pointe work there is the basic consideration of 'placing', each dancer must find her centre of equilibrium; if she is at all off balance, injuries and falls will inevitably follow. The hours of hard work and exercise are designed to help the dancer defy the laws of gravity, to leap high in the air, to perform intricate beating movements of the feet (batterie), to alight softly and surely and with sufficient control to go straight into a fast series of multiple turns (pirouettes), and to acquire harmonious movements of the arms and changes of direction of the head and shoulders (épaulement).

At the age of sixteen or thereabouts the full-time professional dance training commences and during the next couple of years takes up the greater part of the student's day. The culmination comes in the final year when the student will either be accepted into the company or will have to seek work elsewhere, be it in another ballet company or in some other form of show business.

The dancer's instrument, we must stress and stress again, is the human body, and the way in which it can be used depends almost entirely on how it has—or has not—been trained. It is possible to devise very beautiful and striking ensemble works with dancers who have had virtually no training but who can look and move well. A clever choreographer can manipulate them into sculptural poses or groups. Many Nativity plays, for example, have used untrained dancers to very good effect. But the trained body is nearly always more eloquent and permits much greater variety of steps, jumps, turns, lifts and almost acrobatic skills. The classical ballet dancer has a remarkable range of movement that cannot be attempted by ordinary mortals.

An Invitation to the Opera

Barrymore Laurence Scherer

THE great American humorist Robert Benchley reputedly observed that "opera is where a guy gets stabbed in the back, and instead of dying, he sings." Even the most rabid operaphile would have to admit that there's more than a little truth to Benchley's quip, at least on the surface. And certainly a lot of people think opera a bit crazy. In opera the most private moments of a character's existence—the contemplation of love, or death, religious ecstasy or deep sadness—are expressed in song. More often than not, the more intense, the more intimate the emotion, the stronger its musical profile. This can mean anything from Canio the clown's full-throated cry of sorrow in Leoncavallo's *Pagliacci* to the comparative whisper at the moment that Debussy's lovers, Pelléas and Mélisande, kiss for the first and last time.

But opera, if you look at it from the right angle, is not all that far removed from more common expressions of popular culture. The first is the Broadway musical, which is a direct descendant of opera anyway. Can you imagine a successful musical in which the dramatic high points were *not* expressed through song? From *Show Boat* to *Sunset Boulevard,* that's how it's done. Moreover, both *Sunset Boulevard* and Andrew Lloyd Webber's finest work, *The Phantom of the Opera,* are virtual operas in their emphasis on musical continuity and minimum spoken dialogue—not to mention the visual spectacle, which, most appropriately for their highly emotional subjects, is operatic. So, even if you don't think you like opera, you are already well on your way to appreciating it if you are amongst the many fans of those shows.

Even real life has its operatic moments—ceremonial rites of passage such as one's graduation or wedding, and more intimate moments like a dance between lovers or a *candlelit seduction.* Either way, these moments would be completely empty without the right musical underpinning.

That's what opera is all about.

In September 1995 the *New York Times* reported that opera is the fastest-growing performance art in the United States, with an audience rise of 35 percent over the last decade. This must surprise the many pundits who have cried for years that "Opera is dead."

But why should this be? Why, in the age of the multiplex and the Internet, should increasing numbers of people concern themselves over Puccini's Madam Butterfly waiting for her ship to come in? Why should they be touched as Verdi's Aida and Radamès prepare for eternity with a final embrace? Why should spirits soar when Siegfried finally makes his way through the Magic Fire and into Brünnhilde's waiting arms? Why should anyone at the end of the twentieth century care about an entertainment devised in the sixteenth century, and care about it passionately?

Simply, because no popular film, no best-selling novel or even hit play can duplicate the sheer emotional high that opera can offer. That's why those who love opera love it with a particular intensity. Nevertheless, ask ten opera lovers how they fell in love, and you'll get ten different answers. Some people are hooked while attending their first opera; others take their time, progressing from an aria or two to complete works.

As I remember my first operatic exposure, I must have been five, and it was purely accidental. We were visiting my grandparents one Sunday, and as usual, the television was on. Instead of *Meet the Press,* however, there was a live telecast of an opera, performed, I believe, by the NBC Opera Company. I remember that the opera was Puccini's *Madama Butterfly,* for I fully expected to see a real winged insect. There was none. Instead, everyone was singing. I would certainly like to report that the experience transformed me like St. Paul on the road to Damascus. But in truth I was *bored!*

When did the opera bug finally bite? I must have been around seven or eight when I began to notice that certain cartoons on television had particularly catchy music. One favorite opened with Porky Pig working in a blacksmith shop, hammering an anvil to an exceedingly infectious tune. In another that I always anticipated with great pleasure, Sylvester Cat took a final pratfall followed immediately by the ascent of his nine lives accompanied by another piece of music that hit home. In a third, Mickey Mouse skippered a tempest-tossed ship, to music that I found not only infinitely appropriate to the imagery of pounding ocean waves but impossible to forget. Later on I began to discover that the sources were operatic: Porky hammered to the "Anvil Chorus" from Verdi's *Il Trovatore,* the feline ascension was accompanied by the Sextet from Donizetti's *Lucia di Lammermoor,* while Mickey's gale raged to the opening measures of Wagner's overture to *The Flying Dutchman,* an opera drenched in salt water and grog.

Little by little I was feeling my way. By the time I had entered the High School of Music and Art in New York, opera was a vital part of my existence. Moreover, at Music and Art—where I had gone to study art, and ended up taking music courses as well—I met one of the greatest influences on my musical development, Rudolf Cooper, who taught English there. Though I never took a course with him, providence had put me in his homeroom class. One morning shortly into my first semester at "the Castle," I noticed, with wide eyes, a pile of 78s on the floor of Mr. Cooper's wardrobe closet. "Where did you get all those?" I asked. "So you like that old stuff, too?" he responded. "Would you be interested in doing any trading?"

I told him I'd give my eyeteeth for the opportunity. Unfortunately, the handful of 78s I owned at the time contained nothing of interest to a connoisseur. And, as I was to learn, Rudolf Cooper was indeed a connoisseur. It was certainly his generosity of spirit and his essential fineness as a teacher that led him to encourage my interest despite my lack of anything to trade.

Instead of records, he suggested trading me batches of 78s in return for reels of blank recording tape. I got the best of a splendid bargain, for not only did Mr. Cooper expand my awareness of Golden Age singers, he began to broaden my taste in vocal music. From obvious starting points such as Enrico Caruso's recordings of "Vesti la giubba" and "Celeste Aida" we moved into increasingly sophisticated fare.

One day he presented me with a recording of the trio "Qual volutta" from Verdi's early opera *I Lombardi.* I was already fascinated by "forgotten" operas, and I will never forget the effect it had on me. The melody of this piece is one of the sweetest in the entire Verdi canon, and at the climax of this performance, the voices of Caruso and Frances Alda rise higher and higher until they hit a series of repeated high Bs. As I listened for the first time, I was rooted in place, with a lump in my throat the size of an egg. It still has the same effect on me, and I have yet to hear a better recording or performance of this trio, let alone one to equal it.

While I was at Music and Art, I made my first visits to the Metropolitan Opera, during the final season of the old house on Broadway and 39th Street. I bought a seat in the Family Circle for a Saturday matinee performance of Donizetti's *L'Elisir d'Amore* (The Elixir of Love). When the great day came, I arrived at the house to discover that I could not enter through the front door—the Family Circle had its own dingy entrance on the north side of the house. Breathless from a climb up endless iron stairs, I found myself in a dim corridor. As I walked through the doors into the auditorium, my temples were pounding from the exertion and excitement. Before my eyes was a vision I can never forget: the beautiful gold proscenium, the ornate ceiling with its painted cloudborne putti, the wine-colored sea of mohair seats, the great gold curtain, and the stage. There the greats had sung, the greats I was collecting on my 78s—Caruso, Melba, Ponselle, Pinza, Chaliapin. In the pit, Toscanini and Gustav Mahler had conducted. At that point in my life there was no place more hallowed.

By the time I had left Music and Art I was determined to be an opera singer myself. However, though my tenor voice was said to be pretty, it was also pretty small. While I enjoyed my training years as a performer, I'm glad that I eventually realized when to throw in the towel and pick up the pen. Nonetheless, those years behind the footlights were not wasted, because they instilled in me a sympathetic understanding of what it takes to stand before an audience and face the music.

As a critic, few art forms have given me so much pleasure as opera. And though it isn't necessary to listen to a performance or recording as intensively or as comprehensively as a professional critic, it remains that the more you understand, the deeper your enjoyment.

That said, I listen to a variety of elements. I listen to the melodic lines, of course, and follow the story. I listen with a critical ear to the singing and to how it expresses the composer's intentions. On another level, I listen to the components of complex musical sound: to the harmony and the rhythm and to the orchestration, the beguiling combinations of instruments that clothe the music in a lustrous aural fabric of ever-changing color and weight that conveys an expression of its own. I listen to the way the composer works with his thematic material within a single aria or an entire act, repeating it, altering it—in musician's terms, developing it. I listen to the musical architecture of a scene, and to the way each scene relates to the entire act, and each act to the whole opera.

When I am viewing an opera on stage or on video, I watch the acting, the direction, and the physical production just as anyone would at a theatrical presentation. From its inception, opera was theater above all, theater enhanced by music that often expresses what mere words cannot.

Whether a critic or not, when an opera lover listens to an opera, be it a familiar favorite, a brand-new work, or an old one heard for the first time, he or she hopes to be moved by the music, by the story, by the performance. One hopes to be moved to the very marrow of one's bones, for there is no high comparable to the emotional high that comes of a glorious opera wonderfully performed. Your pulse quickens, your muscles tighten, you feel yourself uplifted, occasionally with the happy sting of tears in your eyes. And you can feel that sensation more than once during the course of an opera, for the best operas— dramas and even comedies—are full of these moments.

The key to learning about opera is not to fear what you don't yet know. One of the greatest pleasures of opera is the sheer amount available—in the opera house, on records and video, and on radio and public television. If you haven't heard a particular opera, or even heard of the title, don't be afraid to try it. If you don't want to buy a ticket, or can't find one, there is probably a recording or a video. If you don't want to buy the recording, look for it at your public library, or persuade the librarian to acquire it. If you don't want to take the whole opera in at the first try, go for the highlights. A good way to acquire a broader knowledge is to listen to some recital albums, in which the featured singer performs scenes and arias from a variety of operas. When you hear excerpts you particularly enjoy, you can explore the complete opera later on.

Regardless of whether it is an old or a new work, not every opera appeals to every listener. Moreover, your discernment develops as you go along; you may outgrow some operas that appeal at first, while others will start to attract you as your taste develops. Still others will remain close to your heart forever. But above all, the happiest opera lover is open to everything. If you keep listening, if you remain curious about the unknown, your confidence will grow in leaps and bounds. And the payback in pleasure will be infinite.

from

Jazz is

Nat Hentoff

AS a boy, they seemed to me a different species. I could ask a ballplayer or a movie star for an autograph, but I was speechless when Johnny Hodges or Lester Young walked by. I was in awe of jazz musicians because of their power, because of the mystery of their sinuous but overwhelming power. Nothing else in my experience was so exhilarating, so utterly compelling. The laughter in the music, the intimacy, the range and bite of the life-tales each player told in textures and cadences entirely his own. The irony, the deep blues, and, as I grew older, the sensuousness.

Also, as I grew older, I was finally able to speak and get to know scores of these magical improvisers. And then scores more. I remained—and still am—in awe of the leaping imagination of the best of them. Off the stand they are, of course, like us, variously flawed. And yet to me they are still a different species. I have covered many beats through the years—civil liberties, education, classical and folk music, rock, the courts, films and theater, politics—and still, by and large, I most enjoy being with jazz musicians.

For one thing, they have little patience with euphemism, since they spend much of their working time being direct. Also, being accustomed to change as the only constant in their music, they tend to be more resilient and curious than most—and less likely to be conned by the manipulative conventional wisdom of institutions and institutional figures. And, as you might expect, most jazz people are lively, irreverent, sharp-witted. They see as well as hear a lot.

This book is a selective tribute and guide to the jazz life, the players, and the music. It is not a chronological or a comprehensive history, but rather a personal exploration through variegated seminal figures of the nature of the music (and how it keeps changing). And it is about the nature of those who make the music—temperaments as disparate as those of Louis Armstrong and Charlie Parker. It tells too of the political economy of jazz, its internationalization, the continuing surprises of its further frontiers.

I have been writing about this music for some thirty years, and since I am not a musicologist my approach has been to try to understand the intertwining of lives and sounds, of personal styles and musical styles, of societal dynamics and jazz dynamics. I still find it ceaselessly absorbing—the music, its players, and the society which thinks them marginal as they illuminate it so penetratingly and sometimes so mordantly.

Above all, however, this book is meant to bring pleasure—to bring you to the music of these players and composers, if you have not been there before, and perhaps suggest another dimension if you have been.

I am grateful to all the players in this book for the conversation, as well as musical time, they've given me through the years. They are a brilliant motley, each having lived—or still living—a life obsessed with this spirit-music, its mysteries and infinite seductiveness. And the magnetism works both ways, of course. Once you're inside the music you'll want to keep going deeper and deeper, because it is impossible to get enough of it.

My Musical Career

Robertson Davies

ROBERTSON DAVIES felt that music, which turns the thoughts inward and is conducive to contemplation, was a route to self-knowledge; a journey he described many times as the most important of all. He loved many forms and styles of music and had done so from his youngest days. Therefore, when the Royal Conservatory of Music at the University of Toronto invited him to become a Fellow, he was very grateful for the honor, being acutely aware that he was not an accomplished musician. He made this speech at the ceremony on November 26, 1994.

I AM more grateful than I can express for the honor which you have done me; it is totally unexpected and it comes from a source which I have long held in awe. My admiration for this institution goes back to the days of Sir Ernest MacMillan who, among other accomplishments, made Canadians a perceptive and sophisticated audience for music. That I should, on this occasion, be linked with Miss Lois Marshall, whose art has been one of the great pleasures of my musical experience—as indeed it has been to hundreds of thousands of others—is to me a truly wonderful experience. I thank you warmly, and I wish I could say that I shall strive to be worthy of this distinction—but I know that will be utterly impossible.

Let me explain. It is not that I am ignorant of music, or that I have no career in music. But alas, that career has been so obscure, so ignominious that it hardly deserves to be regarded as a career at all. You are all of you this evening receiving awards that mark your musical achievement, in some degree; doubtless music will be your profession, and doubtless some of you will achieve great things in the musical world and bring refreshment, and perhaps enchantment, to a new generation of listeners. I could never have been included in such a group as yours, because I have, all my life, been among the very worst musical performers in a profession which is not lacking in failures.

I come from a family that was devoted to music and I was brought up in an atmosphere in which music was a very special interest. Everybody sang. Everybody played something. My father played the flute; my mother the piano; one of my brothers was a by no means inglorious performer on that now almost forgotten instrument, the cornet. We were a Welsh family and song was as familiar to us as speech. It was decided that I should excel all the rest as a musician, and as soon as I could sit on a piano stool without falling off I was set to work on that appallingly difficult instrument, and I was kept at it for years, and years and years.

It was obvious to me from the beginning that I had no talent, and the piano, with its array of grinning teeth, was my tormentor. But simply by the process of growing older, I made something that looked like progress, and in my teens I was despoiling the works of Beethoven and Chopin and Schumann. I had, you see, no scrap of that quality which psychologists call "the sensation function." I never knew where anything was. I would place myself at the piano, and bring my hands down on what ought to have been a commanding opening chord, and foozle it every time.

My mother's idol among pianists was Paderewski. I knew that I would never be a Paderewski, so I searched among the other great pianists of the day, looking for a model, and I found one at last who seemed to be just right for me. He was Vladimir de Pachmann. His style was refined, and so was mine. He was distinguished for the fact that especially in the works of Chopin he struck a great number of wrong notes. It was here that I knew I could rival him, and perhaps even excel him. You see, he struck his wrong notes in extremely rapid passages: I worked at my technique until I was certain that I could strike great numbers of wrong notes *in very slow passages.*

Nobody appreciated my style. I remember the dark day when my teacher, who was a very kind and patient man, but also a musician of a high order, said to me: "You know, Davies, it's perfectly clear that you will never be able to play the piano acceptably even if you live to be a hundred. Why don't we stop wasting time and settle to some serious study of musical literature, and it's just possible that after a while you might make some mark as a music critic."

You will understand my dejection. A critic! Could any greater ignominy befall someone so devoted to music as I was? It was as if I were an aspiring tennis player and had been told that some day I might be a ball-boy. But I did as I was told. I tried to understand what I could never hope to perform.

Not, mind you, that I did not have my triumphs. When I was an actor in my young days I was often asked to provide music for plays in which I appeared, and I did. I suppose nobody listens critically to such music. My finest hour came when I was working in a play which was set in the time of Henry VIII, and some offstage music was required on an instrument called the virginal. I expect you all know what a virginal is: it is a young and inexperienced piano. I twangled out a few easy pieces, some of them written by Henry VIII himself, and all went well. Then, suddenly, the British Broadcasting Company decided that it would like to have some parts of our play broadcast over the air, and again I was required to provide the musical accompaniment.

I cannot forget my dismay when I went into the studio and was confronted with a large harpsichord. It was a huge affair, with two sets of teeth and a bewildering variety of pedals. I assumed an air of nonchalance, and tinkered with the thing until I had subdued it to, roughly, the status of the virginal to which I was accustomed. And I got away with it! Nobody found me out and I listened to the subsequent broadcast with a good deal of satisfaction.

And what do you suppose happened? The play was scheduled to go on for an hour, but when it ended there were still ninety seconds before the end of the hour. My guardian angel was hard at work, because some kindly soul at the BBC filled in the time with a record by Yella Pessel, who was one of the great harpsichordists of the day! Afterward, several people said to me, "I never dreamed you could play like that."

I am not a liar. But I am not a fool, either. I always replied, "I'm glad you liked it."

That was the high point of my musical career. After that, I did indeed become a critic, but I wasn't much good because I couldn't bear to write nastily about some wretched performer who had played far better than I had ever been able to do myself. If you can't spray the acid around you are no use as a critic, so I had to take to other forms of writing in which I was able to say what I really felt about music, without having to provide personal examples.

There it is, you see. I stand before you as a failed musician, upon whom nevertheless this kindly institution has bestowed an honor. You are not failed musicians. You are the real thing. Speaking, as it were, from the sidelines, I wish you every success and happiness in a career to which I was never able to aspire.

The Recording

John Fordham

THE first "jazz age" began when the first jazz records were made. Because the raucous, uninhibited sound of the Original Dixieland Jazz Band was available on a Victor recording to anybody with access to a phonograph, the band and the new idiom it introduced became cults within months. But recording technology also caught the unique qualities of jazz on the wing. Because the rhythmic fluidity of the music was hard to notate, as were the unusual inflections in notes, the vibrancy of a jazz performance could not be recaptured from a written transcription. Records became the staple documentation of jazz and, because no two performances of the same piece are ever exactly alike, they also became the key to the elusive idiosyncrasies of improvisation.

When the Original Dixieland Jazz Band opened in New York, recording had already been under way for over three decades, but not for jazz. The technology was limited, and the fact that music could be captured and replayed at will was a new development to which the public was still acclimatizing itself in 1917.

Musicians played into an enormous horn that worked like a loudspeaker in reverse. Its vibrations shook a cutting stylus attached to the horn's tapered end, which drew a groove in a wax cylinder or disk, the undulations in the groove following the variations of frequency. After three stages of molds from the wax, a metal negative was made which acted as a disk stamper.

It all happened too late, and jazz was too much of an underground phenomenon, for the sounds of the honky tonks, the original bluesmen, the first boogie pianists, and the marching bands to be preserved on wax (Although rumors persisted of the existence of a long-lost Buddy Bolden cylinder from 1894). Ragtime pianists and the early stride players were recorded, but on piano rolls—punched reels of paper used to activate automatic player pianos.

Even after the Original Dixieland Jazz Band's million-selling debut, the record business executives still saw jazz and blues as music that appealed only to a black-dominated market—in other words, a segment of society too poor to buy phonographs.

But when the early blues recordings by Mamie Smith and later, Bessie Smith, sold in unexpected quantities, the "race records" industry (disks specifically for sale to non-Caucasians) began and boomed until the economic slump of 1929. The Gennett, Paramount, and Okeh labels were among the pioneers in the field, although the technical difficulties meant that anything from cold weather to rail traffic outside the studio could ruin recording sessions, and the sounds of drummers and pianists were virtually inaudible on the disks.

Electric recording, using a microphone to turn sound waves into electrical impulses activating a motorized cutter, transformed fidelity in the mid-1920s, allowing bands to sound more natural, and it made field recordings made on mobile equipment more reliable, too. But with the Depression of the early 1930s, the recording industry capsized, and the race labels never recovered. A series of mergers between smaller companies and strenuous efforts to capitalize on the runaway success of network radio stabilized the industry. (Initially perceived as a threat to the record business, radio later became a voracious consumer of its products.) The popularity of swing did the rest.

If radio, movie, and recording interests were increasingly coming together, improvements in technology were also encouraging both independent labels and enthusiastic amateurs. The famous Dean Benedetti live recordings of the early career of Charlie Parker were produced on a portable disk-cutting machine, and wire recorders, a precursor to tape, were also often used from the bebop years onward. Ironically, this amateur material turned out to be vital documentation of early bebop because the American Federation of Musicians, fearing the effect of radio on live performance opportunities, instituted a recording ban—in pursuit of a percentage on radio transmissions—that lasted from 1942 to 1944.

Large-size transcription disks and longer-running "V—disks" were also made from broadcast material for troop entertainment in the years of the ban, although most of them represent what the authorities assumed would be popular—swing. After the war, the independent recording companies resurfaced to document both the incandescent bebop and the newly revived Dixieland—labels like Commodore, Dial, Clef, Savoy and Blue Note. Because they were run by jazz enthusiasts alive to the needs of musicians, the output of these companies often saw unusual configurations of players, challenging repertoires, and recordings of great sensitivity. New labels sprang up in the 1950s, like Prestige, Riverside, and Pacific, as plastics technology let grooves become narrower and more tightly packed. The long-playing microgroove disk was born, and the complex, open-ended qualities of improvisation were at last properly documented and more ambitious, extended music written.

Editing technology in those days was used less in jazz than other styles of music. After studios began to use multitrack recorders in the early 1960s, the producer and recording studio featured more prominently in the creative process of the session, and making a disk came to be regarded as a separate artistic discipline. The arrival of the compact disc in the 1980s with its laser technology and the development of sophisticated, noise-reducing equipment resulted in massive reissue programs. Now even the earliest jazz can be heard with the shortcomings of the original studios and engineers greatly reduced.

Duke Ellington

John Fordham

HE did not learn his art in a conservatory or with the encouragement of wealthy patrons but as a Harlem bandleader, where the closest species to a patron was the mobster. But Duke Ellington's wonderful music proves him to be one of the finest composers to have emerged from America in the 20th century. Ellington was among the most expressive explorers of a jazz orchestra's palette of sounds, the idiom's unique melodies and rhythms, and the personalities of soloists. He made distinctions of art and pop meaningless. Although he wrote or cowrote thousands of compositions over a prolific half-century, Duke Ellington did not compose in a study with a piano but furiously scribbled his great works in airport lounges and the back seats of cars, endlessly on the road. Among Ellington pieces are some of the century's most famous songs, but these alone do not explain his genius. Band members like Billy Strayhorn, Johnny Hodges, and Juan Tizol were involved, and it is hard to be certain just how large the leader's contribution was in notes on paper. Ellington was a composer for the 20th century and helped change the way composition works. The vitality and color of his work reflected fast travel, reflexive speed, and relentless deadlines rather than lengthy contemplation. He absorbed himself in improvisation and collaboration, and his relish for throwing a fragment of a tune into rehearsal to see what others made of it gave a mixed input to the massive body of Ellingtonia. Yet nothing would have happened without Ellington, the alchemist.

The pioneer jazz musicians were frequently working-class, but many of those who developed orchestral jazz came from the emerging black middle class. Duke Ellington's childhood was founded on Victorian principles, his father an ambitious coachman turned valet whose work for the rich gave him a vision of the good life which he passed on to his son. Ellington's mother, Daisy Kennedy, was the daughter of a police captain and "a real Victorian lady" according to Duke's sister Ruth. Daisy doted on her son, and a sophisticated manner of speech, elegant clothes, and a sense of self-worth led to the lifelong nickname. But the boy did not show his promise early on.

Duke Ellington married young and had a son (Mercer, with

Edna Thompson) in 1918. A good commercial artist, he started a sign-painting business but preferred the atmosphere of the clubs and dance halls. Although a limited pianist, he could keep up with rags and dance tunes and formed a band with friends, eventually dubbed the Washingtonians. When Ellington learned that some dance musicians in New York were getting rich, the Washingtonians moved base, and their fortunes rose on the wave of the Harlem Renaissance of African-American culture. But the band remained undistinguished and rhythmically conservative until the arrival of two "hot jazz" specialists—trumpeter James "Bubber" Miley, a King Oliver admirer, and the impulsive, impassioned saxophonist Sidney Bechet. They transformed the band with trombonist "Tricky Sam" Nanton, a growl-and-mute specialist and another crucial carrier of the urgent New Orleans message. A five-year stint at New York's Cotton Club backing the "jungle" dance theater routines developed Ellington's conceptual sense and understanding of tone color. The semiclassical composers Will Vodery and Will Marion Cook also helped. During the Cotton Club years, early classics like "The Mooch," "Rockin in Rhythm," and "Mood Indigo" changed jazz. But the Ellington Orchestra often proved it could raise the roof on commercial 1930s swing events, too, and was truly peerless at the atmospheric jazz ballad—for among many fine soloists Duke Ellington employed one of the most sensitive and subtly emotional of saxophonists, Johnny Hodges.

By the 1940s, a musical high point for the band, Ellington was reinventing jazz with more unexpected outcomes than anyone before him could have imagined, producing such glowing music as "Concerto for Cootie," "Warm Valley," "Harlem Air Shaft," and "Take the A Train." He applied rhythmic devices and key changes that were close to classical music to material that could only have come from jazz. Moreover, Ellington's rhythm section was strengthened by a revolutionary bassist, the short-lived Jimmy Blanton.

There was a downturn in the early 1950s, not helped by the brief departure of Johnny Hodges, but in 1956 the band staged a tumultuous comeback at the Newport Jazz Festival, when tenorist Paul Gonsalves delivered twenty-seven consecutive choruses of a careening "Diminuendo and Crescendo in Blue." The upswing led Ellington to write and record again, and the long-playing record invited extended pieces. "Such Sweet Thunder," a dedication to Shakespeare, spliced jazz with classical music;

several long pieces were inspired by his tireless globetrotting, and in later life he wrote religious music. Ellington stayed on the road into his 70s, received innumerable citations, performed at the White House, and represented the boldest, most open-handed and creative face of American culture to audiences the world over.

Music

Lensey Namioka

MUSIC figures in a number of my books. This is not because I'm musically gifted; on the contrary, I have the worst ear in my family. *Yang the Youngest and His Terrible Ear* describes the problems of a boy from a family where everyone else is gifted musically. My ear is not quite as bad as his, but I know just how he feels.

My father composed songs at one time, and some of them became famous, especially a love song for solo voice and piano. One of my sisters said she heard this song at a Hong Kong Karaoke bar.

My eldest sister was picking out tunes on the piano at the age of two, and she eventually became a professor of musicology at Harvard. My other two sisters also play instruments and regularly make music.

A great deal of our family leisure time was spent in some form of musical activity, usually playing the piano or singing. The family practice of unaccompanied singing developed during the war years when we moved around a lot and had no instruments with us. We sang the multiplication table. We also sang more pleasant music, mostly part songs. Father had to write or arrange music to accommodate the voices available. In our case, we four daughters provided two sopranos and two altos, while Father provided the lone male voice.

I continued to sing when I grew up. In college I sang in choirs, and I also belonged to smaller groups singing madrigals and other unaccompanied songs. You might ask why these groups accepted me when I had a poor ear. The fact was that I was a whiz at sight-reading: I might be a bit too high or too low, but I was always *there* at the right time. Maybe the other singers regarded me as sort of a conductor, giving them cues for their entrances.

Mother was the only person in our family who didn't sing. She had a lovely baritone voice, but her ear was even worse than mine. She could read musical notation for the piano, and in fact she was the one who gave me my start on the piano by telling me which note on the staff corresponded to which black or white key. But she couldn't keep a tune. The only piece of music she recognized was the slow movement of Haydn's *Surprise* Symphony.

Mother became involved with Haydn when she was attending a missionary school in Shanghai. The school decided to hold a concert in which some of the students played musical solos, and Mother had been chosen to play in the program not because she was musical, but because she never experienced stage fright. Her piece was a piano arrangement of the slow movement of Haydn's *Surprise* Symphony. This was her first and last public performance of music, and the tune made a deep impression on her.

Mother's solo caused a terrible ruckus in her family. Some of the relatives had opposed sending her to the missionary school in the first place. It was bad enough that a girl of good family should sit in a room with strangers and learn all sorts of foreign subjects. But to go on stage and make music for the public, that was taking the first step toward becoming a singsong girl! The storm eventually blew over because the piano was considered a relatively harmless instrument. Traditionally, opera was considered a vulgar art, and instruments connected with the opera were vulgar. These included a kind of violin, drums, and various percussion instruments. The genteel instruments, those that could be played by gentlemen and ladies, included the *pipa*, or lute, the bamboo flute, and a zitherlike instrument called a *qin*. When the piano was introduced into China from the West, it was called *gang-qin*, or steel *qin* because it also had many parallel strings. Therefore the piano looked respectable to Chinese eyes. By the time my parents were growing up, the piano was the most popular Western instrument in China.

The piano, then, was our family instrument. Father liked to play the music of the Classical and early Romantic composers. His taste was influenced by his music teachers while he was in college, and what he liked best was the music of Haydn, Beethoven, Schumann, Schubert, and Mendelssohn. If his early musical training had been different, he might have grown to like Bach because he had the kind of mathematical mind often attracted to Bach.

When our family moved to America, we had very little money, but Father immediately bought a piano. Mother insisted that a dining table and chairs came first, but the piano came before things like box springs and bed frames. For years we slept on thin mattresses and steel-linked springs balanced on orange crates. But we had the piano.

This didn't mean we could play the piano anytime we wanted, for it was understood that Father always had priority. Even when he wasn't playing, we were nervous about sitting down to play if he was within earshot because he would rush over to correct our mistakes. And he was within earshot almost everywhere in the house, since his ear was unusually acute. Even in his old age, he could hear better than people thirty or forty years younger.

Mistakes in rhythm bothered Father the most. It's because of his stern attitude that we all became very good at counting time. I have trouble with pitch because my ear isn't keen, but I can count time like nobody's business. I never get lost when playing with other people (though sometimes they wish I *would* get lost).

In *Who's Hu?* the mother is a piano teacher. Emma, my protagonist, doesn't have a very good ear but she never gets lost while playing duets with her mother. She is also glad that her mother is too busy playing her own part of notice all of Emma's mistakes.

You'd think that having a father ready to pounce on our every mistake would discourage us from music altogether. Like Emma Hu, we found we could play duets with Father. He would be so busy with his own part that some of our mistakes would escape his notice.

Over the years Father bought an enormous quantity of piano duet music. Some of the pieces were original compositions written for four hands, but most were orchestral music arranged as piano duets. We played overtures by Beethoven, von Weber, Mozart, and Rossini. We played most of the better-known symphonies of Mozart, Haydn, Schubert, and Mendelssohn.

Because I lived at home the longest, I played more duets with Father than any of my sisters. In the weeks before I left home to get married, Father and I went through a marathon of symphonies of Beethoven. When we came to the choral movement of the Ninth, Father sang the bass solo.

While playing duets with Father, it was necessary to obey his rules. Rule Number One was that we didn't play any of the repeats indicated by the composer. We wanted to finish a whole symphony, and doing all the repeats would take too long. There was one exception: we did all the repeats in the slow movement of Haydn's *Surprise* Symphony because that was the one piece of music Mother recognized. She always came over to listen, and we wanted to prolong her pleasure.

Rule Number Two was that we never stopped for mistakes. If I missed a note, if I reduced a passage to complete chaos, still we ploughed on. I remember a terrifying session playing Beethoven's *Eroica* Symphony with Father. In the development section of the first movement, there is a passage that consists almost entirely of crashing chords. To my dull ear, every measure sounds like every other measure. My attention must have wandered. From the kitchen I heard Mother's voice saying, "We'll have to set the table soon. There are fourteen people for dinner tonight."

Suddenly I realized that something was wrong. From the sound of things, I must have skipped a line. We were still playing crashing chords, and I tried to compensate by jumping back to the previous line. But it didn't work, and I could feel the sweat trickling down my back.

Father must have noticed that I was floundering in a morass. Would he stop for me? Never! I continued to play crashing chords, but my crashes were getting feeble. At long last, Father played a recognizable melody, an oboe solo with the principal theme. I finally knew where we were and found my way back into the music. To this day, I can't listen to an orchestra play the *Eroica* Symphony without suffering an anxiety attack.

Besides the piano, a couple of Chinese flutes, and Father's cello, we also owned a number of other instruments. When guests opened the coat closet of our house in Cambridge, they had to be careful not to bring down on them two violins, a clarinet, and a trumpet.

In the late 1940s, Father made a series of recordings of spoken Mandarin for Folkway Records in New York. Upon receiving his first royalty check, he went on a splurge. The size of the check limited his splurging to a pawnshop on Seventh Avenue, where his eye was caught by some musical instruments in the window. He probably thought, "It's time the family branched out and took up something besides singing and piano playing."

He bought four instruments because he had four children, and he saw himself accompanying us on the piano while we played. Why did he choose this particular combination? They were probably what were available in the pawnshop that day. When he came home and distributed the instruments, I wound up with one of the violins.

My eldest sister took the trumpet, but I don't remember which sisters had the other two instruments. Up to now, our family had practiced togetherness whenever possible. If we couldn't find ready-made music, Father would arrange pieces to suit us. But the violin-violin-clarinet-trumpet combination was just too unwieldy, and we had to go our separate ways.

My eldest sister tooted her trumpet for a while, but gave up when the neighbors complained. I was the only one to take lessons. This was not because I was the most musical one of the family—rather the opposite. As soon as I drew my bow across the violin strings, the family decided that I needed help—outside help. Money was tight then, but this was an emergency! We managed to find a music teacher willing to give me lessons at fifty cents a shot. At least it got me and my fiddle out of the house once a week. For some reason my music teacher got sick a lot; my exercise book mysteriously disappeared, and when I declared that I'd rather play the piano than the violin, nobody objected strenuously.

In addition to this assortment of Western instruments, we also had a few Chinese instruments. The one that fascinated me most was a Chinese oboe, called a *suona,* and it was used in religious ceremonies and processions. I found its nasal, plaintive voice strangely moving. Years later the *suona* appeared in a comic scene from my book about Chinese outlaws, *Phantom of Tiger Mountain.*

My craving to play the *suona* was partially satisfied when my eldest sister Rulan (who had married and was living a safe distance away) gave me an oboe for my birthday. I still remember my excitement at putting the oboe reed to my lips for the first time. I huffed and I puffed, but nothing happened. After repeated tries, I finally blew a great big *blaat.* Our cat jumped under the bed, and it was a long time before I could coax it out again.

Playing the oboe was harder than I had thought. The difficulty isn't in blowing hard, but in not being able to release the air as fast as you want. I began to get migraine headaches. Strangely enough, Father also got migraine headaches when he heard my oboe. But he never tried to talk me out of playing, since he believed in encouraging musical activity, even if it hurt.

I gave up the oboe after a while. Some years later, when my daughters were both playing instruments, I took up the cello in order to play music together with them and their friends. Although my cello didn't inflict as much pain as my violin, I noticed that other players began to sidle away when I approached wistfully with my instrument. I gave up the cello and faced the bitter truth that a person with a poor ear should not play a string instrument. A piano is better because it can be tuned by somebody else.

My musical activities continued even when I left home to get married. My husband and I play piano duets almost daily, the same arrangements of classical symphonies that I used to play with my father. We also play four-hand arrangements of string quartets by Mozart and Beethoven.

Only now I have the upper hand: namely the primo part, which used to be my father's. The rules are different, too. We now do all the repeats, and when my husband gets lost, he insists on stopping. He refuses to grope around on the keys until he finds his place again, the way I did with my father.

Another difference is that we always draw the drapes when we play. Our piano can be seen from the street, and we don't want our neighbors to know who is making that awful racket.

My musical life isn't always an awful racket, since my husband and I go regularly to concerts. In my series of books about the musical Chinese immigrant family, the Yangs play string quartets. I feel safest writing about string quartets because that's what I hear most often in concerts, and I also play arrangements of them on the piano with my husband.

The scenes describing music lessons and recitals in the Yang books, however, actually come from my daughters' experiences. They took lessons in the flute and violin respectively and went through the usual torments of children forced to play in recitals. Their love for music managed to survive, however, and today they still play chamber music with their friends. Both of them are very good at sight-reading. One of them told me that when she was auditioning for the orchestra at her university, the conductor said to her, "You sight-read better than you play." Maybe she's a chip off the old block.

from

The Boys from Liverpool

Nicholas Schaffner

FOR most of 1963, the American record business had proved as tough a nut for Brian Epstein to crack as the English had been a year earlier. Despite all the British Number Ones and sell-out tours, nobody in the United States seemed to want to know about his Beatles. After all, rock 'n' roll music was a purely American invention. Who could possibly care about some English imitation?

Capitol Records, being the American branch of EMI, the Beatles' British record company, had the first chance at all their releases. But Capitol wasn't interested, so "Please Please Me," "From Me to You," "She Loves You," and the first album were put out in the United States by tiny companies like Vee-Jay and Swan. All sank without a trace.

"We didn't think there was a chance," admitted John. "We just didn't imagine it at all; we didn't even bother. Even when we came over to America the first time, we were only coming over to buy LP's."

Nonetheless, the American pop-music scene was desperately waiting for someone new and exciting to come along. The Golden Age of Rock 'n' Roll was long over. Many of the great stars were either dead—like Buddy Holly—or had lost their touch. Others, including Elvis Presley, had turned into slick "adult" entertainers, crooning sappy ballads to the rich and middle-aged in Las Vegas.

Except for some of the black "Motown" groups, few of America's early 1960s pop stars could boast any real originality or vitality. Rock 'n' roll was in danger of dying in the land of its birth. It needed a shot in the arm—and fast.

Then, on November 22, 1963, John F. Kennedy was assassinated. This youthful, dynamic President had been especially popular with young Americans, and his sudden loss may have made them feel an unconscious need for a new hero. In any case, the country's mood was certainly very depressed during the last weeks of 1963. Magazines and the TV news urgently needed some light relief from all the grim coverage of the Kennedy murder. They found it in reports of the strange epidemic of mass silliness that appeared to have sent Mother England right off her rocker.

Time, Life, and *Newsweek* all ran profiles on John, Paul, George, and Ringo. Their hair, at least, seemed good for a laugh. The Associated Press defined their sound as "a weird new kind of music that makes rock 'n' roll seem tame by comparison." Still, the stories all suggested that Beatlemania was a purely British brand of nuttiness. Nobody seemed to think it could ever spread to the United States.

Then someone at Capitol Records thought: Why not? The company decided to release the Beatles' fifth single, "I Want to Hold Your Hand," after all—and to follow it with an edited version of *With the Beatles,* retitled *Meet the Beatles.* Brian Epstein once wrote that he was sure all along that "if the Beatles were to make a record that would sell in America, then 'I Want to Hold Your Hand' was that record." The song was easily the Beatles' most original and electrifying yet, full of subtle shifts in the pounding rhythm.

Brian came to New York that November to arrange for the Beatles' first United States visit. An appearance at Carnegie Hall was scheduled, and the Beatles were booked on Ed Sullivan's popular Sunday night variety television show. Sullivan had seen Beatlemania firsthand on a trip to England, but he agreed to let the Beatles top the bill only after a great deal of haggling with Epstein. In exchange for this honor, however, he only paid the Beatles $10,000 for their three February 1964 appearances.

As interest grew, Capitol decided to pour a small fortune into a Beatles "crash publicity campaign." Balding Capitol executives were photographed wearing Beatle wigs, and girls who worked for the company were encouraged to accept free "Beatle hairdo's." Five million stickers reading "The Beatles Are Coming" mysteriously turned up on walls, lamp posts, and phone booths across the fifty states. A million Beatle newsletters tumbled off the press.

Capitol even mailed every disc jockey in the country a list of questions and an "open-ended interview" record featuring John, Paul, George, and Ringo's prerecorded answers. This way any DJ could, whenever he wished, give the impression he was conducting a personal interview with the Beatles.

The boys were on tour in Paris at the end of January when they received the stunning news that "I Want to Hold Your Hand," a mere month after its release, had hit Number One all over the United States. What's more, all the earlier American flops had sprung to life and were racing up the record charts as well, and *Meet the Beatles* was reported to be the fastest-selling LP album ever issued in the United States. The jubilant Beatles threw a celebration dinner in Paris's elegant George V hotel, during which even the staid Brian Epstein was photographed clowning around with a chamber pot on his head as he puffed at his victory cigar.

Still, even after the Beatles had boarded their flight to New York on February 7, they weren't totally convinced that their American success wasn't just a temporary fluke. "Since America has always had everything, why should we be over there making money?" Paul asked Phil Spector, the brilliant young record producer who had become one of the Beatles' first American supporters and friends. "They've got their own groups. What are we going to give them that they don't already have?"

Paul needn't have worried. Though on New Year's Day the names John Lennon, Paul McCartney, George Harrison, and Ringo Starr meant nothing to Americans, already, only five weeks later, millions of them were dancing and swooning in the grip of the most joyous epidemic of mass insanity the country had ever seen.

Wherever one turned the radio dial in New York, there seemed to be no escaping the Beatles' thunderous beat. Between Beatle records, the disc jockeys on local stations like "W-A-Beatle-C" counted down the hours and minutes to the group's arrival. "It's thirty-four Beatle degrees outside at eight-thirty Beatle time—just four hours and fifty minutes to go!"

Over four thousand giddy teen-agers cut classes to pack Kennedy Airport's observation deck—where 110 policemen tried to keep them from getting too unruly. "We've never seen anything like this before," said an airport official. "Not even for presidents and kings." It was also the biggest crowd by far that the boy themselves had yet drawn.

When the Beatles finally stepped out of their Pan-Am jet, their American fans' shrieks dwarfed anything the four boys had heard in Britain or Europe. John, Paul, George, and Ringo were whisked through customs as another crowd of teen-agers clawed at the plate-glass windows. Then they gave their first American press conference.

The reporters who had come to the airport to cover this event didn't expect much. They knew from experience that pop-music stars were generally morons or phonies, or both, who rarely had anything interesting to say. But the reporters were in for a surprise.

"Will you sing something for us?" one asked.

"We need money first," John Lennon shot back.

"What's your message for American teen-agers?"

"Our message," said Paul McCartney, "is buy more Beatle records."

Whatever the question, at least one of the four was sure to be ready with a sharp answer. As *The New York Times* correspondent put it, "The Beatle wit became contagious. Everyone guffawed. The show was on—and the Beatle boys loved it."

"What about the movement in Detroit to stamp out the Beatles?" demanded another reporter.

"We're starting a movement to stamp out Detroit," said Paul.

"Why do you wear so many rings on your fingers?" Ringo was asked.

"Because I can't get them through my nose."

"Don't you guys ever get a haircut?"

"I just had one yesterday," replied George Harrison. Added Ringo, "You should have seen him the day before."

The United States' first attack of Beatlemania was an experience that will never be forgotten by anyone involved. The fans, of course, had a great time; but—in America more than in Britain—many parents, policemen, and commentators were disgusted at the hysteria, the loud music, and above all, what they felt was the four boys' shockingly long hair.

Nobody was more upset than the management of the Plaza, one of Manhattan's most conservative, expensive, and high-class hotels. When the Beatles' suites had been reserved a month before, the Hotel Plaza had been as unfamiliar as most Americans with the names Lennon, McCartney, Harrison, and Starr, and had assumed they were just another group of decent British businessmen. When the truth finally dawned, the Plaza desperately—and unsuccessfully—tried to find the quartet rooms elsewhere. Throughout the rock 'n' rollers' New York stay, the hotel was exposed to all the wild elements of Beatlemania—including swarms of disc jockeys, reporters, and cameramen, plus the hundreds of screaming fans who camped outside at all hours, kept at bay by several lines of barricades and dozens of policemen.

Most Americans got their first taste of the Beatles in action on the February ninth "Ed Sullivan Show." Though the group was nervous—and George Harrison had come down with the flu—the eight hundred lucky Beatlemaniacs in the studio audience more than made up for the rough edges in their idols' performance. They were well aware that their names had been chosen from sixty thousand ticket requests; even Elvis Presley's famous appearance on Sullivan's show had only drawn seven thousand.

Over seventy million Americans tuned in that night—a record audience for a TV entertainment program. Most did so purely out of curiosity, "to find out what all the fuss was about." Few had ever seen a spectacle such as that offered by the long-haired boys from Liverpool and their crazed fans. Millions of the younger viewers, at least, were completely hooked. By the time the show was over, Beatlemania had swept into the most remote corners of the North American continent.

New York's *Daily News* reported the next morning: "From the moment the Beatles began by blasting out 'All My Loving,' the kids bounced like dervishes in their seats to the driving beat. With the Beatle bounce, performed best by wild-eyed girls aged between 10 and 15, but also likely to infect adults, goes a wild screaming as if Dracula had just appeared on stage. The screams reached a pitch dangerous to the eardrums at times when the Beatles shook their shaggy locks."

On February 11 the Beatles traveled to the nation's capital, to perform their first American concert at the Washington Coliseum. After the show, they appeared as guests of honor at a formal charity ball at the British Embassy. Many of Washington's top socialites were there, some armed with scissors with which to snip away locks of the Beatles' famous hair for souvenirs. John Lennon left early in disgust.

The next day the group was forced to return to New York by train, as a snowstorm had grounded all air traffic. Two separate crowds, each numbering in the thousands, welcomed them at Pennsylvania Station and the Hotel Plaza. "In the shrieking pandemonium," reported the *Daily News,* "one girl was knocked down and trampled, another fainted, and a police sergeant was kicked by a horse. At times the cops could not control the mobs, and the Beatle-lovers broke through barricades in wild assaults in the station and the hotel."

The boys were back in town for a pair of concerts at elegant Carnegie Hall. The management, like that of the Plaza, had had little idea of what they were in store for when the shows were booked in late 1963. Rock 'n' rollers, such as Elvis Presley, had always been refused permission to play there. According to *The New York Times,* the show lasted just thirty-four minutes, after which "all four Beatles fled amid a hail of jelly beans. During this time the Beatles appeared to be singing and playing 12 songs," all of them drowned out by fans "who paid from $3 to $5.50 for the privilege of outshrieking their idols."

The following day, to the great relief of the Hotel Plaza and the New York Police Department, the Beatles flew to Miami to spend the last ten days of their visit on what Brian Epstein had originally planned as a holiday in the sun. But the mobs of cameramen, reporters, and fans gave them little chance to relax. In Florida, the group also did their other two Ed Sullivan shows before flying back to London on February 22.

The Beatles' conquest of the United States was accomplished in one lightning attack—over, it seemed, almost before it got underway. Quite aside from their musical talent, the Beatles appealed to Americans because they seemed so strange, and yet at the same time so real. Their long hair and their Britishness made them appear refreshingly unusual in comparison with earlier American pop stars—but so did the fact that they were intelligent and honest human beings.

A Tour of the Watts Towers

Arloa Paquin-Goldstone
& N.J. Bud Goldstone

WELCOME to the famous Watts Towers. The Towers is on the Registry of Historic Places of the National Trust of the United States and is a Cultural Heritage Monument of the City of Los Angeles.

People come from all over the world to see them every year.

All the sculptures you see were built by one man, Sabato "Sam" Rodia, an Italian-American laborer, during every spare moment each day after work on the weekends over a 30-year period from the mid-1920s to 1954. Sam was also known as Simon Rodilla, Simon Rodia, and Don Simon by some neighbors, visitors, or reporters.

The intricate towers and surrounding wall were built on the triangular lot which also held his house. The main vertical legs of the sculptures are slender columns containing internal steel reinforcements, tied with wire, wrapped with wire mesh, and covered by hand with mortar.

The objects and materials embedded in the mortar were all carefully selected from available sources, circa 1920–1950, and the artist's choices are excellent examples of these objects and materials which were popular household and decorative items of the time. Even though these items were quite common in many American households during their time of manufacture, they are now seen as important elements in the history of California (and American) decorative arts of the first half of the 20th century. Many of these items can now be found in antique shops, galleries and even the permanent collections of several museums.

The materials used include glass, mirrors, seashells, rocks, ceramic tile, pottery, and marble. The glass, usually parts of beverage bottles, is predominantly green from 7-UP bottle pieces or blue from Milk of Magnesia. There are none that are clear, such as used in Coca Cola bottles of that era.

The tiles are of many types, with many from the Malibu Potteries in Malibu, California, where the artist was employed. The firm was in business only from 1926 to 1932 and sold its wares through a showroom and warehouse on Larchmont Boulevard. Even though the firm was in business for only a few years, many tiles were produced and can still be found in homes and structures built in Southern California during the late '20's and early '30's. Malibu Potteries produced a full line of tile for almost every architectural purpose, either interior or exterior. The tiles are polychromatic and are "among the most beautiful finely detailed and well executed pieces of their kind manufactured locally" according to architectural historian Kathryn Smith. They can be distinguished by their reproduction of European hand-decorated tiles known as Saracen or Moorish and are primarily abstract and geometric in design.

In addition to the Malibu tiles, the viewer will also find a few areas decorated with tiles from the Batchelder Tile Company. Even though there are fewer Batchelder wares to be found in the Towers, these tiles are as prominent in the history of the decorative arts in Southern California as are those of Malibu Potteries. (The lack of many Batchelder tiles in relation to the number of Malibu tiles found in the Towers gives some credence to statements made by former Malibu employees that Rodia worked there for a time and would go home on weekends with pockets and bags full of discards and broken pieces of tiles.)

The Batchelder Tile Company, later known as Batchelder-Wilson, and Gladding McBean and Co. was originally founded by Ernest A. Batchelder in 1909 in Pasadena. The early Batchelder tiles, those found in the front wall of the Towers, differ stylistically from the Malibu tiles in that they are of the Craftsman Movement and are of a softer, more somber pallette. However, the later Batchelder tiles did move from the Craftsman style into the Spanish Colonial and Pre-Columbian revivals and on into Art Deco. One of these earlier tiles, a Viking Ship in the lower front wall, can also be found in the permanent collection of the Smithsonian Institute.

In addition to the Batchelder and Malibu tiles, the largest Southern California tile company, Gladding, McBean and Company, is most likely represented in the Towers as well.

We are very fortunate today to have in the Towers a repository of elements produced in California during the early 20th Century when California styles, Craftsman and the Spanish Colonial Revival or Mediterranian in particular, produced such a diversity of decorative designs. The tiles and their manufacturers were even the subject of a government study published by the

California State Mining Bureau in 1928. This report, "The Clay Resources and the Ceramic Industry of California," states that "The artistic development of California Decorative tile is an outstanding contribution to ceramic art in the United States. There is perhaps no other region in the world today that produces such a wide diversity of wall and fireplace tile, or that is so well prepared to create new designs for private homes, hotels, stores and office buildings."

That the Towers is so typically Southern California is due in large part to its decorative elements, many of which are products of Southern California's prominence and proliferation in the pottery and tile manufacturing industries of the first half of the 20th century. Just as Rodia brought art and technology together in the makeup of the Towers, the tiles and wares found in them are also a rich history of the meshing of artistic influences and technological advances made in Southern California during the early and mid-20th Century.

Nowhere else was there such an abundance of the raw materials (high quality clays) and the economic climate of growth to stimulate an industry to make use of them as well as a great diversity of architectural design and decorative styles to create a taste for such items. And all Rodia had to do was walk the streets and alleys of Los Angeles to glean this treasured ephemera of our daily lives.

You are standing in front of the entrance to Sam Rodia's Towers and to his house, which was right behind the entrance.

On both sides of the entrance, there is a mailbox with Rodia's initials, "S R" and the street address, "1765 East 107th Street". Although Rodia probably received little if any mail and possibly couldn't read, he built the two mailboxes into the front wall next to his front entrance. Above the entrance, he put the address, again, and his initials, this time with a reversed "s".

Inside the entrance is the decorated facade of the front wall to the house. The house itself is gone, burned in 1955, a year after Rodia left, handing over the deed to his house and towers to a neighbor. All that remains of the house is the front facade, posts along what was the east wall of the house, and the fireplace and chimney.

The canopy over the entrance, between the outside wall and the house, contains rows of pottery objects—unicorns, horses, dolls, and more—placed in the cement.

Along the side of what was the east wall of the house, remain a series of decorated posts. This post contains some of the pieces of broken California pottery also used by Rodia for decorations throughout the sculptures.

Turning eastward from the front door of the house, you enter the patio with its decorated floor from which the sculptures rise. Immediately east of the entrance are two of the small towers.

To the north is the very intricate "Gazebo", with its 40-foot tall spire and inside seating circle. Sit down on the long circular bench and you can view and enjoy the two small sculptures to the south, the chimney to the west, the rear, north wall, and the tallest tower on the east. Rodia has placed a great assortment of embedments in the Gazebo: tiles with hearts, seashells, pottery, colorful bits of glass in green and blue, and a golden bumblebee.

The north wall contains many fascinating decorations and embedments. Beginning at the west corner, you will find rows of corncobs, boots, and other shapes embellishing the colorful panels of the wall. The length of the north and south walls combined is almost 300 feet. The wall is decorated on both sides on the south and on the inside on the north.

The tower east of the Gazebo is the west tower, the tallest at 99 and 1/2 feet high and the last tall tower built by the artist. Rodia built this tall tower and the others without use of a ladder or scaffold! A small man, about 5 feet tall, he waited until the cement hardened on the lower levels and then climbed up using the horizontal rings as his ladder rungs. Over his shoulder was a bag of dampened cement and a bag of decorations, and in one hand was a steel reinforcement. The foundation for this tallest tower is only 14 inches deep. Rodia dug a circular trench in the ground and put 16 pieces of steel—eight 2" × 2" × 1/4" angles and eight 2 1/2" × 2 1/2" × 5/16" T-sections—vertically in the trench at equal distances apart to form the reinforcements for the tower's 16 legs. Then he poured the concrete into the trench, forming a shell which included the 16 pieces of steel for the legs. He filled in the open shell with broken concrete, covered the top of the shell to form the tower base and decorated the outside with his typical embedments. In some areas he added color to the cement or varied the surface finishes.

This tallest tower was subjected to a stress test simulating high wind loads on October 10, 1959 by an author of this article, to prove its strength and thus avoid demolition ordered by the Building and Safety Department of Los Angeles. The test was successful.

The center tower is 97 feet 10 inches tall. The tower consists of two separate sets of legs, forming a tower-within-a-tower design, unlike the west tower.

Between the center and east towers are a series of hearts on a set of connecting members, decorated with bottle glass and tiles.

The eastern tower is 55 feet tall and was the first tower Rodia made. On the north side, he built a ladder-like section extending to the top. This addition allowed easy access to the upper portions. Since the other two tall towers do not have built-in ladders, it may be assumed that Rodia found he could go up and down the sculptures with no trouble, even without a "ladder", by using the horizontal rings.

To the east of the east tower is the "Ship of Marco Polo" sculpture. The ship and its masts and superstructure are like all the Rodia works, different from the others. To the north of the ship, the wall contains sections of translucent glass inserts in orange and yellow which create a vivid display each day at sunset.

Rodia has left us with a wonderfully enjoyable work in the Watts Towers. Hidden among the many decorations are treasures you can find only by close observation. One such treasure, a delicate female form, was placed amidst a rock-filled wall panel in the south wall near the east tower.

Next time you visit the Towers, look for it.

from

Bertice: The World According to Me

Bertice Berry, Ph.D.

THOUGH Terry Evenson was generously helping me, I was determined to carry as much of my own load as possible. I became a resident assistant in the dorms to reduce my housing costs (and get a private bathroom). Doing so put me in touch with Sally Myers.

Somehow she was the only professor at Jacksonville University I could call by her first name. In addition to being director of the women's dormitories, Sally taught art therapy. I was excited by the idea of combining art with healing and enrolled in her class.

When Sally announced an assignment called "pillow fantasy" and told us to bring a pillow to the next class, we all thought that she had reached new heights in her already outrageous teaching techniques. When we arrived that day, she told us to stretch out on the floor. Then she turned out the lights and coaxed us to relax. I was thinking, Free schools and crazy White people.

Sally told us to visualize our ideal creation. It could be anything: a painting, a song, a performance. Her only request was that it be incredible.

I started thinking that maybe Sally wasn't so crazy and that I could get into this. I began to imagine a project where I'd combine information with entertainment. I would have this great delivery. I'd be funny and informative. There would be an audience that would also participate. We would find solutions to their problems through humor, song, and education.

I got lost in the fantasy. After about twenty minutes, Sally instructed us to return from the fantasy but remember it. I expected her to tell us to share the fantasies we'd had. Instead, she told us that we should write an outline of what we'd imagined.

We all wrote furiously, and at the end of class, none of us were finished. Then Sally informed us that what we had written would be our final exam; we had to realize our fantasy. "But it was just a fantasy," someone complained. "Yeah," another student chimed in, "my idea is too complex to produce."

Sally smiled the world's biggest grin and said, "If you can imagine it, you can create it."

At the end of the semester, students brought in some of the most amazing work I'd seen: self-portraits, sets of dishes. My presentation couldn't be carried in a bag.

I organized the class to sit as if they were members of a television audience. I brought in my friends, who performed beautiful music and joined my panel to discuss relevant topics. It was a combination of daytime talk show and late-night variety show. It was a big hit.

I forgot about this experience until I signed the deal for *The Bertice Berry Show*. When I remembered, I marveled at how profoundly Sally had helped me to anticipate what I was going to do years before I had any idea I was going to do it.

Biographical Notes

Bertice Berry, Ph.D. Dr. Berry has overcome racism and family tragedy to become a college professor, award-winning comedian, motivational speaker, writer, singer, TV talk show host and sit-com star. She draws inspiration from folk wisdom, humor and a deep spirituality.

Ray Bradbury (1920–   ) His talents range as far as his imagination. While winning many prizes for his creative writing, Bradbury has also designed space rides at EPCOT, EuroDisney and the U.S. pavilion at the 1964 World's Fair. He has won many honors, perhaps the most unusual was the naming of the Dandelion Crater on the moon of his beautiful short story collection, Dandelion Wine.

David Bodanis Although he is a distinguished science lecturer at Oxford University in England, Bodanis reveals a fascinating, grossed-out world of hidden dust, dirt, and chemicals that abound in our bodies, food, and environment. This field has engrossed him since childhood.

Bruce Brooks (1950–   ) Born in Washington, D.C., Brooks spent most of his childhood in North Carolina and, after his parents' divorce, had to shuttle to new places and new schools, where his knack for storytelling helped him overcome his shyness and make new friends. His fiction and nonfiction have been honored by the American Library Association, Horn Book, the National Council of Teachers of English, the International Reading Association, and School Library Journal.

Julie Checkoway (1964–   ) A graduate of Harvard, the Iowa Writer's Workshop, and the Johns Hopkins Writing Seminars, Checkoway's books have been nominated for the Pulitzer Prize, the National Book Award, and the Pen Award for a First Book of Nonfiction. She has received many awards and honors and teaches Creative Nonfiction at Goucher College.

C. J. Cherryh (1943–   ) Gifted with intelligence and vitality, Cherryh has taught Latin, Greek, and Ancient History and has traveled from New York to Istanbul and Troy, waded in two oceans and four of the seven seas. Although she is an award-winning writer, Cherryh manages to try new things such as riding, fencing, wilderness survival, and ancient weapons, among many other activities.

Beverly Cleary (1916–   ) Born in McMinnville, Oregon, Cleary spent her early years on her father's farm, and later graduated from the University of California, Berkeley, where she met her husband, Clarence. She published her first book, Henry Huggins, in 1950 and has seen subsequent books honored with the prestigious Newberry Medal and the Laura Ingalls Wilder Award, among many others. One of the most beloved of children's writers, her books have sold more than 35 million copies, in part because they express Cleary's realistic, sensitive, and humorous views of growing up.

Bob Costas (1952–   ) Born in New York, Costas began his broadcasting career while he was still a student at Syracuse University. He was an avid and capable athlete, but knew that his size (he's 5'6") would prevent him from a career in the big leagues. So he honed his broadcasting skills and has become one of the most respected and honored sportscasters in the United States. He was the youngest person to be named *Sportscaster of the Year*, and went on to win the award a record six times. He has also won more than ten Emmy Awards for hosting and writing, and his acclaimed interview program, "Later with Bob Costas," won an Emmy for Outstanding Informational Series. He is married and has two children.

Robertson Davies (1913-1995) A man of many talents, he was born and died in Ontario, Canada. Educated in Canada and in England, he joined the Old Vic Repertory Theatre Company in 1938. In addition to being a talented actor, Davies went on to a distinguished career as a musician, teacher, critic, playwright, and award-winning novelist.

Rita Dove (1952–   ) The daughter of a chemist and the wife of a writer, Rita Dove was the first woman and the first African American to be named Poet Laureate of the United States. Her career has been filled with honors: the Pulitzer Prize in poetry, a Fulbright Fellowship, a Rockefeller Foundation Grant to be Writer-in-Residence in Bellagio, Italy, and a Guggenheim Fellow, among others.

Gerald Durrell (1925-1995) An avid naturalist, Durrell referred to himself as a champion of small uglies, all the insects, mammals, and birds he loved from childhood. He devoted his life to writing and the preservation of wildlife. At ten, he left his native England for the island of Corfu where he was greeted with the lush beauty of nature which he celebrated his entire life.

Zlata Filipovic (1980–   ) Her diary about life as an only child in war-torn Sarajevo became a world-wide bestseller when it was published by UNICEF (United Nations International Children's Fund). Enduring bombings, the deaths of friends and pets, Zlata, like Anne Frank, found good things to write about. Her diary has been published in twenty-five countries.

Robert Finch (1943–   ) A contributor to several anthologies of nature writing, Finch has twice been named Conservationist of the Year by the Brewster Conservation Trust. He has also been honored by the United States Environmental Protection Agency. Finch enjoys singing almost as much as he likes writing, and he is a member of the Chatham Chorale.

James Finn Garner (1960–   ) The author of the multi-million-copy best-selling Politically Correct Bedtime Stories, Garner is celebrated for his wildly humorous look at a variety of topics: UFO's, the internet, the millennium, and much more.

Stephen Gardiner (1925–   ) Born in London, the son of two artists, Gardiner graduated with honors from the Architectural Association School of Architecture in 1948. He married an architect with whom he has two children. He has been compelled to explain the field of architecture to the public because he feels that it is a little understood field.

Kathlyn Gay (1930–   ) and Martin Gay With her son, Martin, Kathlyn Gay is the author or co-author of more than thirty-five books on a variety of subjects such as the environment, education, and cults. Ms. Gay has had a varied career: she has been an editor and public relations writer as well as a lifelong activist in her church's social and missionary programs. She has won many regional literary prizes, and two of her books have been nationally honored as ALA Notables.

Whit Gibbons, Ph.D. (1939–   ) and **Anne R. Gibbons** (1947–   ) He is Professor of Zoology at the University of Georgia, and a senior research ecologist at the Savannah River Ecology Lab. She is a freelance editor and co-author with her husband. Together they present fun-filled facts based on finger-tip experience.

Alison Leslie Gold (1945–   ) Gifted with a compassionate and sensitive ear, Gold, also the author with Miep Gies of Anne Frank Remembered: The Story of the Woman Who Helped Hide the Frank Family, paints a poignant picture of life in Nazi-occupied Amsterdam.

Joyce Hansen (1942–   ) A gifted writer and a dedicated preservationist explore the past through archeology. Hansen's book, Which Way Freedom? was named an ALA Notable Book in 1986 and I Thought My Soul Would Rise and Fly was the winner of the Coretta Scott King Award.

Nat Hentoff (1925–   ) Born in Boston, Hentoff did graduate work at Harvard before he accepted a Fulbright Fellowship that took him to the Sorbonne in France. His expertise ranges from music to education and the law. He is recognized as one of the foremost authorities on the Bill of Rights, the Supreme Court and student rights. Hentoff's columns have appeared in The New York Times, The Village Voice, The Atlantic, and The New Yorker, where he was a staff writer for 25 years. He has an honorary doctor of law degree from Northeastern University.

Paul Hillyard Since 1974 Hillyard has been the Director of the Arachnology Section at the British Museum of Natural History. His enthusiasm for his crawly, some might say creepy, subjects began when he was a boy and he has shared his humorous and brilliant insights about them in several books and many magazine articles.

Sue Hubbell (1942–   ) This former librarian has created an inspiring life in the rural beauty of the Ozarks. Now a commercial bee keeper, honey seller and farmer, among other things, Hubbell is a gifted writer whose work has been praised for its careful, understated grace.

Gish Jen (1956–   ) A graduate of Radcliffe College, Jen is the American-born daughter of Chinese, immigrant parents. She grew up in Scarsdale, New York which had left an indelible mark on her. The town had a large Jewish population which, Jen believes, profoundly influenced her life and her writing. She sees deep sympathy between the Jewish and Chinese cultures.

Florence Griffith Joyner (1959-1998) began to run track at seven, and, at fourteen, won the annual Jesse Owens National Youth Games. (The Games were named for the legendary runner who set ten world records and won four gold medals at the 1932 Olympics.) She married Olympic gold medalist Al Joyner in 1987, and set new world records at the 1988 Olympics. Her performances were so impressive that she was voted World Athlete of the Year and earned the unofficial title of The World's Fastest Woman in 1988. Joyner displayed unprecedented glamour with her brightly-colored running suits, long flowing hair and her multi-color fingernails. Her life was cut short by a fatal heart attack.

Gary Kinder (1946–   ) Kinder began researching the story of Ship of Gold in the Deep Blue Sea in 1987, and was aboard the Arctic Discoverer when Thompson announced his find to the public. The author of the best-selling books, Victim and Light Years, Kinder teaches writing seminars to lawyers around the country. He lives in Seattle with his wife and two daughters.

Martin Luther King (1929-1968) The Reverend Doctor King is one of the towering figures in the twentieth century struggle for civil rights, peace and justice—for African Americans and for all people. Awarded the Nobel Peace Prize, he rallied America to the cause of freedom for all in his famous I Have a Dream speech heard by millions around the world. He wrote several prize-winning books, and was assassinated while he was negotiating a labor strike.

Richard Lederer, Ph.D. (1938–   ) He has been in love with words since childhood. A graduate of Haverford College, Harvard Law School, and the University of New Hampshire, Dr. Lederer taught English and media at St. Paul's School for 27 years and turned to full-time writing. The recipient of many honors, he refers to himself as the Wizard of Idiom, Attila the Pun, and Conan the Grammarian.

Aldo Leopold (1887-1948) Born on the bluffs of the Mississippi River near Burlington, Iowa, Leopold was fascinated by the magic and mystery of nature and, as a result, pursued a degree in forestry at Yale University. He was a pioneer in the field of ecology and game management, and is considered the father of wildlife conservation in the United States. Widely published, he received the John Burroughs Medal for his life's work and particularly for his influential book, Sand County Almanac.

Linda Leuzzi The author of more than 200 newspaper and magazine articles, Leuzzi has also written books about American history and the fashion industry. Women in the Fashion Industry was named a Best Book for Young Adults by the New York Public Library.

Barry Lopez (1945–   ) Lopez defines himself as a writer who travels and his travels to Australia, the North and South poles, Asia and Africa have inspired award-winning fiction and nonfiction. He has established a reputation as an authoritative writer on the environment and natural history. Lopez's writing has also been praised for its poetic, descriptive clarity.

William R. Maples Ph.D. (1937-1997) and Michael Browning. Through scrupulous scientific research, Dr. Maples shed light on several notorious deaths, including President Zachary Taylor, Russian Tsar Nicholas II, explorer Francisco Pizzaro, and Joseph Merrick, the tragic 19th century person known as *The Elephant Man*. Maples was also involved in the identification of remains of soldiers from the Korean and Vietnam Wars. Browning is a reporter for The Miami Herald.

Janet Marinelli When she was ten, Marinelli spotted a giant silk moth on her window screen. It was such a beautiful, indelible memory that she has created a summer garden designed to attract the elusive Luna back for a visit. Although she has yet to succeed, she has achieved international recognition as Director of Publishing for the Brooklyn Botanical Garden, one of the most beautiful and distinguished in the world. She firmly believes in the gardener's role in the preservation of the planet.

Joe Namath (1943–   ) Born in Beaver Falls, Pennsylvania, Namath became a star quarterback at the legendary University of Alabama before signing with the New York Jets. He became the first pro football player to pass for more than 4000 yards, and quarterbacked the Jets to an upset victory in Super Bowl III in 1969. He has pursued a career in the movie and broadcasting since his retirement.

Lensey Namioka (1929–   ) Born in Peking, China, Namioka is the daughter of a linguist father and a physician mother. She graduated from Radcliffe College and has an MA from the University of California, Berkeley. Although she had excellent training in mathematics, Namioka says that its only effect on her writing is an urge to economy. Because of her own Chinese heritage and her husband's Japanese roots, Namioka draws heavily on both cultural traditions in her writing.

Jim Northrup (1943–   ) This gifted poet, journalist, and storyteller invites readers to explore the world of today's Ojibway people and offers humorous commentary about his encounters with the immigrant communities (his term for Caucasian Americans).

Gary Paulsen (1939–   ) Born in Minneapolis, Minnesota, Paulsen's inspiration for writing came after a librarian gave him a book to read along with his own library card. He was hooked, and spent hours in his basement reading one book after another. Since then, he has published more than 130 books, three of which have been named Newberry Honor Books. He has also written more than 200 short stories and magazine articles for children and adults. He loves to sail and lives part of the year with his wife on a sailboat in the Pacific. He also collects Harley-Davidson motorcycles.

George Plimpton (1927–   ) Born into a prominent family in New York City, Plimpton graduated from Harvard University and King's College, Cambridge. He is the founder and co-editor of the leading literary journal, The Paris Review. Through the years he has stepped into the role of a quarterback, baseball pitcher, boxer, golfer, hockey goalie, parachutist, race car driver and orchestra percussionist. These colorful, first-hand experiences form the basis for two dozen books and countless articles, and have been the basis of hit movies and TV shows. He is the official fireworks chairman of New York.

Ian Stewart, Ph.D. (1945–   ) Dr. Stewart is Professor of Mathematics at the University of Warwick in Coventry, England. He is an active research mathematician as well as the 1995 winner of the Royal Society's Michael Faraday Meal for outstanding contributions to the public understanding of science. (Michael Faraday [1791-1867] was an English chemist and physicist whose life work was in the field of electricity.)

George Sullivan (1927–   ) Born in Lowell, Massachusetts and graduated from Fordham University, Sullivan is one of the most prolific and informative writers of nonfiction for young adults. He has published more than 200 books on topics ranging from gymnastics to baseball, from sharks and shipwrecks to treasure hunts. His books have won many awards, among them, numerous citations as Best Book for Young Adults from the American Library Association. A talented, all-season tennis player, he is married and has one son.

Roger Swain (1950–   ) Although he trained to be an educator at Harvard, and holds a Ph.D. from there, Swain's interest in rain forest biology planted in him a lifelong interest in horticulture. His career has branched into many areas: TV celebrity as the host of PBS's Victory Garden and award-winning writer of books and magazine articles, as well as a popular lecturer throughout the United States. He is married to Elizabeth Ward Swain, Ph.D. who is an administrator at Harvard University.

Edwin Way Teale (1899-1980) Teale and his wife Nellie bought an overgrown farm in Connecticut and spent the rest of their lives in deep and intimate exploration of the plants and animals on their land. One of the best-loved naturalists of his generation, Teale won a Pulitzer Prize in 1966 for his four book series on the seasons in America. He was also awarded the John Burroughs Medal for distinguished nature writing.

Jenny Elizabeth Tesar (1937–   ) Tesar has published more than thirty-seven books and more than a thousand articles over the past thirty years. The topics range from dentistry to dinosaurs, software to sleep. She has also created more than thirty software products. Tesar holds a B.S. from Cornell University and an M.S. from Oregon State University.

Jim Trelease A prolific and noted author of more than twenty-five reading textbooks, Trelease is well known in the field of educational publishing.

Acknowledgments *(continued from p. ii)*

Don Congdon Associates

Excerpt from "Idea Beast" by Ray Bradbury. Published in *Faces of Science Fiction* by Bluejay Books, 1984. Copyright © 1984 by Ray Bradbury. Reprinted by permission of Don Congdon Associates, Inc.

Bob Costas

"Eulogy for Mickey Mantle" by Bob Costas, August 15, 1995. Reprinted by permission of the author.

Darhansoff & Verrill Literary Agency

From *A Book of Bees and How to Keep Them* by Sue Hubbell. Copyright 1988 by Sue Hubbell. Reprinted by permission of Darhansoff & Verrill Literary Agency.

Delacorte Press, a division of Random House, Inc.

"First Strike," excerpt from *Father Water, Mother Woods* by Gary Paulsen III, illustrated by Ruth Wright Paulsen. Copyright text 1994 by Gary Paulsen. Illustrations 1994 by Ruth Wright Paulsen. Used by permission of Delacorte Press, a division of Random House, Inc.

Detroit Free Press

"Underwater Gold Rush" by Susan Hall-Balduf from *The Detroit Free Press*, July 19, 1998, book reviews. Reprinted by permission of Detroit Free Press.

Dorling Kindersley Publishing

"Duke Ellington" and "The Recording" by John Fordham from *Jazz*. Text copyright © 1993 John Fordham.

Doubleday, a division of Random House, Inc.

From *Dead Men Do Tell Tales* by William R. Maples. Copyright © 1994 by William R. Maples. Used by permission of Doubleday, a division of Random House, Inc.

Rita Dove

Rita Dove's essay was excerpted from *I Know What the Red Clay Looks Like*, ed. Rebecca Carroll. Copyright 1994. Reprinted by permission of the author, Rita Dove.

Dutton, a division of Penguin Putnam Inc.

"An Invitation to the Opera" from *Bravo! A Guide to the Opera for the Perplexed* by Barrymore Laurence Scherer. Copyright © 1996 by Barrymore Laurence Scherer. Used by permission of Dutton, a division of Penguin Putnam Inc.

Ebony Magazine

"Hoop Dreams" from *Ebony* magazine, March 1996.

Farrar, Straus & Giroux, Inc.

"Knowing" from *Making Sense: Animal Perception and Communication* by Bruce Brooks. Copyright © 1993 by The Educational Broadcasting Corporation and Bruce Brooks. Reprinted by permission of Farrar, Straus & Giroux, Inc.

Robert Finch

"Death of a Hornet" by Robert Finch, published in *The Bread Loaf Anthology of Contemporary Essays*, edited by Robert Pack and Jay Parini. © 1989 by Bread Loaf Writer's Conference/Middlebury College. Reprinted by permission of the author.

Franklin Watts, a division of Grolier Publishing

"Edward Toth: Saving Brooklyn's Last Forest," "Sally J. Cole: Preserving the Past, Looking to the Future" and "Jake Blair: Protector of Chesapeake Bay" from *To the Young Environmentalist: Lives Dedicated to Preserving the Natural World* by Linda Leuzzi. Copyright © 1997 by Linda Leuzzi. "Examining Documents" from *Scientific Crime Investigation* by Jenny Tesar. Copyright © 1991 by Jenny Tesar. Reprinted by permission of Franklin Watts, a division of Grolier Publishing.

Acknowledgments

Acknowledgments

Pantheon Books, a division of Random House, Inc.
"The Attic: A Family Museum" by Susan Power, "The Garage" by Gish Jen, and "The Workroom, or, There are Other Tools Besides the Hammer" by James Finn Garner from *Home: American Writers Remember* by Sharon Sloan Fiffer and Steve Fiffer. Copyright © 1995 by Sharon Sloan Fiffer and Steve Fiffer. Reprinted by permission of Pantheon Books, a division of Random House, Inc.

Pocket Books, a division of Simon & Schuster
"The Case for Short Words" and "A Celebration of Libraries" by Richard Lederer is reprinted with permission of Pocket Books, a division of Simon & Schuster, from *The Miracle of Language* by Richard Lederer. Copyright © 1991 by Richard Lederer.

Random House, Inc. and Hutchinson, a division of Random House UK
"Trap-door Spider" and excerpt from "Remarkable Jumpers" from *The Book Of the Spider* by Paul Hillyard. Copyright © 1994 by Paul Hillyard. Reprinted by permission of the publishers, Random House, Inc. and Hutchinson, a division of Random House UK.

Random House, Inc.
"Introduction" from *Jazz Is* by Nat Hentoff. Copyright © 1976 by Nat Hentoff. Reprinted by permission of Random House, Inc.

Rosen Publishing Group
"Programmers" from *Exploring Careers in Cyberspace* by Michael Fulton. Copyright 1998 by Michael Fulton. Published by The Rosen Publishing Group, Inc. Reprinted by permission of the publisher.

Timothy Schaffner for the Estate of Nicholas Schaffner
From *The Boys from Liverpool* by Nicolas Schaffner. Permission granted courtesy of the Estate of Nicholas Schaffner.

Scholastic Inc.
From *Memories of Anne Frank: Reflections of a Childhood Friend* by Alison Leslie Gold. Published by Scholastic Press, a division of Scholastic Inc. Copyright © 1997 by Alison Leslie Gold. Reprinted by permission.

Scribner, a division of Simon & Schuster
From *Bertrice: The World According to Me* by Bertrice Berry. Copyright © 1996 by Bertrice Berry Productions, Inc. Reprinted by permission.

Share Our Strength
"Swims with Frogs" by Roger B. Swain from *The Nature of Nature: Essays from America's Finest Writers on Nature*, edited by William H. Shore. Copyright © 1994 by Roger B. Swain. Reprinted by permission of Share Our Strength, Washington D.C.

Simon & Schuster, Inc.
From *Football for Young Players and Parents* by Joe Namath and Bob Oates. Copyright © 1986 by Namanco Productions, Inc. From *The Secret Family: Twenty-Four Hours Inside the Mysterious World of Out Minds and Bodies* by David Bodanis. Copyright © 1997 by David Bodanis. "Monticello" from *Inside Architecture* by Stephen Gardiner. Copyright © 1983 by Prentice-Hall, Inc. Reprinted by permission of Simon & Schuster, Inc.

Studio Vista, a div of Cassell plc UK
"The Dancer" from *Understanding Ballet* by Mary Clarke and Clement Crisp. Copyright © 1976 by Mary Clarke and Clement Crisp. Published by Studio Vista, a division of Cassell plc UK. Reprinted by permission of the publisher.

Acknowledgments

Jennifer Surridge

"My Musical Career" from *Happy Alchemy: on the pleasures of music and theatre* by Robertson Davies, edited by Jennifer Surridge and Brenda Davies. Copyright © Pendragon Ink, 1997. Reprinted by permission of the editor.

University of Alabama Press

"Silver Ants Sup When the Temperature's Up" from *Ecoviews: Snakes, Snails, and Environmental Tales* by Whit Gibbons and Anne R. Gibbons. Copyright © 1998 The University of Alabama Press. Reprinted by permission of The University of Alabama Press.

University of Connecticut Libraries

"Keeping an Insect Zoo" from *The Junioor Book of Insects* by Edwin Way Teale. Copyright © 1972, 1955, 1939 by E. P. Dutton & Company, Inc. Reprinted by permission of University of Connecticut Libraries.

Viking Penguin, a division of Penguin Putnam, Inc. and Curtis Brown, Ltd.

From *Birds, Beast and Other Relatives* by Gerald M. Durrell. Copyright © 1969 by Gerald M. Durrell. Used by permission of Viking Penguin, a division of Penguin Putnam Inc. and Curtis Brown, Ltd.

Viking Penguin, a division of Penguin Putnam Inc.

"A Story Rescued from the Ashes" from *Hey! Listen To This* by Jim Trelease. Copyright © 1992 by Jim Trelease. From *Zlata's Diary* by Zlata Filipovic, translation copyright © 1994 Editions Robert Laffont/Fixot. Used by permission of Viking Penguin, a division of Penguin Putnam Inc.

William Morris Agency for C.J. Cherryh

Excerpt by C.J. Cherryh, copyright 1984 by C.J. Cherryh, from *Faces of Science Fiction*, coordinated by Mark Bigham, published by Bluejay Books.

John Wiley & Sons

From *The Magical Maze: Seeing the World Through Mathematical Eyes* by Ian Stewart. Copyright © 1997 by Ian Stewart. Reprinted by permission of John Wiley & Sons, Inc.

Note: Every effort has been made to locate the copyright owner of material reprinted in this book. Omissions brought to our attention will be corrected in subsequent editions.